Reducing Stress in Young Children's Lives

Janet Brown McCracken, Editor
Director of Publications 1976–1986
National Association for the Education of Young Children

NATIONAL ASSOCIATION FOR THE EDUCATION OF YOUNG CHILDREN
WASHINGTON, D.C.

National Association for the Education of Young Children
1509 16th Street, N.W.
Washington, DC 20036–1426
202–232–8777 800–424–2460

The National Association for the Education of Young Children (NAEYC) attempts through its publications program to provide a forum for discussion of major issues and ideas in our field. We hope to provoke thought and promote professional growth. The views expressed or implied are not necessarily those of the Association. NAEYC wishes to thank the editor and authors, who donated much time and effort to develop this book as a contribution to our profession.

Library of Congress Catalog Card Number: 86–062564

ISBN Catalog Number: 0–935989–03–X

NAEYC #216

Printed in the United States of America

Contents

To James
as he rises to the challenge

Introduction

Rarely does a day go by when we don't experience some form of stress. Some pressures are inevitable, but others are self-induced or are imposed by others. As parents and teachers, we need to take a close look at how we handle stress, both our own and that faced by our children. Few of us deliberately set out to cause children stress or to teach them how to deal with it, yet we do just that with our every word, action, and reaction.

For example, if we shout, hit, or curse at the least bit of irritation, our children will use similar behaviors when they encounter obstacles. On the other hand, if we talk about problems with those involved, or find similar constructive ways to deal with stress, our children will also soon adopt these methods. What children learn from us, negative or positive, will infuence how they handle stressful situations the rest of their lives.

Growing up means meeting a variety of challenges, many of which can cause stress. Some of those challenges are expected as part of life—how to deal with fears, power, sex, death. In addition to these typical human developmental stresses, two other sources of stress are common in the lives of most children today.

First of all, American families are moving, working, falling apart, and reforming at an unprecedented rate. These changes affect children as well as adults. In addition, our often unrealistic expectations, and our ever-changing world, impose other stresses on children.

How then, as adults, can we help children successfully deal with each of the problems they face today, so that they will have the strength and skills to face the challenges of tomorrow? We can give children a priceless legacy—the opportunity to give, and therefore get, the most joy in life.

In this book you will find some of the best work in the field of human development on how adults can help children learn to cope with stress. Each of the chapters previously appeared in *Young Children*, the professional journal of the National Association for the Education of Young Children. These articles—all popular because they are so practical—are assembled here for your convenience, so that other adults and children might reap the rewards of understanding, and constructively dealing with, stress.

Janet Brown McCracken
September 1986

List of Articles

reprinted from *Young Children*

Almy, M. (1984, May). Reaffirmations: Speaking out for children. A child's right to play. *39*(4), 80.

Carlsson-Paige, N., & Levin, D. E. (1986, March). *The Butter Battle Book:* Uses and abuses with young children. *41*(3), 37–42.

Fassler, D. (1980, September). The young child in the hospital. *35*(6), 19–25.

Furman, E. (1978, May). Helping children cope with death. *33*(4), 25–32.

Haiman, P. E. (1984, November). Viewpoint. There is more to early childhood education than cognitive development. *39*(1), 8.

Hale-Benson, J. (1981, January). Research in review. Black children: Their roots, culture, and learning styles. *36*(2), 37–50.

Honig, A. S. (1986, May & July). Research in review. Stress and coping in children. Part 1, *41*(4), 50–63; Part 2, *41*(5), 47–59.

Hyson, M. (1979, July). Lobster on the sidewalk: Understanding and helping children with fears. *34*(5), 54–60.

Ideas that work with young children. Why Not Holiday Performances? (1985, March). *40*(3), 17.

Jalongo, M. R. (1983, July). Using crisis-oriented books with young children. *38*(5), 29–36.

Jalongo, M. R. (1985, September). When young children move. *40*(6), 51–57.

Kamii, C. (1984, May). Viewpoint. Obedience is not enough. *39*(4), 11–14.

Koblinsky, S., Atkinson, J., & Davis, S. (1980, November). Sex Education With Young Children. *35*(1), 21–31.

Kostelnik, M. J., Whiren, A. P., & Stein, L. C. (1986, May). Living with He-Man: Managing superhero fantasy play. *41*(4), 3–9.

Krogh, S. L., & Lamme, L. L. (1985, May). "But what about sharing?" Children's literature and moral development. *40*(4), 48–51.

Lane, M. (1984, September). Reaffirmations: Speaking out for children. A child's right to the valuing of diversity. *39*(6), 76.

Liebman, T. (1984, September). "When will you be back?" We bring generations together! *39*(6), 70–75.

McAfee, O. D. (1985, September). Research report. Circle time: Getting past "Two Little Pumpkins." *40*(6), 24–29.

Meddin, B. J., & Rosen, A. L. (1986, May). Child abuse and neglect: Prevention and reporting. *41*(4), 26–30.

Merrow, J. (1985, July). Viewpoint. Self care. *40*(5), 8.

Roopnarine, J. L., & Honig, A. S. (1985, September). Research in review. The unpopular child. *40*(6), 59–64.

Skeen, P., & McKenry, P. C. (1980, July). The teacher's role in facilitating a child's adjustment to divorce. *35*(5), 3–12.

Skeen, P., Robinson, B. E., & Flake-Hobson, C. (1984, January). Blended families: Overcoming the Cinderella myth. *40*(2), 64–74.

Smith, C. A., & Davis, D. E. (1976, September). Teaching children non-sense. *31*(6), 438–447.

Soderman, A. K. (1985, July). Dealing with difficult young children: Strategies for teachers and parents. *40*(5), 15–20.

Trawick-Smith, J., & Thompson, R. H. (1984, July). Preparing young children for hospitalization. *39*(5), 57–63.

Veach, D. M. (1977, May). Choice with responsibility. *32*(4), 22–25.

Wallinga, C. R., & Sweaney, A. L. (1985, November). A sense of *real* accomplishment: Young children as productive family members. *40*(1), 3–7.

White, B. P., & Phair, M. A. (1986, January). "It'll be a challenge!" Managing emotional stress in teaching disabled children. *41*(2), 44–47.

Ziegler, P. (1985, March). Saying good-bye to preschool. *40*(3), 11–15.

Part 1.
Coping with the expected challenges

When we know what to expect, we can prepare ourselves. When we know how children grow and learn, we can anticipate some of the successes—and some of the challenges—children will face on their way to adulthood. Our understanding will also enable us to work *with* children, rather than in ways that only make it more difficult for them to build skills and attitudes that will serve them well all their lives.

This book begins with some of the most universal sources of stress for children—their fears, dreams, bodies, and loss of loved ones. All of us have been afraid of the dark, or of monsters under our beds, or of something. Pretending to be all-powerful superheroines or superheroes may be one way of dealing with such fears.

Many other issues also need to be dealt with beginning in early childhood, if children are to appreciate life to its fullest extent. Children's attitudes about themselves and others are shaped from the moment they are born, possibly before. Their concerns about their bodies—sex, health, pain—must be sensitively

handled in the early years so children will continue to deal positively with these difficult issues throughout their teens and adulthood. When we work with children, we need to be aware, and help children to be aware, that life includes many goodbyes and greetings. It is essential to help children find appropriate ways to cope with the strong feelings they have, and will continue to have, at times of painful separations.

Lobster on the Sidewalk: Understanding and Helping Children With Fears—*Marion C. Hyson* ● Living With He-Man: Managing Superhero Fantasy Play—*Marjorie J. Kostelnik, Alice P. Whiren, and Laura C. Stein* ● Sex Education With Young Children—*Sally Koblinsky, Jean Atkinson, and Shari Davis* ● Preparing Young Children for Hospitalization—*Jeffrey Trawick-Smith and Richard H. Thompson* ● The Young Child in the Hospital—*David Fassler* ● Saying Good-Bye to Preschool—*Patricia Ziegler* ● Helping Children Cope With Death—*Erna Furman* ● Using Crisis-Oriented Books With Young Children—*Mary R. Jalongo*

Lobster on the Sidewalk

Understanding and Helping Children with Fears

Marion Carey Hyson

One day when Jeff was almost 3, he and his mother met a neighbor outside their apartment building. The neighbor, just back from shopping, was carrying a large brown bag.

"Come here, Jeff," the neighbor called. "Let me show you what I bought." She reached into the bag and placed a live lobster on the sidewalk. As it moved slowly toward Jeff, waving its claws in the sunlight, he screamed with panic. The apologetic neighbor rushed the lobster to its waiting pot.

At Jeff's day care center several weeks later, Jeff sat on the floor while his teacher showed the group a new book about the sea. While turning the pages, she came to a delicate illustration of a lobster. Jeff's eyes widened. He jumped up and tried to close the book.

"Jeff!" the teacher said. "There's nothing to be afraid of!"

"There's nothing to be afraid of!" Generations of teachers and parents have said it, and generations of children have just as firmly rejected it. A lobster, a friendly babysitter, a new hairdo, a vacuum cleaner—such "harmless" things can cause reactions ranging from mild worry to outright panic. Where do these fears come from, how do they de-

velop, and what can be done to help children overcome them?

The origins of fear

Fear is not confined to children. We are all afraid of something, but our fears come in many sizes and many degrees of realism. When you think about it, a totally fearless person would be foolhardy...or dead. Some fears are clearly sensible and protective. No one scoffs at a person who is cautious about crossing the street, who backs away from the edge of a cliff, or who shrinks from the pain of surgery.

Sometimes an imaginary-sounding fear turns out to have a basis in fact. Children are often unable to reveal traumatic experiences, so adults tend to dismiss their concerns as imaginary. But there are far too many children who have to worry about very real and disturbing events: being bitten by rats, being abandoned, being abused.

Other fears are less directly tied to present dangers. Some people theorize that many of our most basic human fears—of sudden, looming movements, of loud noises, of being alone or enclosed—are leftover survival reactions from our early ancestors (Bowlby

1973). Even today such reactions may occasionally save us from harm.

Other fears are less easily explained because they do not seem to have a reasonable cause. Why should anyone be afraid of a lobster on the sidewalk, or a worm, or a Halloween costume? Such reactions are easier to understand if we recognize the role of cognitive processes in producing fearful responses. We fear not what will harm us, but what we *think* will harm us. We interpret an event in the light of our past experiences, our present understanding, and the total situation, and on that basis we *infer* that the event is either harmless or dangerous. The same stimulus—that lobster on the sidewalk—might cause reactions ranging from amusement to interest to fright in people of different ages or with differing experiences.

If what we fear is partly determined by our interpretation of events, it is understandable that children have more

Marion Carey Hyson, Ph.D., is a kindergarten teacher at Charlestown Play House, Phoenixville, Pennsylvania. She is a former nursery school, high school, and college teacher. Her doctoral research dealt with the development of coping strategies by young children.

"irrational" fears than adults (Maurer 1965; Bauer 1976). But irrationality is in the eye of the beholder. Piaget and others have demonstrated that, in many respects, children's thinking operates differently than adult thinking. Both its content and structure are constantly changing as the child assimilates new experiences and accommodates thinking to those experiences. An event that seems innocuous to an adult may quite logically appear menacing to the young preoperational child. Thus, not only do children exhibit more fears than adults, but the *content* of these fears changes as the child develops.

The following sketches of some children and their fears may illustrate the cognitive processes and emotional needs that influence developmental changes related to fears.

Louis and the babysitter. Seven-month-old Louis sat in his high chair, banging a spoon against the tray. Suddenly his happy expression changed to one of sober alertness and then to fear and distress. He turned his head and began to wail. Marge, his babysitter, was confused. What had she done to upset Louis?

Fear of strangers is one of the first fears parents and caregivers notice in infants. Before 7 or 8 months, Louis often showed distress when he was hungry, wet, or tired, but it could not be said he showed fear. What's happening now?

The child's changing *interpretation* of the situation influences the appearance of fearful behavior during the first year of life (see Lewis & Rosenblum 1974). In the second half of that year, changes occur in infants' awareness of the unfamiliar (Kagan 1974; Shaffer 1974). Louis has recently acquired a memory or mental representation of his mother and other familiar people. Once he has such a standard to draw upon, he becomes aware of Marge's status as an unfamiliar person who does not match this mental image or schema. Sometimes, especially if the mother is holding the child in well-known surroundings, this kind of unfamiliarity causes the baby to become more interested (Sroufe 1974). But if the newness —the discrepancy between the familiar

and the unfamiliar—is too great, or if other aspects of the situation contribute to wariness, the baby may "evaluate" the situation as threatening rather than interesting.

Paco and the haircut. Mrs. Velez, a teacher at 18-month-old Paco's day care center, had always worn her black hair long and loose. One Monday morning she appeared with a new, much shorter hairdo. Paco stared at her, burst into tears when she spoke to him, and refused to come near her for the rest of the day.

As children enter their second and third year, their fearful reactions increase and extend beyond the fear of strangers. While there are many individual differences in the kinds of things toddlers may find fearful, Paco's reaction to his teacher's haircut illustrates the fear of transformations or changes in familiar things.

Understanding how children interpret such transformations helps explain their distressed reaction. Objects and people have an identity that is maintained despite surface changes. A table is a table whether it is viewed from above or underneath, and Mrs. Velez is Mrs. Velez whether her hair is long or short—a self-evident truth to an adult, but difficult for young children like Paco to grasp. He can not be sure that his teacher is really the same person with a new haircut. The same thinking process influences toddlers' fears of other transformations—Halloween masks, wigs, new glasses, a doll with a missing arm, a slowly collapsing balloon.

Amanda and the vacuum cleaner. Two-year-old Amanda runs to hide in her crib whenever her mother vacuums, and now she will not go near

the machine even when it is turned off. Her mother has tried to explain how it works, but nothing seems to help.

Our technological society depends on inanimate objects that perform obediently at human command. But toddlers see these lifeless gadgets as less docile than they really are. Young children attribute their own feelings and motives to everything around them, including inanimate objects like vacuum cleaners (Piaget 1929). To Amanda the vacuum cleaner is a noisy, all-devouring creature that will consume her like a piece of household debris. The toilet, chiming clocks, fire engines, water hoses, and escalators also appear threatening to some young children as a result of their egocentric and animistic interpretation of the object's function (see Fraiberg 1959).

Peter and the monster. Four-year-old Peter was having a hard time napping at school. After one tearful session, he confided to his teacher that he was afraid that a monster was hiding in the closet and would come out if he closed his eyes.

Unlike Paco and Amanda's concrete fears, the fears of older preschoolers often appear in response to imaginary dangers—monsters, ghosts, bad dreams, Frankenstein. The influence of television provides only a partial explanation, since younger and older children may be exposed to the same material and react differently.

The appearance of these imaginary fears is again related to children's intellectual development. Peter can symbolize or mentally represent what he has never seen (Piaget 1951). This ability enormously extends his potential for learning. But in these years

---

Specific information that allows children to anticipate and predict what will happen in a scary situation will give them an increased feeling of control over their lives.

---

during which children are just beginning the "conquest of the symbol" (Elkind 1974), the dividing line between symbol and referent, between fantasy and reality, is thin indeed.

Songs, stories, television—or the child's own imagination—may produce inventions that blur the distinction between "real" and "just pretend." Often these creations are strikingly wild and fierce. Peter had been having a hard time with his own aggressive feelings; his angry outbursts scared him more than they scared his classmates. Like many 4-year-olds, he is both fascinated by and fearful of aggression. No wonder his imaginary world is populated by untamed monsters.

Shawn and the tornado. Shawn is 8. She has never told anyone, but she is afraid of tornadoes. Every time she sees dark clouds on the horizon, she expects to see a funnel snake down and roar toward her house.

At Shawn's age, more realistic fears begin to take the place of the monsters and ghosts of a few years before. Natural disasters such as tornadoes, floods, and fires, or concerns about injury and illness, worry the schoolage child (Maurer 1965; Bauer 1976), who has begun to differentiate more clearly between what is pretend and what is real. Still, the dangers Shawn and her contemporaries fear are unlikely to occur. She does not yet think in terms of the probability of an event; if a tornado happened somewhere else, she feels it could happen to her. Again, her developing cognitive abilities will gradually help her make a less egocentric and more accurate assessment of potential dangers.

* * *

These examples suggest a pattern in the developmental sequence of children's fears. Fears begin in infancy with unfamiliar versions of concrete objects or persons. In the later preschool years imaginary, symbolic fears appear. In the school years children's attention shifts to more concrete, realistic concerns. These changes seem to be tied to important changes in the cognitive processes through which children interpret and evaluate the significance of a po-

tentially threatening event, as well as to changes in the social and emotional issues that dominate children's needs.

Individual fear patterns

The trends just described provide an overview of general developmental changes in children's fears, but each child has an individual pattern.

Some children are, from their earliest months, more aware of and sensitive to visual novelty. This tendency may, especially in boys, predict later fearfulness (Bronson 1970). Paco, who was so upset by his teacher's haircut, is always the first to notice a new toy or a chair out of place.

Individual experiences and concerns may influence the intensity and the content of fears. Shawn's home was damaged by a windstorm several years ago.

Once a fear is established, it may persist because of the emotional rewards or "secondary gains" a child receives. Peter's monster worries, while genuine, also provide him with his teacher's undivided attention and concern.

Jeff's reaction to that lobster illustrates both developmental and individual patterns of fear. Although an adult would realize the lobster meant no harm, Jeff's interpretation was quite different. Jeff had no mental slot for this unfamiliar creature—the lobster was unassimilable to his limited experience. Using his own motives as an egocentric standard by which to judge the lobster, Jeff sized up its forward movement and waving claws as signs of hostile intentions. Since Jeff had been a biter, he was inclined to see others as possible biters, too. Later, at his day care center, Jeff reacted to the picture—the symbol—as if it were real. The picture *was* the lobster. It is likely, too, that Jeff received a few "secondary gains" from the whole episode in the form of extra lap time from mother and teacher.

Recognizing fear

Although most young children have fears, it is not always easy to recognize when a child is afraid. While an infant

will usually cry loudly when frightened, older children's reactions are more varied. One child who is afraid of dogs may scream and run away from an approaching dog; another may stand frozen in panic. It isn't hard to tell that these children are afraid, but other signs are more difficult to detect. The child who shows an exaggerated fascination with dogs, constantly asking about them and looking for them, may be as worried as the others. Or the child who shows no reaction in a situation where fear would be expected may be deeply fearful under that unconcerned exterior. It takes careful observation and sensitivity to children to recognize when fear is being expressed.

Helping with fears

Knowing the kinds of fears to expect in children, and understanding the reasons for those fears, what can adults do to help?

One thing to do is to wait. Children's fears, even those intense enough to be classified as phobias, usually disappear without any special treatment (Miller et al. 1972). Jerry's fear of the toilet, for instance, will very likely disappear as he gets older. He will acquire information and experience—after hundreds of visits to the bathroom where he never is flushed away. His animistic beliefs about toilets will gradually change to a recognition that toilets differ from people in a number of significant ways. The desire to hold on to his bodily products (and therefore the fear of the instrument that whisks them out of sight) will become less powerful. As the reasons for his fear disappear, so will the fear itself.

In the meantime, sensitive adults may be able to help children cope with their fears by using the following techniques:

● Talk about fears. Although reassurances and rational explanations will not always help, children who can put their worst fears into words (or maybe into drawing pictures) may be better able to manage them. Sometimes a good book can pave the way to a helpful discussion.

● Provide opportunities for dramatic play. One of the many functions of play in children's development is the chance it gives them to re-create and master scary feelings and experiences. Through play, the child who is afraid of being left with a sitter may become a parent leaving the child-doll at home and then returning; the child who is afraid of the doctor can sometimes be seen gleefully giving shots to all the stuffed animals. Turnabout is indeed fair play.

• If a child is afraid of a specific object, try presenting it in smaller, less threatening forms first. For example, introduce a tiny puppy before a full-grown German shepherd, toy fire engines before a visit to see real ones, a dishpan of water before a swimming pool. Therapists find that this sort of gradual desensitization works well in treating serious phobias (Marks 1969). Teachers can use similar techniques informally.

• Focus on underlying cognitive skills. A child who is afraid of masks, for example, may need many concrete experiences with object permanence (the concept that a person or thing retains its identity even when it is transformed or out of sight). Even older children enjoy peek-a-boo, hide-and-seek, or games in which small objects are hidden and found again. A good way to begin with an especially fearful child is to let the child control the hiding and the finding, putting a cloth over the teacher's face and removing it.

• If a child's fears seem to be centered around a particular conflict or need, it may be more helpful to work on that need than on the fear itself. An understanding teacher can help Peter deal with his own angry feelings through talk, play, or constructive problem solving. Better awareness of and control over his own aggression may reduce Peter's fear of the monster's symbolic aggression. In the process, the monster may go somewhere else to live.

• If the child's fearful behavior seems to be persisting because of the secondary gains that are rewarding it, the child can be helped to achieve those rewards through other channels. By hugging Amanda when she is not afraid (as well as comforting her when

she is frightened, of course), her teacher can give Amanda the affection she needs without selectively reinforcing her fearful behavior.

• Broaden the range of a child's coping skills (Murphy and Moriarty 1976). A baby has only one reaction available when frightened—crying. As children grow older, they begin to develop alternative ways of dealing with fear and stress. The more alternatives they have, the better they can cope with their feelings. Adults can help children increase their sense of control over their lives. Vague reassurances ("Don't worry about the doctor, dear") will not help much. Specific information that allows children to anticipate and predict what will happen in a scary situation ("These are the things the doctor will do when she arrives. Here are the kinds of instruments she will use.") will give them an increased feeling of competence (Kanfer, Karoby, and Newman 1975). Knowing and practicing alternative behaviors also reduces a child's sense of panicked helplessness. Teachers can help children practice "What could you do if a big dog came up to you? If it started to thunder? If you got lost?" The point is not to come up with a specific answer, but to help children think of many solutions to problems. Then, when confronted by a potentially threatening event, they have options: They can back away, shout, close their eyes, hold someone's hand, ask questions.

Just as children like Jeff, Paco, and Amanda are active participants in the creation of their own fears, they can be active participants in overcoming them. It is easy to forget that most children *want* to grow up and become competent and effective people. By understanding how children interpret their world, with its opportunities and dangers, adults can help them in this task.

Bibliography

Bauer, D. H. "An Exploratory Study of Developmental Changes in Children's Fears." *Journal of Child Psychology and Psychiatry* 17 (1976): 59–74.

Berecz, J. M. "Phobias of Childhood: Etiology and Treatment." *Psychological Bulletin* 70 (1968): 694–720.

Bowlby, J. *Separation*. Attachment and Loss, vol. 2. New York: Basic Books, 1973.

Bronson, G. W. "Fear of Visual Novelty: Developmental Patterns in Males and Females." *Developmental Psychology* 2 (1970): 33–40.

Bronson, G. W. "Infants' Reactions to Unfamiliar Persons and Novel Objects." *Monographs of the Society for Research in Child Development* 37, no. 3 (1972): serial no. 148.

Dunn, J. *Distress and Comfort*. Cambridge, Mass.: Harvard University Press, 1977.

Elkind, D. *Children and Adolescents: Interpretive Essays on Jean Piaget*. 2nd ed. New York: Oxford University Press, 1974.

Fraiberg, S. *The Magic Years*. New York: Scribner, 1959.

Kagan, J. "Discrepancy, Temperament, and Infant Distress." In *The Origins of Fear*, ed. M. Lewis and L. A. Rosenblum. New York: Wiley, 1974.

Kanfer, F. H.; Karoly, P.; and Newman, A. "Reduction of Children's Fear of the Dark by Competence-Related and Situational Threat-Related Verbal Cues." *Journal of Consulting and Clinical Psychology* 43, no. 2 (1975): 251–258.

Lewis, M., and Rosenblum, L. A., eds. *The Origins of Fear*. New York: Wiley, 1974.

Marks, I. M. *Fears and Phobias*. London: Academic Press, 1969.

Maurer, A. "What Children Fear." *Journal of Genetic Psychology* 106 (1965): 265–277.

Miller, L. C., et al. "Comparison of Reciprocal Inhibition, Psychotherapy, and Waiting List Control for Phobic Children." *Journal of Abnormal Psychology* 79 (1972): 269–279.

Murphy, L. B., and Moriarty, A. E. *Vulnerability, Coping, and Growth*. New Haven, Conn.: Yale University Press, 1976.

Piaget, J. *The Child's Conception of the World*. London: Routledge & Kegan Paul, 1929.

Piaget, J. *Play, Dreams, and Imitation in Childhood*. New York: Norton, 1951.

Shaffer, H. R. "Cognitive Components of the Infant's Response to Strangers." In *The Origins of Fear*, ed. M. Lewis and L. A. Rosenblum. New York: Wiley, 1974.

Sroufe, L. A.; Waters, E.; and Matas, L. "Contextual Determinants of Infant Affective Response." In *The Origins of Fear*, ed. M. Lewis and L. A. Rosenblum. New York: Wiley, 1974.

Wolman, B. *Children's Fears*. New York: Grosset and Dunlap, 1978.

Living
With
He-Man
Managing Superhero Fantasy Play

Marjorie J. Kostelnik
Alice P. Whiren
Laura C. Stein

*J*onathan runs into the classroom, charges over to the block cabinet, and selects a long, thin board. He shoves it under his sweater, takes a fighting stance, and announces, "I have the power." He laughingly advances toward his playmates, who run from him, leaping, shouting, and giggling. Another day of superhero play has begun.

*S*uperhero play is a common event in the lives of young children, and there is little doubt they find the role exhilarating. Teachers and some parents are not so enthusiastic. We often object to the rowdy nature of the play and feel frustrated when children have difficulty shedding the superhero image during nonpretend activities such as eating, sitting at group time, or resting. As a result, we may seriously question the advisability of allowing such play. In fact, many of us forbid children to take on superhero roles and actively squelch such play whenever we see it.

In this article we will examine why children find superhero play so attractive and discuss how it relates to children's development. In addition, we will make a case for why this

Marjorie J. Kostelnik, Ph.D., is Associate Professor and Program Supervisor of the Child Development Laboratories, Michigan State University, East Lansing, Michigan.

Alice P. Whiren, Ph.D., is Associate Professor in the Department of Family and Child Ecology, Michigan State University, East Lansing, Michigan.

Laura C. Stein, M.S., is a child development specialist in the Department of Family and Child Ecology and head teacher of the Child Development Laboratories, Michigan State University, East Lansing, Michigan.

play should be allowed and suggest strategies to make superhero play a constructive experience for children.

Origin of superheroes

The modern day superhero/superheroine evolved in the United States after World War I, flourished throughout the 1940s and 50s, and has enjoyed renewed life in recent years. Children first met superheroes in pulp magazines and comics, then through the radio and movies, and finally through the current crop of Saturday morning cartoons. The roster includes such favorites as Buck Rogers (1929), Superman (1938), Batman (1939), Mary Marvel (1940), Wonder Woman (1941), Captain America (1941), Luke Skywalker (1976), Princess Leia (1976), and He-Man (1983).

Each of these characters has been endowed with powers and qualities which embody the best of human nature and which have ensured their appeal over time. These superheroes and superheroines

- Are unquestionably good. Their virtues are absolute. They are wise, fearless, clever, and strong.
- Possess powers children wish they themselves had. They demonstrate incredible speed, strength, or endurance in addition to being able to fly, swim under water for miles, or change the shape of their bodies.
- Solve every problem and overcome all obstacles. They never have to settle for the unsatisfactory compromises that characterize the real world. Their solutions are always accepted.

Young children meet challenges and demonstrate physical prowess through superhero play.

Glossary of terms

collective symbolization—The collaboration of all children in a group who agree on a theme; assign new meanings to roles, situations, and objects; and who share all the meanings with the group.

instrumental aggression—The physical encounter resulting from disputes over rights, privileges, or possessions. The aggression is a by-product of the interaction, rather than its aim.

object substitutions—The substitution of one object for another. For example, a stick becomes a spoon or a weapon; a towel becomes a magic cape or a healing blanket.

situation substitutions—The *reality* of the situation is altered by time, location, and circumstances. For example, the block corner becomes a space ship.

transformations—The process of altering objects, time, situations, and roles mentally, through pretend play. For example, the child transforms herself into a superheroine, one who travels through space (on a large block) and heals the sick and injured with a powerful blanket (the towel).

- Are in control. Others look to them for guidance and are eager to do their bidding. No one tells them what to do.
- Know what is right. They never make a mistake and are not subject to the doubts, frustrations, and weaknesses which plague ordinary mortals.
- Receive accolades and recognition from powerful adults. There is no doubt that they are well-liked members of their society. Everyone wants to be their friend.

Benefits for children

It is not surprising, then, that children find the superhero image an attractive one to imitate. Children have little power in a world dominated by adults and they are well aware of this. Yet, through their play, they can take on a powerful, potent role through which they can dominate a villian or a situation with no real risk to themselves (Curry, 1971). With relative ease, they can shift from the restricted role of child to the boundless world of superhero. Feelings of fear, vulnerability, and uncertainty can be overcome and transformed through playful demonstrations of courage, strength, and wisdom (Slobin, 1976).

Thus, superhero play gives children access to power and prestige unavailable to them in daily experiences (Pulaski, 1976). It helps them build self-confidence at a time when they are struggling with real-life obstacles which are not always so predictably vanquished: dressing themselves, making friends, toilet training, eating without spilling, and otherwise meeting adult expectations and standards. This imaginary achievement of control over one's own and others' lives is gratifying (Walder, 1976) and enables children to play out wishful fantasies (Peller, 1971).

Superhero fantasy also gives children the opportunity to pretend to be someone they admire and would like to resemble but whom they are as yet unequipped to imitate fully in real-life encounters. Additionally, it allows children to take on the attributes of those they fear, enabling them to become master of the fear for the moment (Peller, 1971). This explains why some choose loathsome personalities to portray such as Jabba the Hutt or Dracula. In this way, children may exhibit a love-hate relationship with the character, one day reveling in its repulsiveness, the next day expressing antipathy or trepidation.

In addition, because superheroes are *all good* and antiheroes are *all bad,* children have clear, precise models for imitation. The cues such characters offer for emulation are obvious and easy to follow (Slobin, 1976). This is not at all the case with real-life models whose behavior is often too ambiguous and complex for children to figure out easily. In this way, superhero play helps children create a way to experiment with ideals and values. It enables children to make concrete ideals which our society prizes but which are abstract and difficult to grasp, such as honor, justice, courage, honesty, and mercy.

Finally, as with all other types of dramatic play, children improve their language skills, problem solving, and cooper-

ation. They benefit from opportunities to build shared social relationships with peers and to establish, follow, and change the rules they set up in a particular episode. Sensorimotor skills, divergent thinking, and creativity are also enhanced when children pretend with one another (Edmonds, 1976; Saltz & Brodie, 1982; Saltz & Johnson, 1977).

The nature of superhero play

Just as in any other kind of dramatic play, the flow of superhero play episodes is determined to a considerable extent by children's ages, dramatic play skill, information about the theme, amount of uninterrupted time available, location, materials for props, and playmates. Transformations using realistic props occur at about the age of 2 (Fein & Appel, 1979) while object and situation substitutions appear later (Overton & Jackson, 1973).

The ability to take on a role is learned gradually during the first 4 years, until an experienced child is able to select relevant gestures, voices, and actions suited to one or more characters. When collective symbolization (Fein & Appel, 1979) occurs, it is because all the children in the group are able to produce all the transformations on objects, situations, and roles, as well as to negotiate the play arrangements.

Difficulties, as perceived by adults, are more likely to arise from the players' lack of skills or knowledge than as a result of the play theme chosen. For example, less skilled players sometimes attach themselves to the superhero play of more experienced players and become lost or confused in the fast action segments. The just pretend of some children's play may be perceived by others as frightening reality.

On some occasions, children may become involved in incidents of instrumental aggression (Feshbach & Feshbach, 1972) as they struggle over establishing turns, rights to possessions, or staking out the territory in which the play will take place. It should be noted that instrumental aggression reaches its peak during the preschool years (Hartup, 1974), a period which coincides with the most obvious manifestations of superhero play.

Superhero themes

The dominant themes of capture and rescue, submit or vanquish, and attack and flee are not unique to superhero play, but evolve naturally from children's interactions in dramatic play.

For instance, Garvey's study (1976) of children's social play episodes reveals three standard plots that appear in a general sequence. First, children enact simple *domestic scenes,* such as cooking, tucking the baby in bed, setting the table, or putting the garbage out. Eventually children move into a second motif, *the rescue.* In such situations, one child announces that the pet is sick, or the doll is dead, or there is no food in the house. Other players then come to the rescue, offering care, sympathy, food, and suggestions.

A third theme which subsequently develops involves the *sudden threat.* This generally results from the appearance of a monster. Children alternately or simultaneously play the role of victim and/or defender, fleeing or attacking as warranted. Such episodes can end triumphantly with children announcing, "I got him," or tragically, "He ate me—I'm dead." In addition, it is not unusual for children to select some neutral person, often an adult or nonparticipating child, who is designated as the monster and from whom everyone runs (Arnaud, 1971). The game becomes an exhilarating combination of chasing and shrieking with children eventually taking over the role of monster themselves.

Rough-and-tumble play

As these play themes develop, behaviors such as running, leaping, shouting, and wrestling are typical. Children spend much of their time engaged in mock battles and feigned attacks. When such behaviors are accompanied by "play face," laughing and smiling, they are referred to as rough-and-tumble play (Blurton-Jones, 1976). Rough-and-tumble play is an important part of the daily activities of young children and is not confined to superhero play alone. It occurs most often among children who know each other well. In fact, newcomers and less accepted peers have more difficulty joining rough-and-tumble play than any other play form (Garvey, 1976).

Adults sometimes mistake the rough-and-tumble nature of superhero play as aggression. However, the jumping up and down, laughter, and interrupted attack movements (a child may strike out and shout "pow" but will not make contact with the other player) which occur are all inconsistent with real fighting (Blurton-Jones, 1976).

The actual cue to real aggression is when children frown, scowl, or cry, or when they do not stop an attack until victims show clearly that they are hurt (Perry & Perry, 1976). Rough-and-tumble superhero play, on the other hand, is accompanied by smiles, laughter, and/or a clear statement of intent, "Let's play fight." Thus, the same motor behaviors may be present in both types of interactions, but it is the expression on the child's face which signals the difference.

Young children learn many things through rough-and-tumble play with age-mates which are not possible in adult-child relations (Hartup, 1982). For instance, children learn aggressive skills: how to defend themselves, or how to make another person angry. They also learn aggressive controls: how to dissipate their own anger, how to resist the temptation to attack someone else, or how to turn a conflict situation into one of compromise. Children learn these appropriate aggressive reactions only in contacts with individuals who are their equal in size and developmental status.

Mastery play

Finally, a vital aspect of superhero play involves children's opportunity to meet challenges and demonstrate physical prowess: hanging upside down from the monkey bars, jumping off the stairs, taking the steps two at a time, or riding bikes without using hands. Activities like these lead to the mastery of new skills and a feeling of control. Such mastery play occurs throughout early childhood, beginning with physical mastery of the environment, and eventually leading to intellectual mastery of words, ideas, and problems of logic (Berger, 1980).

Young children, especially, practice such skills **within the context of pretend play.** This is true regardless of whether the character jumping over the crate is Superman, a prancing pony doing tricks in the circus, or a mother rushing to save her baby.

Strategies for adults

While we often agree that the benefits of superhero play are desirable, we may still object to superhero play for fear that things will get out of hand, that the classroom will be disrupted, or that children may be injured. This concern often stems from our observation that children misinterpret the superhero role as one of simply zapping all the bad guys.

Superhero play enables children to make concrete ideals which our society prizes but which are abstract and difficult to grasp, such as honor, justice, courage, honesty, and mercy.

Rod Gilbert

While it is true that superhero play can disintegrate into conflict or escalate into actions beyond children's ability to reverse, **such difficulties are likely to arise in other dramatic play episodes as well.** Remember, children develop their play themes around their understanding of roles and situations. Although children have some information about superheroes from television, books, movies, or conversations with peers, they may need an adult to translate the competence, power, and virtue of the superhero into their own play episodes. Children's mistaken notion that the superhero's power is used to knock everybody flat is no less a misconception than other still developing understandings they may have, such as that firefighters use their hoses to start fires, or that mail originates in the post office. These misconceptions can be corrected when children are given more information.

Here are some suggestions about how teachers and parents can give children the information and environment they need to make superhero play a constructive experience.

Help children recognize the humane characteristics of the superheroes they admire. Children can become so caught up in the strength, courage, and power of their superhero that they fail to see the qualities of kindness, helpfulness, and generosity which are also part of the heroic personality. Point these out to children at opportune times. Discuss ways in which they can be kind and sensitive to the needs of others. Praise children when they exhibit such behaviors and draw parallels between their acts and those of the heroes they admire. For example, you might make a comment such as "Kendra, you must have felt as helpful as Superwoman when you carried the chairs to the table for our snack!"

Some ways to manage superhero play:

- help children recognize humane characteristics of superheroes
- discuss real heroes and heroines
- talk about the pretend world of acting
- limit the place and time for superhero play
- explore related concepts
- help children develop goals for superheroes
- help children de-escalate rough-and-tumble play
- make it clear that aggression is unacceptable
- give children control over their lives
- praise children's attempts at mastery

Discuss real heroes and heroines with children. Introduce them to people such as Johnny Appleseed, Martin Luther King, Jr., Elizabeth Blackwell, Jackie Robinson, and Helen Keller. Point out the attributes that make them heroic. Talk about ways all people can be superheroes.

Talk with children about the pretend world of acting when they report watching programs in which live performers portray superheroes. Describe all the safety preparations entertainers make before they pretend to fly, leap from tall buildings, or jump over speeding cars. Discuss with children ways to pretend to carry out such feats and the precautions they must take in their play.

Limit the place and time in which superhero play is allowed. Determine where and when superhero play will be permitted. Acceptable locations may be outside or indoors in spaces free of obstructions. Permissible times may be during free choice or recess as opposed to lunch or rest time. Tell toddlers what the limits are. Older children can help decide what the rules will be—this is a good opportunity to include children in the decision-making process.

Once determined, rules must be applied consistently. It is confusing if on one occasion children are told flying belongs outside and on another are asked to show a visitor how beautifully they fly at a time and in a space previously forbidden! Avoid prohibiting superhero play altogether. When we forbid such play, we deprive children of the opportunity to choose what to play and where. Children need to balance the demands of the real world with their desires to pretend.

Build on superhero characteristics to help children explore related concepts. Children's interest in superheroes can serve as a springboard to enhance their understanding of the natural world. Children who play Batman may find a study of bats and bat caves interesting. Activities about animal flight, travel, or X-rays can result from children's fascination with Superman or Wonder Woman. Talk with children about why the spider motif is so appropriate for Spiderman—introduce information about spiders and their webs. The Star Wars series is a good starting place from which to talk about intergalactic travel, life in space, and the peaceful uses of space.

Help children develop goals for the superhero to pursue. Any dramatic play episode can deteriorate if the children define roles and characters and then are at a loss for what to do next. This dilemma can lead to nonproductive activity. Our role at this point is to help children restructure the play constructively. We can assist children in figuring out a plan or scenario within which the superheroes can pretend. For instance, they might plot a rescue operation that requires a specific series of actions or a treasure hunt, complete with superhero-made maps and digging tools.

Help children de-escalate rough-and-tumble play that is in danger of becoming truly aggressive. Potential aggression can be avoided when adults observe children as they play and watch for early signs of difficulty (Caldwell, 1977). If children stop laughing; if their voices become strident or complaining; if their facial expressions show fear, anger, or distress; and if their verbalizations move out of the realm of pretend into real menace, aggression is imminent.

You must intervene when aggression is about to erupt, either by becoming directly involved in the play yourself or by redirecting it. You may need to give children information, offer assistance, help them reevaluate their goals, break the task into more manageable steps, or offer a way for them to take a break before resuming their play.

Teach children to give a clear message when they want the play to stop. Children can learn to say, "I'm not playing" or "Let's not play anymore" or "I'm getting scared for real," as a signal to halt a play episode which is on the brink of chaos.

When the play goes awry, help children understand what happened. Frequently, children are surprised when one of them is injured or frightened during play. We can provide valuable information when we say, "Jennifer didn't know you were playing," or "That was a real hit, not a pretend hit."

Provide a safety zone for children who wish to escape from the superhero play. For some children, the intensity of play may be too much. Adults can work with children to establish a place for retreat where neither heroes nor villains are allowed.

Make it clear that aggression is unacceptable. When physical or verbal aggression occurs during superhero play, step in immediately. Stop children's aggressive acts and make it clear that such behavior will not be tolerated. Express your concerns and give a reason for why a particular action is unacceptable. Suggest specific alternative behaviors for younger children to pursue. Help older children generate their own ideas for a more constructive way to achieve their aims. Clearly state the consequences for continued aggression and carry them out immediately should children persist.

Provide opportunities for children to exercise control over their lives. Adults bestow power to children when they offer real choices for them. Children may select clean-up jobs, with whom to play, which pair of mittens to wear, or how they will solve a particular problem. While such issues may seem insignificant to adults, they represent important decisions to children. When we frequently offer choices, we show confidence in children's ability to take on responsibility, not only in the fantasy world of superhero play, but in everyday living.

Present appropriate challenges to children throughout the day. It is important for children to feel competent as they interact with people and materials. Children who are bored because activities are too easy and those who are frustrated by materials which are too advanced will find it difficult to experience the satisfaction that comes from accomplishment. Such children may find superhero play to be one of the few avenues available to develop their skills. Providing challenging activities will not eliminate superhero play, but will help children achieve a sense of mastery in both pretend and real situations.

Praise children's attempts at mastery. Children benefit when their efforts to improve their skills are acknowledged. It builds their confidence and self-esteem when adults appreciate the hard work children put into buttoning their coats, making a puzzle piece fit, constructing a tower, writing

As with all other types of dramatic play, children improve their language skills, problem solving, and cooperation through superhero play.

Subjects & Predicates

Aggression is imminent in children's play if

- children stop laughing
- their voices become strident or complaining
- facial expressions show fear, anger, or distress
- talk moves from pretend into real menace

To interrupt aggression, you must become involved or redirect the play. You can

- give children information
- offer assistance
- help children reevaluate goals
- break the task into more manageable steps
- offer a way for them to take a break

their name, or making a new friend. Comments such as, "You're really trying hard" or "You've been working a long time" show children these accomplishments count and they can receive recognition for real situations.

Offer support and comfort to older children who discover flaws in their heroes. As children mature, they often select real people to be their heroes or heroines. In time they may recognize these people are not perfect. Kind words from an understanding adult can ease the disillusionment and pain such a discovery often brings. Adults can share with older children similar experiences from their own lives. In this way, adults and children can build bonds of mutual understanding.

Conclusion

Superhero play is a specialized form of dramatic play that has considerable appeal for young children. While we encourage children's involvement in other dramatic play themes, superhero play is often seen as too noisy, chaotic, or violent. Yet superhero play is not all bad. It offers numerous opportunities for children to gain a sense of mastery and empowerment, as well as providing other developmentally appropriate benefits commonly associated with dramatic play.

While we do not suggest that you actively promote superhero play, plan superhero units, or discourage other forms of

dramatic play, we do hope you will keep an open perspective when superhero play arises naturally from children's interactions with one another. The strategies outlined here can help you feel more comfortable with this dramatic play theme.

References

Arnaud, S. (1971). The dramatic play of six- to ten-year-olds. In N. E. Curry & S. Arnaud (Eds.), *Play: The child strives toward self-realization.* Washington, DC: National Association for the Education of Young Children.

Blurton-Jones, N. (1976). Rough-and-tumble play among nursery school children. In J. Bruner, A. Jolly, & K. Sylva (Eds.), *Play: Its role in development and evolution* (pp. 352–363). New York: Basic Books.

Berger, K. S. (1980). *The developing person.* New York: Worth.

Caldwell, B. M. (1977, January). Aggression and hostility in young children. *Young Children, 32* (2), 4–13.

Curry, N. E. (1971). Five-year-old play. In N. E. Curry & S. Arnaud (Eds.), *Play: The child strives toward self-realization* (pp. 10–11). Washington, DC: National Association for the Education of Young Children.

Edmonds, H. (1976). New directions in theories of language acquisition. *Harvard Educational Review, 46* (2), 175–195.

Fein, G., & Appel, N. (1979). Some preliminary observations on knowing and pretending. In N. R. Smith & M. B. Franklin (Eds.), *Symbolic functioning in childhood* (pp. 87–100). Hillsdale, NJ: Erlbaum.

Feshbach, N., & Feshbach, S. (1972). Children's aggression. In W. Hartup (Ed.), *The young child: Reviews of research. Vol. 1.* Washington, DC: National Association for the Education of Young Children.

Garvey, C. (1976). Some properties of social play. In J. S. Bruner, A. Jolly, & K. Sylva (Eds.), *Play: Its role in development and evolution* (pp. 570-583). New York: Basic Books.

Hartup, W. (1982). Peer relationships. In C. B. Kopp & J. B. Krakow (Eds.), *Child development in a social context* (pp. 516–575). Reading, MA: Addison-Wesley.

Hartup, W. (1974). Aggression in childhood: Developmental perspectives. *American Psychologist, 29,* 336–341.

Overton, W. F., & Jackson, J. P. (1973). The representation of imagined objects in action sequences: A developmental study. *Child Development, 44,* 309–313.

Peller, L. (1971). Models of children's play. In R. Herron & B. Sutton-Smith (Eds.), *Child's play* (pp. 110–125). New York: Wiley.

Perry, D. G., & Perry, L. C. (1976). A note on the effects of prior anger arousal and winning or losing a competition on aggressive behavior in boys. *Journal of Child Psychology and Psychiatry, 17,* 145–149.

Pulaski, M. A. (1976). Play symbolism in cognitive development. In C. Schaefer (Ed.), *Therapeutic use of child's play* (pp. 27–42). New York: Aronson.

Saltz, E. D., & Brodie, J. (1982). Pretend-play training in childhood: A review and critique. In D. J. Pepler & K. H. Rubin (Eds.), *The play of children: Current theory and research* (pp. 97–113). New York: S. Karger.

Saltz, E. D., & Johnson, J. (1977). Training disadvantaged preschoolers on various fantasy activities: Effects on cognitive functioning and impulse control. *Child Development, 48,* 367–380.

Slobin, D. (1976). The role of play in childhood. In C. Shaefer (Ed.), *Therapeutic use of child's play* (pp. 95–118). New York: Aronson.

Walder, R. (1976). Psychoanalytic theory of play. In C. Shaefer (Ed.), *Therapeutic use of child's play* (pp. 79–94). New York: Aronson.

Sex Education with Young Children

Sally Koblinsky, Jean Atkinson, and Shari Davis

Michael (age 3) is watching Katherine (age 3) undress for swimming. As she begins to pull up her bathing suit, he stoops down to stare at her genital area. Student teacher Mary approaches the children with a frown on her face. Taking Michael by the hand, she states, "That's not nice. Go over and play with the boys."

The previous incident, recorded in Oregon State University's Child Development Laboratory, illustrates the anxiety and discomfort many teachers and parents experience in responding to children's sexual curiosity. Although early childhood is considered to be an important period in the formation of sexual attitudes (Gagnon 1965; Woody 1973), most adults have little background knowledge for dealing with children's sexual feelings and behaviors. A review of early childhood education texts reveals that the topic of sex education is generally omitted or limited to a discussion of plant reproduction.

Many teachers and parents want to learn more about children's emerging sexuality. Their daily experiences with children have increased their awareness of how much sexual learning occurs in the early years. Between the ages of 2 and 6, children become aware of genital differences between the sexes; express curiosity about reproduction and birth; develop childhood romances; and engage in various types of sex play. Although many of us associate the topic of sex education with adolescence, young children ask more sex-related questions than do children in any other age group (Hattendorf 1932; Strain 1948).

Because young children are curious about human sexuality, more extensive teacher training is clearly needed in this area. Although parents remain the primary sex educators of their children, teachers may facilitate the child's sexual learning and supply guidance for anxious mothers and fathers. We have been exploring ways in which teachers and parents may complement one another's efforts in providing responsible sex education. The Oregon State University Early Childhood Sex Education Project was initiated in the spring of 1978. We asked 150 parents of 3- to 5-year-old children in our Child Development Laboratory and community day care centers to complete questionnaires dealing with their attitudes toward sex education and responses to children's sexual behaviors. Meetings were held with parents to discuss early sex education and to explore parental expectations concerning the teacher's role in this process.

In response to the concerns of both parents and teachers, we have attempted to develop guidelines for sex education with young children. These guidelines are based upon our research (Koblinsky, Atkinson, and Davis 1979) and that of others, as well as the wisdom of fellow early childhood educators.

Guidelines for teaching

Genital differences

By the age of 3, most children can distinguish between males and females (Gesell and Ilg 1949; Kreitler and Kreitler 1965). Although early distinctions are generally based on clothing and hairstyles, children soon become inquisitive about genital differences between the sexes. Such curiosity may be revealed in questions like "Why is Megan different?" or "Why don't I have a thing like Philip?" Adults who straightforwardly respond to those questions may provide a foundation for healthy and open communication about sexuality.

Use correct vocabulary. Children need correct terms for labeling their genitals, just as they need correct terms for other body parts (Calderone 1966; Gordon 1974). Such terms not only help them to learn about human anatomy, but also give them a vocabulary with which to ask questions.

Slang or nicknames such as pee pee or wiener are generally inappropriate for genitalia. Not only will children have to relearn new terms, but they may also suffer embarrassment when they use family words in the presence of their peers.

Adults frequently wonder about what terms to use in explaining genital differences. Our research indicates that

Sally Koblinsky, Ph.D., is Assistant Professor, Family Studies and Consumer Sciences, San Diego State University, San Diego, California.

Jean Atkinson, M.S., is a Doctoral student in Human Development and Family Studies, The Pennsylvania State University, University Park, Pennsylvania.

Shari Davis, M.S., is a Doctoral student in the Department of Family Life, Oregon State University, Corvallis, Oregon.

adults are more likely to provide children with labels for the male genitals than the female (Koblinsky, Atkinson, and Davis 1979). This finding probably reflects the greater visibility of the male organs. Moreover, adults may have difficulty deciding which female organs (vulva, vagina, clitoris, labia, uterus) should be introduced to children. While young children may be confused by too many different labels, they need to know that both males and females possess unique and equally valuable genitalia. Therefore, one response to questions about body differences might be to say "Girls and boys are made differently. Girls have a vagina and boys have a penis."

Provide natural opportunities for children to observe each other. One natural place for children to learn about body differences is in the bathroom. Some early childhood programs have shared bathroom facilities so that girls and boys can use them together. This provides an especially good opportunity for a teacher in the bathroom area to clear up misinformation and model an accepting attitude about body differences. The following anecdote from our preschool illustrates this point:

The teacher is helping David to use the toilet. Sara comments, "He gots a penis just like my brother." The teacher replies, "That's right. David and your brother have penises because they are boys." Sara replies, "Yup! And I got a bagina." "That's right," responds the teacher, "you have a vagina."

Children's curiosity about genital differences may also lead them to question why boys and girls usually urinate differently. Here again, one might stress the differences in male and female anatomy. An adult could respond, "A boy stands up because he urinates through his penis. But a girl's urine comes out from an opening near her vagina. It doesn't stick out like a penis, so she sits down." Child-size toilets make it possible for boys to stand up, because some are not yet tall enough to reach adult facilities.

Regardless of how casual and open a teacher's attitude, there will always be children who have received strict modesty training at home. Teachers need to respect the needs of these children and their parents. Placing a portable screen or divider in the bathroom may help the modest child to feel more comfortable.

Use classroom resources when discussing body differences. Brenner's book, *Bodies* (1973, see Bibliography) provides an excellent introduction to the subject for preschool and elementary children. Black and white photographs depict clothed and unclothed children using their bodies to eat, sleep, defecate, bathe, and read. Another good book, *What Is A Girl? What Is A Boy?* (Waxman 1975, see Bibliography) uses both photographs and drawings to illustrate biological sex differences from infancy through adulthood. Magazine pictures and other photographs of nude children may also be posted on walls as conversation sparkers.

Amy Miller

Children deserve an accurate explanation of reproduction.

Another excellent stimulus for discussing body differences is anatomically correct dolls or puzzles (Constructive Playthings, Childcraft, Horsman). While such dolls may initially create a stir, children soon seem to enjoy differentiating between the girl and boy babies.

Reproduction and birth

In addition to learning about body differences, children often display curiosity about reproduction. Children begin the questioning process at about the age of 3 with "Where do babies come from?" This question is typically followed by "How does it get there?" or "How does it get out?" (Selzer 1974). Observations of pregnant women often stimulate curiosity about the origin of babies (Koblinsky, Atkinson, and Davis 1979). Children who are about to experience a birth in their own family are particularly likely to question teachers about reproduction.

Begin by finding out how much the child knows. Because young children will have encountered different information, it is important to determine how much they know. Therefore, a good rule to follow when answering questions is to ask a question. Throw the question back to the child by asking, "Well, where do *you* think babies come from?" or "How do *you* think it got there?"

Children often come up with remarkable and totally erroneous responses even though they have received accurate information. In our program, a child whose mother worked for Planned Parenthood gave the following explanation:

The baby grows and grows inside the mommy until she gets so big that the baby just about pops out! Then the mommy goes to the hospital to have the baby pop out. And if *you* go to the hospital, you'll have a baby too!

Although her mother had explained the birth process in great detail, Debbie's understanding was influenced by her level of cognitive development. Debbie, like other young children, is in Piaget's stage of preoperational thought and thus interprets information in

terms of her own past experiences (Piaget 1929; Bernstein 1978). Just as balloons expand until they pop, babies will grow so big that they pop out of the mother. Debbie also uses transductive reasons to connect unrelated events. She reasons that anyone who goes to the hospital will return with a new baby.

Because children's ideas are influenced by their cognitive maturity, teachers should avoid laughing at fanciful explanations. Teachers should look for ways of correcting mistaken concepts, rather than telling children they are wrong. For example, a teacher overhearing Debbie's explanation might respond, "That's an interesting way of putting it, Debbie. You're right.... The baby does come out of the mother. Do you know where the baby comes out?" If the child is unable to answer, the teacher might describe the birth process or suggest that they look through a book on birth together. This approach enables the teacher to acknowledge the child's correct information as well as clear up any misinformation.

Give accurate information about reproduction. Our research indicates that adults explain the origin of babies in different ways, but the most common response is that they come from the mommy's tummy (Koblinsky, Atkinson, and Davis 1979). Some adults also explain that the baby began as a small seed. Few adults mention the uterus or union of sperm and ovum, and even fewer deal with the topic of sexual intercourse.

A major problem with these more common adult responses is that they are inaccurate. Babies do not grow in tummies, and they do not sprout from seeds! Children deserve a more accurate explanation of reproduction. Good responses are simple and contain correct terminology. These points are illustrated in the following suggested exchanges between a child and an adult:

Child: Where do babies come from?
Adult: Babies come from a place inside the mother called the uterus. That's where they grow until they're ready to be born.
Child: How does the baby get out?
Adult: There's an opening between the mother's legs called the vagina. When

the baby's ready, the opening stretches enough to let the baby come out.
Child: How does the baby get in there?
Adult: The mother has a tiny ovum inside her uterus. The father has a tiny sperm. When the sperm and the ovum come together, the baby starts growing.
Child: How does the daddy get the sperm in the mommy?
Adult: The father and mother lie very close together and put the father's penis inside the mother's vagina. The sperm come out through the father's penis.
Child: Why can't a man have a baby?
Adult: They aren't meant to. A man's body doesn't have a uterus where babies grow. The man's part is to help make the baby and to help care for it after it's born.

As teachers discuss reproduction and birth, they should remember that these processes are not easily understood the first time around. They must be prepared to answer children's questions again and again and to present the information in a variety of contexts. With an open exchange of information, children will gradually bring their understanding of these events closer to reality.

Use books to explain reproduction and birth. Sex education books (see Bibliography) are especially helpful because they include pictures illustrating concepts that teachers cannot demonstrate. It is important to leave these books out on the shelf, right alongside children's other favorites, so that children may look at them again and again. Easy availability reinforces the notion that sexual curiosity is natural and healthy.

Avoid using plants and animals as substitutes for discussing human reproduction. Young children are greatly interested in reproduction and are intrigued by all new babies. Therefore, teachers are encouraged to plan experiences that familiarize children with the principles of reproduction in plants, fish, rodents, and other animals (Holt 1977). However, there is some risk in attempting to use other species to convey an understanding of human reproduction and birth. Children may have considerable difficulty generalizing from plants and animals to human

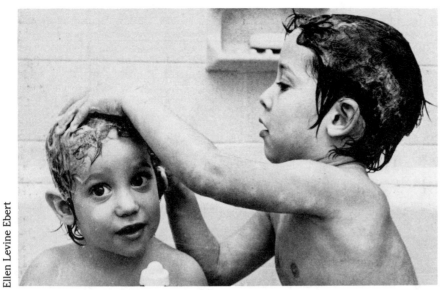

While young children may be confused by too many different labels, they do need to know that both males and females possess unique and equally valuable genitalia.

beings or vice versa. The following exchange illustrates the confusion that can be created by using analogies from the animal kingdom:

Adult: How would the lady get a baby to grow inside her?

Child: Um, get a duck. Cause one day I saw a book about them, and ... they just get a duck or a goose and they get a little more growned ... and then they turn into a baby. (Bernstein and Cowan 1975, p. 87)

It is likely that this child had been read the popular book, *How Babies Are Made* (Andry and Schepp 1968). Although this book provides accurate information, it reviews reproduction in flowers, chickens, and dogs before it discusses humans. Because children are used to hearing stories in the once-upon-a-time to happily-ever-after sequence, it is easy to understand why children might reason that humans were once ducks or flowers.

Individualize discussions about reproduction. It may be best to use a less formal instructional approach than might be used for concepts like colors

or community helpers because young children vary widely in their knowledge of sexuality. When a teacher explains reproduction and birth, children will need an opportunity to ask questions. In one-to-one encounters or small groups, fewer of their questions are likely to go unanswered. Parents' concerns can also be responded to more easily when talking with individual children.

Masturbation

Masturbation is now widely accepted as natural and healthy for both children and adults (Arnstein 1976; Selzer 1974). Children will touch or rub their genitals because this behavior is pleasurable or soothing. Experienced teachers know that young children may absentmindedly fondle their genitals when they are tired, bored, or listening to a story. Children may also clutch their genitals when they are tense or nervous. Although some teachers may feel uncomfortable, adults will handle these situations most effectively if they adopt a relaxed approach to masturbation.

Ignore masturbation in most classroom situations. A teacher will probably notice that the child's behavior usually does not bother anyone else in the classroom.

Avoid negative responses. Adults should refrain from scolding or punishing children for engaging in masturbation. Responses like frowning or pulling the child's hands away from the genitals may communicate that these organs are bad or dirty. Criticisms or threats can lead children to develop unhealthy feelings of anxiety and guilt which can persist throughout life.

It is probably most difficult to refrain from scolding children when they are using masturbation as an attention-getting device. When a child masturbates to bring on laughter from others, you may say firmly and matter-of-factly, "Please put your penis back in your pants. That's where it belongs unless you're going to the bathroom."

Stress that there is a better time and place for masturbation. At times this behavior may interfere with other activities and may be bothersome to the entire class. A teacher might then take the child aside and explain, "I know that feels good, but other people don't like to see you play with your penis/vulva. You can do that when you're by yourself." This response acknowledges the pleasurable aspects of masturbation but also conveys the inappropriateness of its public display. However, teachers will need to be especially aware of any cultural prohibitions specific to their group of children.

Consult the child's parents if masturbation becomes compulsive. Compulsive masturbation, like compulsive scratching or nail biting, may be a symptom of deeper emotional problems. Should a teacher encounter a child who masturbates compulsively, we advise the teacher to discuss such behavior with the child's parents. The discussion may clarify factors contributing to the behavior and may inform teachers about the way masturbation is handled at home. Compulsive masturbation may be a reaction to family stress and may suggest that the child needs more time and attention from others. Parents and teachers can work together to help the child overcome anxiety and find other means of satisfaction.

Sex play

Like masturbation, sex play is an extension of childhood curiosity about body differences and functions (Pomeroy 1976). Children engaged in sex play typically examine one another's bodies and may attempt to place objects into genital openings. Sex play often occurs within the context of children's games, such as doctor or house. Teachers may discover these games in a quiet corner of the classroom or outdoor play area.

Acknowledge children's curiosity. Teachers' responses to children engaged in sex play will vary according to assessments of each situation. It may be sufficient to acknowledge the children's behavior and redirect their interest. A teacher might respond, "Oh, you were just looking to see how boys and girls are different. That's the way we are made. Now, how about a game of hide and seek?" In some cases, sex play may appear to be motivated by unanswered questions about body differences. A teacher may then suggest that children join her in the story corner to review appropriate books on the human body.

Explain potential consequences. If children's play involves inserting objects into each other's genital openings, it is important to discuss the potentially dangerous consequences of this behavior. After acknowledging children's natural curiosity, a teacher may explain that this practice could hurt another child. Use a familiar example, like putting pencils in someone's ears, to suggest the harmful effects of placing objects in body openings.

Discuss consideration for others. If children repeatedly engage in sex play, despite efforts to distract them or satisfy their curiosity, teachers may wish to bring up the issue of consideration for others. A teacher might respond, "I know you're curious about each other's bodies, but it bothers people to see you

playing like that. I'd prefer that you didn't do it here." In asking children to stop this behavior out of respect for others, avoid trying to instill a sense of guilt. Severe scolding or hysterical outbursts may have long-term negative effects on later sexual adjustment.

Obscene words

Almost all adults have encountered children using such bathroom language as "This juice looks like pee" or "You're a poop face!" While such statements are generally accepted as normal experimentation with language, teachers may experience real discomfort when children begin using the more offensive four-letter words. Adults often fear that use of obscene language will become rampant among children. Consequently, many teachers express concern about the proper method of handling obscenities in the classroom.

Ignore obscene language whenever possible. Because children are likely to experiment with any new words they hear, it is best to let a spate of obscene language run its course. Extreme teacher reaction will probably increase children's interest in using these words rather than reduce it. Some children may be scolded for using these words at home, and repeating them at school may help children get them out of their systems.

Explain the word's meaning when it is appropriate. Because children often parrot an offensive word without any idea of its meaning, teachers may question children about what a specific word really means to them. Should their responses indicate a lack of understanding, teachers may define the word and use it matter-of-factly. The following anecdote from our preschool illustrates how this strategy may diffuse the potency of a four-letter word for the child:

John screams that Billy is a "shithead." The teacher asks John, "Do you know what shit means?" John shakes his head. The teacher explains, "Shit is another word for bowel movement. Is that the word you wanted to use!" "No!" John exclaims, "I didn't want to say that!"

Stress the offensive nature of obscene language if it persists. When children's repeated use of obscene language disturbs classroom activities, teachers may need to take firmer measures. Children should be told that obscene words offend many people, and that the times and places for their use are limited. The teacher might respond, "Most people don't like to hear words like that. I don't want you to use them here at school."

General recommendations

Involve parents. It is extremely important to consider the specific backgrounds and concerns of parents because they remain the primary sex educators of their children. Early childhood educators must recognize that their own beliefs and values about sex education may not be shared by many parents. In some communities, sex education is a volatile issue. Consequently, efforts must be made to open discussions in which both parents and teachers can air views about the best ways of responding to children's sexual curiosity.

Teachers who represent their general philosophies of education at an initial get-acquainted parent meeting may allocate a portion of the program to discussing sex education. Parents should be encouraged to share their own ideas about handling sexual behaviors and should feel free to question the rationale behind any program policies. Placing an emphasis on an *exchange* of information will facilitate the development of mutual strategies for educating young children about sexuality.

Many parents seek extra help from teachers in communicating to their children about sexual issues. Therefore, we suggest planning at least one parent meeting to deal exclusively with the topic of sex education. Such meetings can be used to present information on normal psychosexual development and to address parental anxieties about specific behaviors. Meetings should be planned for a time when both mothers and fathers may conveniently attend. Teachers who feel uncomfortable directing a session on this topic may wish

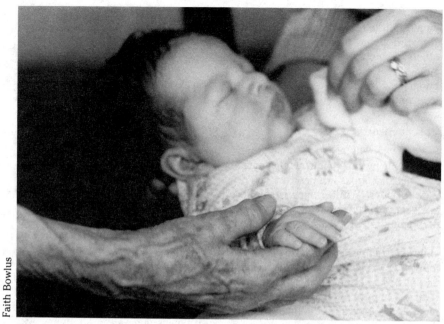

Faith Bowlus

Because parents remain the primary sex educators of their children, it is extremely important to consider their backgrounds and concerns.

to solicit the services of speakers from a family planning agency or other community service organizations.

Parent involvement may play a crucial role in linking the young child's family experiences with those encountered in the school environment. Moreover, parents who establish family communication about human sexuality in the early years increase the likelihood that their children will approach them with sexual questions in the future. Finally, parents who develop an early concern for educating children about sexuality are likely to become active proponents of quality sex education programs in elementary and secondary schools.

Encourage staff members to participate. Lectures, group discussions, films, and other resources may be used to explore early childhood sexuality with all staff members. Time may be spent examining the ways in which teachers transmit sexual information and values to young children. Staff meetings provide an ideal opportunity to practice answers to children's questions about body differences and birth and to role play responses to specific sexual behaviors.

Examine personal sexual values. We believe that teachers must feel positively about their *own* sexuality before they attempt to discuss this sensitive subject with children. Therefore, discussion groups or values-clarification exercises may be used to explore sexual values and to increase comfort in responding to sexual issues. A relaxed and accepting attitude is just as important as the information provided.

Be a positive role model. Although we have focused on responding to children's overt sexual behaviors, sex education involves more than teaching facts about genital differences and birth. Indeed, sexuality is an integral part of the personality and involves the whole sense of what it is like to be a male or female. Teachers and parents are important role models for young children. Teachers who demonstrate warmth, affection, and support for others provide children with positive models for interpersonal behavior. The affective component of sexuality may also be stressed by reading children stories that describe the love, loyalty, and trust in human relationships.

Evaluate staff efforts. It is important

to seek feedback from both teachers and parents about the effectiveness of sex education strategies. Efforts should be made to encourage a free exchange of feelings, attitudes, and personal experiences. Teachers may wish to evaluate their personal effectiveness as sex educators by answering such questions as "What have I learned?" "What have I relearned?" "How do I now feel about responding to various sexual behaviors?" It is wise to plan a specific time for dealing with sex education because the staff may be reluctant to bring up this subject in routine meetings.

Conclusion

Sex education is an important but often unrecognized component of early childhood programs. All children express curiosity about sexuality, and they deserve honest and thoughtful responses. The early childhood educator with a background in sex education may play a vital role in helping children experience the joy and responsibility of their sexuality.

Bibliography of recommended sex education books for preschoolers

Suggested age levels are designated with overlapping age ranges as follows: **N**—nursery, up to age 5, **K**—kindergarten, ages 4–6, **P**—primary, ages 5–9.

The Birth of Sunset's Kittens. Carla Stevens. New York: Young Scott, 1969. NKP

Black and white photographs illustrate the birth of kittens. The text includes correct terminology for body parts and the birth process and subtly relates the birth of kittens to the child's own birth.

Bodies. Barbara Brenner. New York: Dutton, 1973. NK

Beautiful photographs of males and females from all age groups and cultural backgrounds are used to explore the fascinating topic of bodies and what they can do. The text stresses the uniqueness of each child's body.

Did the Sun Shine Before You Were Born? Sol and Judith Gordon. Fayetteville, N.Y.: Ed-U Press, 1974. NKP

With a focus on the family, the book explains male-female genital differences, intercourse, conception, and the birth process with multicultural illustrations and suggestions for parents and teachers.

Girls Are Girls and Boys Are Boys: So What's the Difference? Sol Gordon. Fayetteville, N.Y.: Ed-U Press, 1979. P

The differences between boys and girls are explained in terms of body build and function, rather than play, clothing, or career preferences. Masturbation, menstruation, intercourse, birth, and breast-feeding are discussed. The illustrations are multicultural.

How Babies Are Made. Andrew C. Andry and Steven Schepp. New York: Time-Life, 1968. KP

Simple, eye-catching illustrations enhance a long book that covers sexual differences, intercourse, and the birth process. Children may be confused by the sequential presentation of plant, animal, and human production.

How Was I Born? Lennart Nilsson. New York: Delacorte, 1975. P

A story of conception, prenatal development, and childbirth is told in a sequence of beautiful photographs by the author/photographer. The text is clear and scientifically accurate and may be edited for younger children. The photos depict body differences in the sexes from early childhood to adulthood.

Making Babies. Sara Bonnett Stein. New York: Walker & Co., 1974. NKP

One of the *Open Family* series, the book presents a simple description of pregnancy and birth with vivid photographs of the fetus. There is a separate text for children and adults on each page, with the adult text suggesting strategies for responding to children's sexual curiosity.

What Is a Girl? What Is a Boy? Stephanie Waxman. Culver City, Calif.: Peace Press, 1975. NKP

Black and white photographs depict body differences between the sexes from infancy through adulthood. The book points out that, despite anatomical differences, both boys and girls can have the same names, enjoy the same activities, and feel the same emotions.

Where Did I Come From? Peter Mayle. Secaucus, N.J.: Lyle Stuart, 1973. P

An amusing text with cartoon-like illustrations explains body differences, sexual arousal, intercourse, conception, fetal development, and the birth process. The text may be too long for some children.

Where Do Babies Come From? Margaret Sheffield. New York: Knopf, 1972. NKP

A beautifully and sensitively illustrated book that discusses intercourse and fetal development and depicts natural childbirth and genital differences in infancy, childhood, and adulthood.

The books listed in this bibliography are available from the publisher or at your local bookstore.

Sources for anatomically correct dolls and dressing-undressing puzzles:

Constructive Playthings
P.O. Box 5445
Kansas City, MO 64131

Childcraft Education Corp.
20 Kilmer Road
Edison, NJ 08817

Horsman Dolls, Inc.
200 Fifth Avenue
New York, NY 10010

References

Arnstein, H. "How Sex Attitudes Develop." *Day Care and Early Education* 3, no. 5 (May–June 1976): 11–14.

Bernstein, A. *The Flight of the Stork.* New York: Dell, 1978.

Bernstein, A., and Cowan, P. "Children's Concepts of How People Get Babies." *Child Development* 46 (1975): 77–91.

Calderone, M. S. "Sex Education and the Very Young Child." *The PTA Magazine* 61, no. 2 (October 1966): 16–18.

Gagnon, J. "Sexuality and Sexual Learning in the Child." *Psychiatry* 28 (1965): 212–228.

Gesell, A., and Ilg, F. L. *Child Development.* New York: Harper & Brothers, 1949.

Gordon, S. "Three Short Essays Toward a Sexual Revolution." *The Humanist* 34, no. 2 (March–April 1974): 20–22.

Hattendorf, K. W. "A Study of the Questions of Young Children." *Journal of Social Psychology* 3 (1932): 37–65.

Holt, B-G. *Science with Young Children.* Washington, D.C.: National Association for the Education of Young Children, 1977.

Koblinsky, S.; Atkinson, J.; and Davis, S. "Early Childhood Sex Education Project, 1979." Unpublished research report. Corvalis, Ore.: Oregon State University Family Life Department, 1979.

Kreitler, H., and Kreitler, S. "Children's Concepts of Sexuality and Birth." *Child Development* 37 (1965): 363–378.

Piaget, J. *The Child's Conception of the World.* New York: Harcourt, Brace, 1929.

Pomeroy, W. B. *Your Child and Sex: A Guide For Parents.* New York: Dell, 1976.

Selzer, J. G. *When Children Ask About Sex.* Boston: Beacon, 1974.

Strain, F. B. *The Normal Sex Interests of Children.* New York: Appleton-Century-Crofts, 1948.

Woody, J. D. "Contemporary Sex Education: Attitudes and Implications for Childrearing." *Journal of School Health* 43 (1973): 241–246.

Preparing Young Children for Hospitalization

Jeffrey Trawick-Smith and Richard H. Thompson

Teacher: What happens to a person who goes to the hospital?

Child: Well, you get shots.

Teacher: Anything else?

Child: Well, they might cut you open, like if you swallow a puzzle or something and you have to have an operation.

Teacher: What else happens to a person who goes to the hospital?

Child: Well, you might die. My grandpa went to the hospital and they cut open his tummy and he died.

Teacher: How would you feel if you went to the hospital?

Child: Sad.

Teacher: Why would you feel sad?

Child: Because you wouldn't know anybody.

Teacher: Are there any other reasons you would be sad?

Child: Yes. Because I don't want shots.

Young children contemplate a hospital experience with much anxiety and uncertainty, yet each year 4.5 million children are hospitalized (Select Panel for the Promotion of Child Health 1981). In one group of 40 five-year-old children selected for a research project, 9 had already been hospitalized! It is well documented that hospitalization and illness produce great emotional stress in children (Thompson and Stanford 1981). These experiences are most traumatic for children younger than age 6, due to their cognitive abilities and social and emotional vulnerability of this developmental period (Prugh et al. 1953).

Early childhood educators and health professionals can attend to the emotional needs of children before, during, and after a hospital experience by reducing stress and anxiety through programs in hospitals (often called Child Life programs), classrooms, and work with individual children.

Hospital-based preparation programs

Hospital-based preparation programs have been effective in helping children to cope successfully with the trauma of a hospital experience. Skipper and Leonard (1968) found reduced levels of stress in both parents and children when mothers were given more information about the hospital and were provided opportunities to express feelings concerning the hospital experience.

Wolfer and Visintainer (1975) obtained similar results from a preparation strategy in which children, as well as parents, received more information and opportunities for self-expression. Other researchers have identified specific techniques which have been successful in lessening the stress of hospitalization. For example, providing children who were to have casts removed with descriptions of the sights, sounds, and feelings of this procedure was emotionally beneficial (Johnson, Kirchhoff, and Endress 1975).

Melamed and Siegel (1975) demonstrated the utility of a hospital film in reducing fear in children before surgery and after discharge. Fassler (1980a) discovered that a hospital story followed by a discussion of fears and doubt associated with hospitalization and a dramatic play period within a mock hospital play setting all contributed to lower anxiety levels in hospitalized children. An important finding of this study was that the emotional support of nurturing adults, even in the absence of these specific, hospital-related activities, still reduced children's stress.

Providing information, opportunities for expression of feelings, and emotional support from adults appear, then, to be effective strategies in promoting the emotional health of the hospitalized child.

Limitations of these programs

While some hospitals have programs incorporating these strategies, many hospitals do not. Those that have programs may lack funding and other resources to reach all of the children in need of these services. A broader based effort is needed in some communities.

Many children encounter a hospital for the first time in an emergency room. Thus, there is little opportunity to implement a hospital-based preparation program before medical treatment has begun. Traditional preparation pro-

---

Jeffrey Trawick-Smith, Ed.D., is Assistant Professor, Eastern Connecticut State University, Willimantic, Connecticut.

Richard H. Thompson, Ph.D., is Research Associate, Association for the Care of Children's Health, Child Life Research Project.

grams focus on the inpatient hospital population. These activities cannot meet the needs of the growing number of children requiring outpatient care or treatment in ambulatory care clinics.

Often the anxiety level of children who are soon to be hospitalized is so high that a hospital preparation program staffed with strangers may not be fully effective. An earlier educational program, presented in a familiar environment by familiar people and before children are faced with the possibility of hospitalization, might more effectively reduce uncertainty concerning the hospital. When children who have completed this program eventually enter a hospital, they may respond with less anxiety to hospital activities.

Therefore, early childhood educators can develop preparation programs in their classrooms in an effort to familiarize all children with the hospital experience. These should in no way replace preparation efforts provided by hospitals to individuals just prior to their admission. Instead, these classroom programs should complement the activities of medical, nursing, and other health personnel who provide well-child care.

Classroom preparation programs

This classroom episode illustrates the need for careful planning and reliance on child development principles and hospitalized child literature in designing a preparation program.

A young teacher was informed that a 3-year-old in her class was soon to have surgery. She was aware that dramatic play was often an important element in a hospital preparation program so she collected materials commonly used by hospital personnel to create a mock hospital in the dramatic play area. Children were given access to this area at free play time.

What happened? Children used syringes as rockets. Batman tied up monsters with strips of gauze. A doctor chased patients around the room with a shot to punish them for being bad. Another doctor tied bandages around an old doll's head so tightly that the head popped off. Clearly, several important

features beyond providing materials should be included in a good preparation program. Before they are expected to have meaningful and emotionally useful hospital play, children need to be acquainted with real hospital settings.

Hospital visitation

Children tend to play about what they already know (Piaget 1962). Thus, the first step in implementing a classroom hospital program should be to help children learn about what happens in a hospital. Discussion could center on the sights, sounds, and smells of the hospital in an accurate, but positive, portrayal of hospital life.

Films or books such as *The Hospital Book* (Howe 1981) are needed to help children visualize what they might encounter. Children will be able to recall their own visits to clinics or medical offices, and can share their experiences with familiar items such as tongue depressors, stethoscopes, and scales.

A field trip to a hospital may be considered. Teachers should consult with the hospital staff when planning such a visit. All adults accompanying the children should be aware of any hospital regulations. Parents and teachers must also be prepared to expect a variety of emotional responses the children may exhibit during or after the visit. Children should be clearly informed that this is a brief visit and all of the children will return to school and their homes. This will help dispel the common childhood myth that once inside a hospital, a child may never leave.

A field trip to a hospital should provide children with an accurate view of a few meaningful medical procedures and the hospital environment. While there is a concern that children may be unnecessarily exposed to anxiety-producing events during such a tour, Thompson and Stanford (1981) emphasize the benefits of familiarity with the hospital personnel, equipment, and environment of a carefully monitored visit. The primary goal of a hospital visit is to accustom children to a strange setting and to discuss feelings associated with a hospital encounter. Children should view commonly visited treatment and admission areas such as

a hospital room, the X-ray department, the surgery waiting room, a recovery room, and the outpatient waiting room if it will not disturb children or those waiting. The tour could also include a visit to the playroom if one is available. A brief play experience in this area would be useful. Pointing out bathrooms and other familiar areas would demonstrate to children that everyday life routines continue in the hospital.

Brief interactions with various health personnel should be arranged. A discussion of their clothing or medical equipment would be useful. The warmth and caring of these individuals as well as their role in children's lives should be emphasized.

Children should become familiar with common medical instruments. An opportunity to handle and explore those which are safe and commonly used would enhance their understanding of hospital procedures.

The hospital tour should not intrude on patients or personnel. Neither would benefit, for example, from the children's curious intrusion into private hospital rooms. Visits should be conducted by hospital staff accompanied by as many familiar teachers and parents as is feasible. Their assistance is much needed and their own fears and uncertainties may be reduced.

Children's feelings should be carefully observed during and after the visit. The importance of observation and intervention by a perceptive and nurturing adult is illustrated in the following incident during a hospital tour.

A teacher noticed that one of her 4-year-old students was becoming increasingly withdrawn during a tour of the laboratory. She asked him if he would like to leave the area and he nodded. In the hall, the following conversation took place:

Child: I didn't like that blood room.
Teacher: Can you tell me what made you afraid?
Child: Is there a man in that machine that takes your blood?
Teacher: No. A nurse takes a little bit of your blood with a syringe, remember? Then it is put into the machine to check it.

The child seemed satisfied with this clarification. He continued on the tour, walking close to his teacher, but without obvious anxiety.

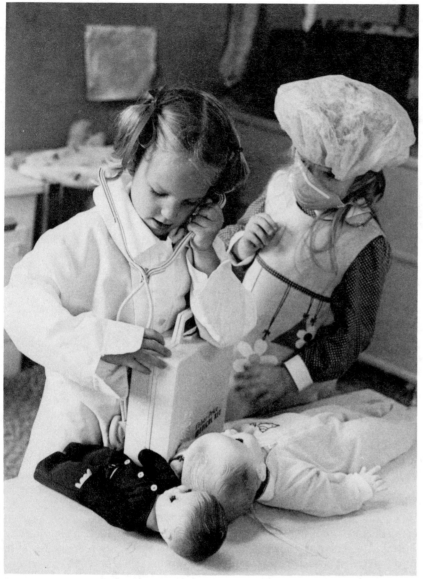

Elaine M. Ward

Dramatic play is an excellent medium for the expression of fears and uncertainties about the hospital.

Other hospital experiences

If you do not believe the children in your group are ready for a tour or if your local hospitals do not provide tours for groups of young children, other methods of portraying the hospital environment may be substituted. Films and other visual materials have been found useful in aiding children in coping with hospitalization (Melamed and Siegel 1975). Hospitals and other medical organizations sometimes provide these, such as the Mister Rogers *Let's Talk About the Hospital* materials (Family Communications 1977). Children should view such materials with nurturing caregivers who can immediately clear up misunderstandings, discuss or expand upon information presented, and respond to children's questions and expressions of emotion.

Books are also useful in presenting the hospital experience (see Fassler 1980b). Altshuler's annotated bibliography, *Books That Help Children to Deal with a Hospital Experience* (1978), reviews some children's books dealing with this topic. Two especially realistic books are *Jeff's Hospital Book* (Sobol 1975) and *A Hospital Story* (Stein 1974). *The Hospital Book* (1981), mentioned earlier, is excellent. Children's librarians will be happy to assist you in your selection. A variety of pamphlets for both parents and children may be obtained from the Association for the Care of Children's Health (see Resources).

The teacher should select books that are well written and are appropriate for the developmental level of young children. Books should portray the hospital experience accurately but in a nonthreatening way. If a child in class is facing a specific medical procedure, an effort should be made to locate books focusing on it. For example, books about the removal of a cast or tonsillectomy are available. Books are most helpful when children are encouraged to ask questions and share feelings openly while these are being read.

Self-expressive activities

A second fundamental element in the successful preparation program is the provision of opportunities to express fears and ideas concerning the hospital within a nurturing and accepting environment. Some activities could take place before and/or after more concrete hospital experiences.

Traditional circle time can facilitate self-expression. Guidelines for meaningful group interaction should be followed when conducting these discussions (see Leeper, Skipper, and Witherspoon 1979). The use of medical instruments, pictures, and other concrete materials encourages children to focus on hospital-related topics and stimulates their expression of feelings.

Teachers must respond to children's comments and give honest but age-appropriate answers to sometimes difficult questions. Hospitalization is frightening and the teacher should recognize this as a legitimate emotion.

Play activities

Young children often express concerns through play rather than directly in conversation. Axline (1969) describes the power of a child's play in gaining mastery over feelings:

> By playing out ... feelings he brings them to the surface, gets them out in the open, faces them, learns to control them, or abandons them. When he has achieved emotional relaxation, he begins to realize the power within himself to be an individual in his own right, to think for himself, to make his own decisions, to become psychologically more mature, and by so doing, to realize selfhood. (p. 16)

Open-ended and creative play is especially helpful in achieving this mastery of feelings and realization of individual power, since these involve the most direct expression of self. Block play, art activities, sand and water play, and dramatic play are excellent opportunities to express thoughts and feelings. Miniature hospital vehicles, furniture, or personnel could be placed in the block area, for example, to stimulate construction play or dramatization which is relevant to the topic. Medical instruments could be provided for use in the water or sand play areas. Syringes, for example, make for fascinating but perhaps messy water play.

Drawing and other art activities allow meaningful self-expression. Children might be guided toward hospital-related themes by asking them to "draw a person who has been admitted to the hospital." This might elicit interesting and emotion-rich portrayals of hospital life. Asking children about these drawings allows verbal expression and gives the teacher insight into areas of misunderstanding or concern. Drawing self-portraits has been found an effective component of a successful program to prepare children for upcoming surgery (Fassler 1980a).

Dramatic play is a common spontaneous and self-initiated activity in early childhood. As such, it serves as an excellent medium for the expression of fears and uncertainties about the hospital. After a visit to the hospital or a story or film presenting hospital procedures, opportunities should be provided for children to play out these experiences in the dramatic play area.

A realistic and attractive hospital environment could be designed in a special section of the room. Genuine hospital instruments should be used, unless the anxiety level of children becomes too great. Toy replicas may be less threatening substitutes for use with very anxious children. Materials such as surgical masks, old X-rays, stethoscopes, blood pressure gauges, gauze bandages, and empty syringes may be borrowed from a physician's office or purchased from a medical supply house.

A hospital bed may be fashioned out of a nap cot. This encourages children to occasionally play the role of patient, as well as doctor or nurse. Inventive teachers or children might construct cardboard hospital equipment such as X-ray machines or respirators (see Fiarotta and Fiarotta 1977).

Provision of dramatic play materials may not be sufficient to ensure high quality dramatic play, however (Smilansky 1968). Teachers can judge the level of their involvement needed to stimulate hospital-related play, clear up misconceptions, and heighten the vocalization of feelings. By pretending with children, the adult can contribute to the complexity or organization of the play or the accuracy of hospital-related themes. For example, adult statements like the following increase the complexity of hospital play: "Oh my! This baby is running a high fever! We'd better take her to the doctor."

Adults can encourage children to try on a diversity of hospital-related roles with comments such as "Who would like to be the anesthesiologist?" Playing with children, adults can elicit expression of feeling with questions like "How does the baby feel now that his mother has to leave him alone for a while?" By a similar technique, the adult can add accuracy to play situations: "I'm going to give the doll an injection right in his arm, because that's where the nurses often give them."

Once the adult has enriched the hospital play of children with such interactions, it is important to withdraw from the setting and allow children to continue the theme by themselves. The intent of adult intervention is not to direct children's play, but to foster more sophisticated and accurate self-directed dramatization of hospital life.

Parent involvement

Involving parents in the hospital preparation program is important (Skipper and Leonard 1968; Wolfer and Visintainer 1975). Teachers can give parents outlines of the program, including an overview of activities and materials used. A list of hospital-related terms and concepts, discussed in the classroom, could be provided to contribute to follow-up discussions at home. A bibliography of children's books, as well as reference books for parents, can be assembled and distributed to families. Preparation of a list of local resources and services of medical facilities might be beneficial. The names of helpful professionals in the community, such as Child Life workers, pediatric nurses, clinical psychologists, or play therapists, could be available on request.

Because providing parents with opportunities to express feelings about the hospital has had a positive influence on the emotional state of children as well as adults (Skipper and Leonard 1968; Wolfer and Visintainer 1975), two-way interaction between parents and teachers is extremely important. Parents should be invited to participate in classroom activities and tours. Special parent support groups can be organized to facilitate discussion of the hospital experience.

Conclusion

Medical personnel are becoming increasingly concerned with the affective aspects of health and recovery. Early childhood educators can contribute to the effectiveness of the growing number of Child Life programs by preparing young children in their classrooms. Medical personnel and educators should collaborate on these activities in a joint effort to ensure the emotional well-being of all young children.

References

Altshuler, A. *Books That Help Children Deal with a Hospital Experience.* Washington, D.C.: U.S. Government Printing Office, 1978.

Axline, V. *Play Therapy*. New York: Ballantine Books, 1969.

Family Communications. *Let's Talk About the Hospital: A Guide for Hospital Staff.* 1977. Family Communications, 4802 Fifth Ave., Pittsburgh, PA 15213.

Fassler, D. "Reducing Preoperative Anxiety in Children: Information Versus Emotional Support." *Patient Counseling and Health Education* 2 (1980a): 130–134.

Fassler, D. "The Young Child in the Hospital." *Young Children* 35, no. 6 (September 1980b): 18–25.

Fiarotta, P., and Fiarotta, N. *Be What You Want To Be.* New York: Workman, 1977.

Johnson, J. E.; Kirchhoff, K. T.; and Endress, M. P. "Altering Children's Distress Behavior During Orthopedic Cast Removal." *Nursing Research* 24, no. 6 (1975): 404–410.

Leeper, S. H.; Skipper, D. S.; and Witherspoon, R. L. *Good Schools for Young Children.* 4th ed. New York: Macmillan, 1979.

Melamed, B. G., and Siegel, L. J. "Reduction of Anxiety in Children Facing Hospitalization and Surgery by Use of Filmed Modeling." *Journal of Consulting and Clinical Psychology* 43 (1975): 511–521.

Piaget, J. *Play, Dreams and Imitation in Childhood.* New York: Norton, 1962.

Prugh, D. G.; Staub, E.; Sands, H. H.; Kirschbaum, R.; and Lenihan, E. A. "A Study of the Emotional Reactions of Children and Families to Hospitalization and Illness." *American Journal of Orthopsychiatry* 23 (1953): 70–106.

Select Panel for the Promotion of Child Health. *Better Health for Our Children: A National Strategy.* Washington, D.C.: U.S. Public Health Service, 1981. (NTIS no. PB81-242869)

Skipper, J. K., and Leonard, R. C. "Children, Stress and Hospitalization: A Field Experiment." *Journal of Health and Social Behavior* 9, no. 4 (1968): 275–287.

Smilansky, S. *The Effects of Sociodramatic Play on Disadvantaged Preschool Children.* New York: Wiley, 1968.

Thompson, R. H., and Stanford, G. *Child Life in Hospitals: Theory and Practice.* Springfield, Ill.: Charles C. Thomas, 1981.

Wolfer, J. E., and Visintainer, M. "Pediatric Surgical Patients' and Parents' Stress Responses and Adjustments as a Function of a Psychological Preparation and Stress Point Nursing Care." *Nursing Research* 24 (1975): 244–255.

Resources

Association for the Care of Children's Health
3615 Wisconsin Ave., N.W., Washington, DC 20016
(ACCH has recently developed a "School Kit" for teachers to use in helping children learn about hospitals and health care. They also publish a brochure, "Children and Hospitals: A Guide for Teachers," and an educational resources brochure.)

Family Communications, Inc.
(Producer of "Mister Rogers' Neighborhood")
4802 Fifth Ave., Pittsburgh, PA 15213

Children's Books

Howe, J. *The Hospital Book.* Photographed by M. Warshaw. New York: Crown, 1981.

Sobol, H. *Jeff's Hospital Book.* New York: Walck, 1975.

Stein, S. B. *A Hospital Story.* New York, Walker, 1974.

The Young Child in the Hospital

David Fassler

Certainly there is nothing in the practice of medicine so barbarous and so fraught with psychological danger as the prevalent custom of taking a child into a strange white room, surrounding him with white-garbed strangers, exhibiting queer paraphernalia and glittering knives, and at the height of his consternation pressing an ether cone over his face and telling him to breathe deeply. The anxiety stimulated by such horrors is probably never surpassed in the child's subsequent life. (Menninger 1934)

Despite Menninger's emphatic declaration, the acknowledgment of the possible emotional implications of early childhood hospitalization is a relatively recent phenomenon. Prior to the 1950s, attending to the emotional needs of hospitalized children was considered an interference in the process of efficient medical treatment. The job of hospitals was seen as the treatment of illness.

The resulting emphasis on medical efficiency produced policies and practices which often seemed to interfere with children's emotional development. Children were physically restrained for long periods of time; explanations of procedures were rarely offered; and visiting hours were brief and infrequent. In addition, hospital staff often worsened the child's difficulties through apparently unfeeling and inappropriate actions. Beverly (1936) describes an intern who said, "Give me the scissors and I will cut them out," in front of a child awaiting a tonsillectomy, and a nurse who warned a post-tonsillectomy child to stop crying or she would be returned to the operating room to have her throat tied up. Jackson (1942) reports observing a nurse who remarked to a 4-year-old boy that his eyes were so beautiful that she would like to have them. She told the child that when he was asleep under anaesthetic she would take them out and exchange them for hers. In such an environment, the emotional trauma of hospitalization may well have produced consequences far more serious than the original physical illness.

The situation has changed dramatically in recent years. Most hospitals have adapted their policies to provide the child with increased emotional support. Pre-hospitalization orientation, therapeutically trained staff, liberal visiting policies, and rooming-in for parents are some of the innovations gaining widespread acceptance. However, despite these and other improvements, the hospitalization experience remains difficult and confusing for many young children. This is partly due to the wide variety of internal fears and misconceptions each child has about hospitalization and medical procedures, some of which are initiated by well-meaning but misinformed adults. Parents, teachers, and other caring adults can help make hospitalization less threatening and traumatic by attempting to view the situation from the

David Fassler is an M.D. candidate at Yale University School of Medicine, New Haven, Connecticut. He has worked extensively with children in both pediatric and psychiatric settings.

child's perspective, understanding the related and often confusing emotions, and providing an environment conducive to questions and discussion.

The child's view of hospitalization

One of the misconceptions most commonly encountered in work with young children concerns the reasons for their hospitalization and surgery. Hospitalization is often viewed by children as a punishment for real or imagined wrongs. In work with children awaiting tonsillectomy procedures (an increasingly rare event), the following explanations for the condition were encountered:

"I drank water too fast and got the hiccoughs."
"I sang too loud and hurt my throat."
"I went outside without my raincoat."
"I sucked my thumb. It must have messed them up."

One girl on kidney dialysis told the following story:

This is a picture of my living room. I was sitting down watching a circus picture show. I got up and started turning around. After a while, I started to get a chest pain. I told my mother I had a chest pain. She said I shouldn't have gone around so fast. She took me to the hospital and they told me I had kidney problems.

A young boy constructed the following elaborate fantasy to explain the hospitalization and tonsillectomy of a doll figure in his play with hospital toys:

He was on his way to school. He saw this dog and ran after him. Then he was in the woods and there was a giant who said it was his dog, but he could have a magic bird. But it flew away and the giant got mad and made it so the boy couldn't talk, and he went home and his Mommy said he was bad and had to go to the hospital and have his tonsils out.

Although the boy did not believe his own hospitalization to be the result of such an event, the elements of punishment and externally imposed controls are evident in his story.

Many children believe that an injury sustained in one part of the body can easily cause damage elsewhere. These children often focus on a physical fight

as the event which precipitated their illnesses and hospitalization. A boy hospitalized for a heart ailment drew a self-portrait and told the following story:

This is me in a fight. My friend hit me and my bones got weak. See my heart? You can see it beating through my shirt. My legs are hurting so my Daddy had to carry me to the hospital.

Another boy was firmly convinced that his hospitalization for a tonsillectomy was the result of repeated aggressive interactions with his brother. This belief was uncovered when the child was questioned about the black eye and scar in his self-drawing. He offered the following explanation:

He fights with me all the time.... That's all he knows how to do.... I got a black eye 'cause my brother hit me. Then I couldn't hear. That's why I had to come to the hospital and get my tonsils out.

It is important to explain to children that illness often occurs without negligence or physical injury and that the purpose of hospital care and treatment is not punishment. Young children should never be made to feel guilty about their illnesses or hospitalization.

Children also may focus on rejection and abandonment by parents as the reasons behind the hospitalization. One boy who had been hospitalized for several weeks for observation and tests related to a stomach disorder drew a picture of his mother as a monster and explained, "She doesn't like me. She wants me to stay in the hospital." A young girl on kidney dialysis told the following story:

My brother would beat on me all the time, and I wanted to get away. See, my mother couldn't take care of us so she went away, and my brother would beat on me.... I wished something would happen to me so I could go away to the hospital, and then I got kidney trouble.

Again, patience and careful explanation of the actual reasons for the hospitalization, along with increased emotional support and parental attention, can help alleviate such fears. Frequent visitation is important for young children. Rooming-in of one or both parents can greatly reduce the anxiety a child experiences in the hospital and should be strongly encouraged. Especially during prolonged hospitaliza-

tions, sibling visitation can help maintain a sense of family unity for children and the parents.

Inconsistent or erratic visitation can worsen a child's feelings of abandonment. If parents leave the hospital, they should be honest with the child as to when they expect to return. If plans are changed, the child should be informed. If a parent is unable to visit on a particular day, an effort should be made to reassure the child by telephone that she or he has not been forgotten.

Another major group of children's misconceptions centers on inaccurate information about the parts of the body involved in operations. The size, location, and multiplicity of organs seem to be areas of considerable confusion. For example, most children hospitalized for tonsillectomies believe it is the uvula (the central tag-like structure visible at the back of the throat) which is being removed. Such a misconception can be damaging, especially when the child checks after the operation and discovers that the uvula is still there. A child could conceivably wonder what was removed instead.

Adenoids are very small glands associated with the tonsils. They are often removed during tonsillectomy procedures. One young girl was convinced that there were exactly 30 adenoids, existing in 3 varieties: thin and elongated, dot shaped, and large round spheres.

Misunderstandings of the need for routine hospital procedures create additional anxieties in many hospitalized children. Blood tests, for example, seem particularly frightening and confusing. One child thought his blood test was performed to remove the bad blood. Another believed the blood was saved, mixed with medicines, and put into other people. A 6-year-old girl explained, "The doctors look at your blood, and they can see what you're thinking." All of these fantasies make the procedure even more threatening and anxiety-provoking.

The operation itself is a source of considerable confusion for many children. Using hospital toys, a young boy created the following story:

You get on a table and nurse tells you to count until you get tired and fall asleep.

Then the doctor comes with a pliers and pulls out your tonsils. He looks with a flashlight to make sure he gets it all. Sometimes you wake up before he's done. Then you have to count some more.

This story is probably the result of the child's synthesis of various explanations concerning the operation. The product is a rather frightening scenario in which the doctor "pulls tonsils" as one might pull teeth, and the anesthesia is inadequate. It is likely that such expectations are considerably more disturbing than the operative procedure itself.

Another type of fantasy involves death fears associated with the hospital. Many children develop such fears following the death of a relative who had been hospitalized. In their minds the hospital becomes associated with death. One girl was able to express such ideas through projective play with hospital toys. She organized a funeral scene and told the following story:

This man is in the hospital because he got shot. They operate on him, but he dies anyway. Then they have to take him to the place where they put people who die in the hospital. They get there, and then they throw him over the edge. Then they go back and operate on more children.

Such a fantasy could understandably increase the child's anxiety about hospitalization.

Hospitalization can be a frightening and emotionally confusing experience for a young child. To prevent lasting psychological difficulties, it is important to correct a child's misconceptions and provide accurate, understandable information and reassurance. Adults can help by discussing hospitalization and related fears openly and honestly with children. However, it is not always easy for the child to express thoughts and fantasies. Fortunately, a number of tools are available to aid such communication.

Techniques and procedures for communication

The use of children's books dealing with hospital-related themes is one of

The children's quotations contained in this article represent material drawn from work with children on the pediatrics wards of the following hospitals: Jacobi Hospital, Bronx, N.Y.; New York University Institute of Rehabilitation Medicine, New York, N.Y.; Albert Einstein Hospital, Bronx, N.Y.; Middlesex Memorial Hospital, Middletown, Conn.; Boston Children's Hospital, Boston, Mass.; and Yale-New Haven Hospital, New Haven, Conn.

the most valuable resources in work with hospitalized children. In addition to providing factual information about hospitalization and medical procedures, such stories can help initiate discussions of children's own fears and feelings. An annotated list of books for this purpose is included at the end of this article.

After reading one of these stories, children can be encouraged to discuss the events depicted and to create original stories based upon their own thoughts and experiences. The following questions apply to most hospital stories:

Why do you think the child had to go to the hospital?

How do you think the child felt?

What happened during the operation?

How did the child feel after the operation?

What kinds of things do you think were scary to the child in the hospital?

How do you think the child felt about staying overnight in the hospital?

What kinds of things happened to the child in the hospital?

Why did the doctors and nurses take blood and urine tests and X-rays?

How was the hospital in the story different from this hospital?

How do you think the child felt when it was time to go home?

Through such questions, children often begin to express their own feelings about hospitalization. Adults should be flexible in such discussions and should pursue any topic in which the child seems interested. Misconceptions should be corrected, but children should never be criticized or ridiculed for their ideas. The use of books with hospitalized children is discussed in greater depth by Fassler (1977).

Not all children can verbalize their thoughts and feelings about hospitalization. For these children, projective drawings and toy play provide valuable alternative modes of expression. Children can be encouraged to draw pictures of themselves, people in hospitals, doctors, nurses, hospital equipment, operations, and specific body parts such as tonsils, adenoids, appendixes, hearts, or kidneys. The stories children formulate based upon their drawings often provide additional information about their thoughts and ideas and can be used to initiate further discussion.

The child's conception of the events surrounding hospitalization, medical procedures, and surgery can be explored by encouraging the child to act out these events with dolls, puppets, or hospital toys. Although any set of toys can be used, I have found the Playmobile System Doctor and Nurse Kit (Schaper Manufacturing Company, 1107 Broadway, New York, NY 10010) especially well suited for these purposes. This noteworthy set includes an operating table, hospital beds, and a wheelchair. Using these toys, a child's conception of the events which take place during an operation can be explored in detail. The adult can also become incorporated into the child's projective toy play. Children and adults can take turns playing the role of doctor, nurse, patient, or parent. In this manner adults can provide additional information and correct any misconceptions the child may have expressed.

In addition to emotional support and information from parents and teachers, the child may be able to attend a hospital orientation program. Many hos-

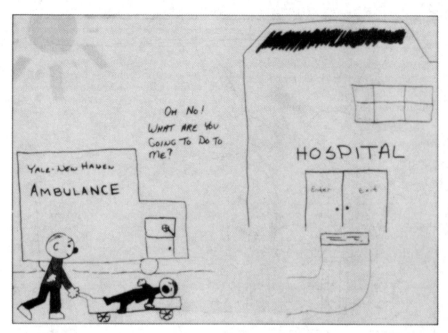

Drawings by Andrea Patalano, 11 years old.

pitals now offer prehospitalization visits or classes which can be extremely beneficial to both parents and children. It is essential, however, to explore children's understanding of the explanations received and the procedures and equipment encountered during such visits. Children may be frightened by a wheelchair or an IV bottle, or they may misunderstand an explanation of the

need for a blood test. By discussing the visit with the child, an adult can ensure that no new fears or misconceptions have been generated.

Last, we can help children by making the hospital a less mysterious place. Class visits to the pediatric wards of local hospitals in conjunction with discussions and individual projects could be encouraged. Physicians and hospital staff can be invited into schools to speak with children about hospitalization and illness. Such activities are preventative measures with the potential to help children cope more effectively with the emotional aspects of any hospitalization experiences they may later encounter.

Preparation of this article was supported in part by a summer research grant from Yale University School of Medicine. The author wishes to thank Drs. Solnit, Lewis, and Wessel at Yale; Dr. Belfer at Boston Children's Hospital; and Dr. Pessin at Bronx Children's Psychiatric Center for their continuing support and encouragement.

Books useful for initiating discussions about hospitalization with children

Rey, M., and Rey, H. *Curious George Goes to the Hospital.* Boston: Houghton Mifflin, 1966.

Hospitalization results from a swallowed puzzle piece. Should be used carefully to explore ideas and misconceptions concerning the reasons for hospitalization. Includes illustrations of an X-ray machine, IV bottle, operating room, and hypodermic needle.

Shay, A. *What Happens When You Go to the Hospital.* Chicago: Reilly and Lee, 1969.

The story of a young girl's tonsillectomy with descriptive photographs. Karen cries and expresses fear of hospital procedures. Illustrations include wheelchairs, traction, hospital bracelets, blood tests, and X-ray equipment. Only book to include a photograph of tonsils.

Sobol, H. *Jeff's Hospital Book.* New York: Walck, 1975.

Sensitive story about a young boy undergoing eye surgery. Illustrated with photographs, including a realistic portrayal of the operation. The book presents accurate information and deals with the boy's feelings and fears.

Stein, S. B. *A Hospital Story.* New York: Walker, 1974.

Realistic portrayal of the experiences surrounding a young girl's hospitalization for a tonsillectomy. Jill cries and expresses feelings of pain. Illustrated with photographs including depictions of hospital beds, wheelchairs, an operating room, an IV bottle, the induction of anesthesia, and a blood test.

Weber, A. *Elizabeth Gets Well.* New York: Crowell, 1970.

The story of Elizabeth's appendectomy. Colorful and detailed illustrations depict an operating room, IV bottle, blood test, X-ray machine, and cast saw. Feelings of fear and pain are acknowledged. Only children's book to show blood as bright red.

For younger children

Bemelmans, L. *Madeline.* New York: Viking, 1939.

Madeline is hospitalized for an appendectomy. There is little real information about the hospital, but the book can be used to introduce the subject with young children.

Bruna, D. *Miffy in the Hospital.* New York: Methuen, 1976.

A nonthreatening presentation of Miffy's visit to the hospital for a tonsillectomy. Fear and pain are acknowledged, but no information about the hospital is given.

Tamburine, J. *I Think I Will Go to the Hospital.* Nashville, Tenn: Abingdon, 1965.

At first, Susie does not want to go to the hospital for a tonsillectomy. She changes her mind after she visits the hospital and acts out the procedures with her pets. The story ends before her operation.

References

Beverly, B. "Effects of Illness on Emotional Development." *Journal of Pediatrics* 8 (1936): 533–543.

Fassler, D. "Experiences with Children and Books in Hospital Settings." *Journal of the Association for the Care of Children in Hospitals* 6 (1977): 12–16.

Jackson, E. "Treatment of the Young Child in the Hospital." *American Journal of Orthopsychiatry* 7 (1942): 56–57.

Menninger, K. "Polysurgery and Polysurgical Addition." *Psychoanalytic Quarterly* 3 (1934): 173–199.

Bibliography

Adams, M., and Berman, D. "The Hospital Through a Child's Eyes." *Children* 12 (1965): 102–104.

Altshuler, A. "Children's Books on Hospitalization." *Library Journal* 98 (1973): 1018–1021.

Azarnoff, P. "Mediating the Trauma of Serious Illness and Hospitalization in Childhood." *Children Today* 3 (1974): 12–17.

Bergman, T. *Children in the Hospital.* New York: International Universities Press, 1965.

Beuf, A. H. *Biting Off the Bracelet.* Philadelphia: University of Pennsylvania Press, 1979.

Brodie, B. "Views of Healthy Children Towards Illness." *American Journal of Public Health* 64 (1974): 1156–1159.

Doak, S., and Wallace, N. "The Doctors Wear Pajamas." *Journal of the Association for the Care of Children in Hospitals* 3 (1975): 8–20.

Freud, A. "The Role of Bodily Illness in the Mental Life of Children." *Psychoanalytic Study of the Child* 7 (1952): 69–81.

Geist, H. *A Child Goes to the Hospital: The Psychological Aspects of a Child Going to the Hospital.* Springfield, Ill.: Charles C. Thomas, 1965.

Haller, J., ed. *The Hospitalized Child and His Family.* Baltimore, Md.: The Johns Hopkins Press, 1967.

Irwin, I., and Kovacs, A. "Analysis of the Children's Drawings and Stories." *Journal of the Association for the Care of Children in Hospitals* 8 (1979): 39–48.

Jessner, L.; Blom, G.; and Wildfogel, S. "Emotional Implications of Tonsillectomy and Adenoidectomy on Children." *Psychoanalytic Study of the Child* 17 (1952): 126–169.

Oremland, E., and Oremland, J., eds. *The Effects of Hospitalization on Children: Models for Their Care.* Springfield, Ill.: Charles C. Thomas, 1973.

Petrillo, M., and Sanger, S. *Emotional Care of Hospitalized Children: An Emotional Approach.* Philadelphia: Lippincott, 1972.

Plank, E. *Working with Children in Hospitals.* Cleveland, Ohio: The Press of Case Western University, 1971.

Robertson, J. *Young Children in Hospital.* New York: Basic Books, 1958.

Shore, M., ed. *Red Is the Color of Hurting: Planning for Children in the Hospital.* Bethesda, Md.: National Institute of Mental Health, HEW #1583, 1967.

Solnit, A. "Hospitalization: Aid to Physical and Psychological Health in Childhood." *American Journal of Diseases of Children* 99 (1960): 155–163.

Stainton, C. "Preschooler's Orientation to Hospital." *Canadian Nurse* 70 (1974): 38–40.

Wessel, M., and LaCamera, R. "Care by Parent: Further Advantages." *Pediatrics* 44 (1969): 303–304.

Wolfer, J., and Visintainer, M. "Psychological Preparation for Surgical Pediatric Patients: The Effect on Children's and Parent's Stress Responses and Adjustment." *Pediatrics* 56 (1975): 187–202.

Saying Good-Bye to Preschool

Patricia Ziegler

"O, we're not off yet, if that's what you mean," replied the first swallow. "We're only making plans and arranging things. Talking it over you know—what route we're taking this year, and where we'll stop, and so on. That's half the fun."

"Fun?" said the Rat, "now that's just what I don't understand. If you've got to leave this pleasant place, and your friends who will miss you, and your snug homes that you've just settled into, why, when the hour strikes I've no doubt you'll go bravely, and face all the trouble and discomfort and change and newness, and make believe that you're not very unhappy. But to want to talk about it, or even think about it, till you really need...."
(p. 156, 1969)

Kenneth Grahame
The Wind in the Willows

*   *   *

Leaving preschool for kindergarten is one of many separations that children meet with a combination of delight and anxiety. Children learn, grow, and are pleased when they are ready for elementary school, but at the same time they may feel anxious about leaving the school, friends, and teachers they know and love.

Other children will change preschool programs, possibly for more hours than their first experience. These children, who share the anxieties of those leaving for kindergarten, may not feel the same sense of accomplishment. How can parents and teachers help ease this important transition for young children?

Teachers and parents carefully plan the first few weeks of children's entry into early childhood programs because we know both children and their parents need time to adjust to their separation. If we are truly committed to meeting the needs of the families we serve, however, we must plan the final weeks of children's attendance, with its potential confusion and loneliness, just as creatively and cooperatively.

Dimensions of school-leaving

Children's separation from a child care or nursery school program may be the most abrupt and permanent break with the past they will experience until they leave home as young adults. Insights from research and the increasing mobility and instability of families in our society sensitize early childhood educators to the importance of bonding, attachment, separation, and loss for young children.

Children who have been prepared or who have had previous separations seem to be able to handle new separations more positively. Two-year-olds briefly prepared by their mothers before leaving for early childhood centers adapted better and played longer and with more toys (Adams and Passman 1981). Similarly, children found later separations easier when they had been cared for by someone they know, stayed with grandparents, spent the night at a friend's house, or had other happy separations (Stacy, et al. 1970; Uphoff 1982).

Our experiences at the Cornell Nursery School also indicate the value of preparation and experience in helping children adjust to separation from early childhood programs. Some children leave during the school year, and we observe how different techniques of handling these separations affect children. We also ask parents to observe their children during the summer between nursery school and kindergarten to help us understand how we can assist families in adjusting to end-

Patricia Ziegler, M.S., is a lecturer at the College of Human Ecology, Cornell University.

of-school changes in the future. These examples highlight some typical separations.

Bob, a distrusting four-year-old, came to school on Wednesday with his parents during group time. Bob's parents announced that he already knew it was his last day of school and they had just stopped to say good-bye, because they were moving right away to a new home. Earlier in the week the children and teachers had been talking together about the end of school which would be on Friday. Bob could not believe both his parents and his teachers' incongruous stories, so his feelings of uncertainty and distrust about his world were once again reinforced.

On the other hand, when Amy and her mother returned to New Zealand several weeks before the end of school, her mother discussed their plans with our teachers. We talked about school ending for everyone soon, and helped Amy feel more comfortable about leaving. Amy and her best friend made duplicate doll houses so they could continue their friendship by exchanging furniture and ideas by mail.

Four-year-old Judy enjoyed her summer following the end of nursery school. She lived in the country and her mother planned activities and included friends so that school-leaving became a way to branch out into the larger community. They took trips to nursery school friends' houses and then to each elementary school that these friends would attend in the fall.

David, however, insisted that everyone else was still at school and spent a good part of his summer lonesome and depressed.

What can we learn from these and other children's reactions when they leave their familiar group for another, possibly very different setting? First, we can attempt to understand the complexity of the separation experience for children and adults.

Separation is not a unitary experience: in considering the consequences which follow separations we must pay due regard to a host of variables, including the reasons for the separation, the pattern of care during the separation, the child's age and maturity, and the quality of family relationships both before and after the separation. (Rutter 1979, p. 147)

We must take these considerations into account as we work with parents and children who leave our early childhood programs.

Involve parents

Abruptness can cause great difficulty for children. At the age of four or five, children are still developing concepts of time, distance, and change. They need to deal with the idea of separation gradually so they can begin to anticipate how leaving school will change their lives.

Parents can help prepare children for an anticipated separation by sharing their plans with their children and the children's teachers at least a month before the change. Review your school policies to ensure that incentives exist so that parents are encouraged to advise the school well in advance of the child's departure.

Parents are young children's social planners (Ascher, Renshaw, and Hymel 1982). Many early childhood programs reach wide geographic areas that serve several elementary schools. In order for children to maintain contact with their friends when they leave for kindergarten, parents must arrange visits, help place phone calls, or mail children's letters. Provide families with a list of children's friends' telephone numbers and addresses to facilitate these contacts.

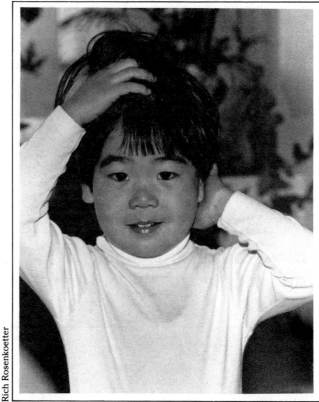

Rich Rosenkoetter

Children's separation from preschool may be the most abrupt and permanent break with the past they will experience until they leave home as young adults.

Parents who see how intense early separations can be are more likely to help young children adopt these and other coping skills that will be important to them as they manage separations throughout life. You may want to discuss the topic with individual families or with parents as a group.

Plan for school-leaving

In good early childhood programs, the basic ingredients for successfully dealing with separation are always present. Teachers who are aware of the importance of school-leaving can channel activities that build on the trust and open relationships they have created with the children.

● Extend the trust between children and adults when dealing with leave-taking. An abrupt departure such as that experienced by Bob will result in mistrust and uncertainty. When adults talk with children about their ambivalence about separations and how they might cope with them, children can begin to understand how to say good-bye and accept separation.

• Call attention to the children's growth. Identify their strengths to help them figure out how they can meet new situations, make friends, and find their special niche at their new schools. As children get to know themselves, they become better able to adapt to new situations, and they will do so with courage.

• Encourage children to express their worries. When they can talk about their concerns and be acknowledged by an empathic listener, some worries may be alleviated. This also gives teachers and parents a chance to add to children's information about their new situation. If possible, visit the new facility with the children, and point out the availability of eating areas, bathrooms, spaces for keeping prized possessions, and other considerations that may concern children.

Photographs offer many opportunities to discuss leave-taking.

Enrich the curriculum

Especially in full-time child care, children leave throughout the year. Some may move to another full-day situation, some may return home to be with a parent and possibly a new sibling, and still others will find different arrangements. In almost all types of programs, the greatest enrollment changes occur when children leave for kindergarten, either in the spring or summer.

These curriculum suggestions can easily be adapted to any individual or group separation situation. Learning opportunities such as these are a natural extension of a good curriculum, so the goal should be to make each activity as meaningful as possible for all the children in your group.

Understand growth. Many children leave their preschool group because of growth. Teachers can help children chart their growth in a number of ways.

• Take frequent photos of children. Prints can easily be kept in chronological order in an album, and are readily available to the children. A projector, screen, and individual viewer will be needed to ensure children easy access to slides. Children can note physical changes, remember activities that they used to do, or identify new skills. "That teddy bear shirt fits my doll! I remember when I wore it, too!" "I can put my cot away all by myself now!"

• Height and weight charts enable children to see their growth recorded. Handprints are another visible indication to children of the changes in their bodies. New shoes are the perfect time for children to talk about how much they are growing!

• Seeds or plant cuttings offer an array of opportunities to observe and direct growth. Beans sprouted on paper towels or an amaryllis bulb shooting up leaves and a flower stalk all dramatically demonstrate changes in nature.

• Animals can also add to children's understanding of the growth process. Baby chicks hatched in the incubator in April will move to the farm in May as their wingfeathers develop.

• Many books and stories can help children understand the nature of change and growth (Bernstein 1977). Some of these children's books are listed in Table 1.

Serve as a role model. Children often experience new feelings. Adults help when they express similar feelings of their own and show appropriate ways to react to these new or confusing emotions. Children will thus expand their pool of possible acceptable responses in similar circumstances (Maccoby 1980).

• Volunteers, student teachers, or staff may leave throughout the year. These adults can talk to the children about their plans and feelings, either informally or in groups. A flannel board, puppets, role playing, or stories may help ease the transition for the children. If the adult is to be replaced, the new person might be introduced informally in a brief visit.

• Adults also can demonstrate appropriate approaches and attitudes when a child or group of children is leaving. Many of these approaches can be planned with the group.

Plan together. Preschool children can demonstrate appropriate empathic responses (Rubin and Everett 1982), and their learning will be more meaningful when they work with adults to suggest good-bye activities for a staff member or child leaving the group.

• A thank you letter to a special visitor is often written by the group. After a firefighter comes, for example, children can write a note of thanks. Such an activity will help children recall the visit and what was special about the person. Letter writing demonstrates a common way of maintaining contact with a person we may not see again.

• A book of drawings or a group mural may be given to a

Table 1. Selected children's books on leaving school.

Caudill, Rebecca. *A Pocketful of Cricket.* New York: Holt, Rinehart & Winston, 1964.

Cohen, Miriam. *The New Teacher.* New York: Macmillan, 1972.

Cohen, Miriam. *Will I Have a Friend?* New York: Macmillan, 1967.

Howell, Ruth. *Everything Changes.* New York: Atheneum, 1972.

Krauss, Ruth. *The Growing Book.* New York: Harper & Row, 1964.

Osborne, Judy. *My Teacher Said Good-Bye Today: Planning for the End of the School Year.* Cambridge, Mass.: Spaulding Co., 1978.

Tobias, Tobi. *Moving Day.* New York: Knopf, 1976.

Waker, Bernard. *Ira Sleeps Over.* Boston: Houghton Mifflin, 1972.

Watson, Wendy. *Moving.* New York: Crowell, 1978.

Zolotow, Charlotte. *Janey.* New York: Harper & Row, 1973.

Zolotow, Charlotte. *A Tiger Named Thomas.* New York: Lothrop, Lee, & Shepherd, 1965.

Parents who see how intense early separations can be are more likely to help young children adopt coping skills to manage separations throughout life.

Elaine M. Ward

departing volunteer, student teacher, staff member, or child as a reminder of shared times. The dollhouses Amy and her best friend made were a personal extension of this type of activity.

• A letter received from a former friend or teacher gives another perspective to the meaning of letters. These letters can be shared together, and children may recall their own memories. Some children may wish to respond with a drawing or letter. Letters from former staff might be shared with parents as well as the children.

Prepare children to leave. When a friend leaves, it is usually less troubling than when the child leaves, but it helps prepare the child for her or his own departure. Some children may leave individually, or groups may depart in other programs or at specific times of the year.

• An excellent book for groups leaving at the end of the school year is *My Teacher Said Good-Bye Today* (Osborne 1978). It includes many photographs of children preparing for leaving school and describes how one teacher worked with her group. Discussions can revolve around what next year might be like, why children are leaving, who will still be at the school, and how they can still see their friends.

• Conferences with parent and child help everyone exchange plans, ideas, and feelings. It also enables adults to say good-bye. Teachers will want to explain to children that they are almost finished with preschool, that they will be missed, and why it is time for them to go to a new school.

• Calendars and maps may help children gain a sense of time and space. Each child might plan a day to be sure of one last chance to engage in a favorite activity. Children and teachers can paste markers on the map to show the location of their houses, their school, and their new schools.

• Photographs taken by children have special significance. A child can talk with a teacher to decide what to take pictures of—favorite items, areas, or friends, and how they will be missed when the child leaves.

• Photographs taken by adults offer many opportunities to discuss leave-taking. Children might request pictures of groups of friends or events. The photos accumulated over the year can be shared with all the children in individual books. Class pictures are always treasured, too.

• Children can learn how to use the telephone to keep in touch with school friends and teachers.

• Dramatic play will inevitably follow discussions about leaving school. Packing boxes, floor maps, cars, trucks, and school buses are some appropriate props. Most important of all are the time, the freedom, and the activities that allow children to play out their thoughts, fears, ideas, and anticipations as they work toward understanding.

Keep in touch. A few activities after the last day of school can help children and teachers maintain contact.

• A telephone-your-teacher time may be most helpful. Send a note home with each child indicating specific convenient times for children to call within the first few days after school has ended.

• Group picnics, either during the summer or in the fall, give everyone a chance to get together in a cheerful and fun way. Such an occasion might be an annual event, especially when siblings attend the same program, because this provides a sense of continuity for everyone involved.

Children, parents, and staff find both the preparation for separation and the reunions to be a source of comfort and joy as they build their fond memories of good times shared together.

Bibliography

Adams, R. E. and Passman, R. E. "The Effects of Preparing Two-Year-Olds for Brief Separations from Their Mothers." *Child Development* 52, no. 3 (September 1981): 1068–1070.

Ascher, R.; Renshaw, D.; and Hymel, S. "Peer Relations and the Development of Social Skills." In *The Young Child: Reviews of Research,* eds. S. G. Moore and R. Cooper. Vol. 3. Washington, D.C.: National Association for the Education of Young Children, 1982.

Baumrind, D. "Childcare Practices Anteceding Three Patterns of Preschool Behavior." *Genetic Psychology Monographs* 75 (1967): 43–88.

Bernstein, J. *Books to Help Children Cope with Separation and Loss.* New York: Bowker, 1977.

Bowlby, J. *Maternal Care and Mental Health.* Geneva: World Health Organization, 1951.

Bronfenbrenner, U. "Children and Families: 1984?" *Society* 18, no. 2 (January-February 1981): 38–41.

Bronfenbrenner, U. *Is Early Intervention Effective? A Report on the Longitudinal Evaluations of Preschool Programs.* Bethesda, Md.: Office of Child Development, U.S. Department of Health, Education and Welfare, 1974.

Chess, S. and Thomas, A. "Infant Bonding: Mystique and Reality." *American Journal of Orthopsychiatry* 52, no. 2 (April 1982): 213–222.

Clarke, A.M. and Clarke, A.D.B. *Early Experience: Myth and Evidence.* London: Open Books, 1976.

Cochran, M.M. and Brassard, J.A. "Child Development and Personal Social Networks." *Child Development* 50, no. 3 (September 1979): 601–616.

Cohen, M.D., ed. *When Children Move from School to School.* Washington, D.C.: Association for Childhood Education International, 1972.

Douglas, J.W.B. "Early Hospital Admissions and Later Disturbances of Behaviour and Learning." *Developmental Medicine and Child Neurology* 17, no. 4 (August 1975): 456–480.

Eckhardt, L. and Prugh, D. "Preparing Children Psychologically for Painful Medical and Surgical Procedures." In *Psychological Aspects in Pediatric Care,* ed. E. Gellert. New York: Grune & Stratton, 1978.

Hoffman, L.W. "Effects of Maternal Employment on the Child—A Review of the Research." *Developmental Psychology* 10, no. 2 (March 1974): 204–228.

Hymovich, D.P. and Chamberlin, R.W. *Child and Family Development: Implications for Primary Care.* New York: McGraw-Hill, 1980.

Kennell, J.H. and Bergen, M. "Early Childhood Separations." *Pediatrics* 37, no. 2 (February 1966): 291–298.

Lamb, M.E. and Lamb, J.E. "The Nature and Importance of the Father-Infant Relationship." *Family Coordinator* 25, no. 4 (October 1976): 379–385.

Maccoby, E. *Social Development: Psychological Growth and Parent-Child Relations.* Harcourt Brace Jovanovich, 1980.

Marantz, S.A. and Mansfield, A.F. "Maternal Employment and the Development of Sex-Role Stereotyping in Five- to Eleven-Year-Old Girls." *Child Development* 48, no. 2 (June 1977): 668–673.

McCord, G.; Osborne, J.; Turner, R.; and Ziegler, P. *Growth Through Separation: Planning for School Leaving.* Urbana-Champaign, Ill.: University of Illinois Press, 1981.

Moore, S.G. and Cooper, C.R., eds. *The Young Child: Reviews of Research.* Vol. 3. Washington, D.C.: National Association for the Education of Young Children, 1982.

Osborne, J. *My Teacher Said Good-Bye Today: Planning for the End of the School Year.* Cambridge, Mass.: Spaulding Co., 1978.

Provence, S. and Lipton, R. *Infants in Institutions: A Comparison of Their Development with Family-Reared Infants During the First Year of Life.* New York: International Universities Press, 1962.

Quinton, D. and Rutter, M. "Early Hospital Admissions and Later Disturbances of Behavior: An Attempted Replication of Douglas' Findings." *Developmental Medicine and Child Neurology* 18, no. 4 (August 1976): 447–459.

Radin, N. "The Unique Contribution of Parents to Childrearing: The Preschool Years." In *The Young Child: Reviews of Research,* eds. S.G. Moore and C.R. Cooper. Vol. 3. Washington, D.C.: National Association for the Education of Young Children, 1982.

Rubin, K.H. and Everett, B. "Social Perspective-Taking in Young Children." In *The Young Child: Reviews of Research,* eds. S.G. Moore and C.R. Cooper. Vol. 3. Washington, D.C.: National Association for the Education of Young Children, 1982.

Rutter, M. "Separation Experiences: A New Look at an Old Topic." *Journal of Pediatrics* 95, no. 1 (July 1979): 147–154.

Schachter, F.F. and Strage, A.A. "Adults' Talk and Children's Language Development." In *The Young Child: Reviews of Research,* eds. S.G. Moore and C.R. Cooper. Vol. 3. Washington, D.C.: National Association for the Education of Young Children, 1982.

Schwartz, P. "Length of Day Care Attendance and Attachment." *Child Development* 54, no. 4 (August 1983): 1073–1078.

Spitz, R.A. "Hospitalism: An Inquiry Into the Genesis of Psychiatric Conditions of Early Childhood." *Psychoanalytic Study of the Child Yearbook* 1 (1945): 53–74.

Stacey, M.; Dearden, R.; Pill, R.; and Robinson, D. *Hospitals, Children and Their Families: The Report of a Pilot Study.* London: Routledge & Kegan Paul, 1970.

Thomas, A. and Chess, S. *Temperament and Development.* New York: Brunner/Mazel, 1977.

Tulkin, S.R. and Kagan, J. "Mother-Child Interaction in the First Year of Life." *Child Development* 43, no. 1 (March 1972): 31–41.

Uphoff, M., M.D. Personal communication in classroom lecture, 1983.

Wallerstein, J.S. and Kelley, J.B. "Parental Divorce—The Preschool Child." *Journal of American Academy of Child Psychiatry* 14, no. 4 (Autumn 1975): 600–616.

Yarrow, M.R.; Scott, P.; deLoeuw, L.; and Heinig, C. "Child Rearing in Families of Working and Nonworking Mothers." *Sociometry* 25, no. 2 (June 1962): 122–140.

This article is based on an NAEYC Conference presentation that included Gretchen McCord, Judy Osborne, and Ruth K. Turner. I gratefully acknowledge their part in the awareness and learning together that formed the foundation for these ideas.

Helping Children Cope with Death

Erna Furman

Perhaps there are some among you who find the topic of death particularly trying because you have recently lost a loved one or because you suffer from old bereavement wounds that are still sore and painful. To those who are hurting and struggling to cope, I extend my sympathies and also my apologies lest this article contain thoughts that might inadvertently make things harder for you.

Many of us go through life for long periods without thinking about death. When it suddenly strikes very close to us, it comes as a shock, not only because it always represents a loss but also because we get the horrible feeling that "this could be me; this could happen to me, to my family, to my children and friends." We have a tendency to deal with this fear by adopting one of two extreme attitudes. We may feel the impact as though the tragedy had really happened to us. We put ourselves in the shoes of the bereaved or of the dying and feel so overwhelmed and anxious that we are unable to extend ourselves appropriately to those who need our help. At the other extreme, we shield ourselves and behave as if "this is not real; this did not happen to me; I don't want to hear, read, or talk about it." This reaction, too, prevents us from extending a helping hand because it keeps

us from coming to terms with our own feelings. Often we waver from one extreme to the other until, hopefully, we reach a kind of middle ground where we are able to feel, "There but for the grace of God go I; it is not me but it could be." When we arrive at this hard-to-reach point we begin to be able to think and feel with others and to help them as well as ourselves.

Many years ago at the Hanna Perkins (therapeutic) Nursery School, we were working without thinking about death. Then within one year, two mothers of young children died, leaving their families as well as therapists, teachers, peers, and friends stunned. We had to cope with the immediate reality and struggle to come to terms with what had happened. But this was only the beginning. In the course of the next few years, we found that, without having sought cases of bereavement, we had in intensive treatment 23 children of all ages who had lost a parent through death. Each analyst who treated a bereaved child and worked with the family found it so difficult and painful that we turned to each other to share and learn together. We hoped that in this way we would be better able to understand and help our patients and, perhaps, formulate some thoughts that might be of general interest and serve to assist others (Furman 1974). I would like to share with you some of the things we

learned, trying to pick out what might be particularly helpful to teachers of young children.

As you know, it does not take the death of a parent to bring children to an encounter with death. Many grandparents, siblings, relatives, and pets die. There are also many daily events which bring children face to face with death, be it a passing funeral procession or a dead worm in the backyard. The worst bereavement is the death of a parent. It is a unique experience distinct from all other losses, such as divorce or separation, and distinct from other experiences with death. Many nursery school teachers may be fortunate enough never to have a pupil whose parent dies, but they are surely called upon to help with some less tragic bereave-

Erna Furman, *B.A., is a faculty member of the Cleveland Center for Research in Child Development and Assistant Clinical Professor, Department of Psychiatry, Case Western Reserve University Medical School, Cleveland, Ohio.*

This article is adapted from a talk given in May 1975 at the Seventh Annual Workshop of the Cleveland Center for Research in Child Development for Preschool Educators of North Eastern Ohio.

ments and the many daily encounters with death—the ants a child steps on or the dead mouse someone brings for show-and-tell (Hoffman 1974).

Our bereaved children came to treatment with many different symptoms. Parental death is unique; it happens to unique people who respond in unique ways. Our patients most often responded in a disturbed, unhealthy fashion, sometimes at the time of the bereavements, sometimes not until many years later. But we were deeply impressed that some children only about 2 years of age, because of very optimal circumstances, could master their tragic loss. By contrast, we had much older patients who could not master it at all. I do not mean to imply that the 2-year-olds master this stress more easily; on the contrary, it is harder. Nor is it short-lived for them; it lasts longer. I am not speaking of the degree of pain and anguish, but the ability to master ultimately. To me that means that these children were upset, struggled and suffered, but were able to mourn their parents and to progress in their development. The danger of parental bereavement does not lie in the formation of isolated symptoms or difficulties. The main danger is that it may arrest or distort a child's development toward becoming a fully functioning adult. Many of the factors involved touch upon the role of the teacher and offer an opportunity to develop in children those qualities which will enable them to master a future bereavement or to help them and their peers to cope with a current loss or minor encounter with death.

Helping children understand death

The first crucial factor is children's ability to understand death in its concrete manifestations, that is, to understand that death means no life, no eating, no sleeping, no pain, no movement. Those children who at the time of bereavement already had a rather good grasp of the concrete facts of death had a much easier time. We found that children from toddler age on show interest in dead things. They find dead insects or birds. When they can tell that a sibling is different from a teddy bear, that one is animate and the other not, they can also begin to understand what *dead* means. For example, when the toddler plays with a dead fly and notes that it does not move, it helps to confirm the child's observation by using the word *dead* and explaining that the fly will never move again because it is dead. Most young children have not yet been helped to acquire this kind of basic concrete understanding of what *dead* means, how things die, and what we do with the corpse. It is much easier to acquire concrete understanding of death from insects or small animals, since they do not have great emotional significance for the child; this knowledge paves the way for later understanding of death in people.

McDonald (1963) studied the responses of the peers of our two bereaved Hanna Perkins Nursery School pupils. She found that children's first interest focused on what death is. They could not direct themselves to the aspects of loss, empathy, or sympathy for a peer's loss until they could understand concretely what death means. McDonald also noted that each of the children's questions required a special effort of thoughtful awareness and listening by the teachers. Initially, and without knowing it, teachers closed their eyes and ears and implied, without words, that death was not a welcome topic. Once their attitude changed, the children's questions just poured out. It is very difficult for all of us to talk about death, even dead insects. Most of us were not helped in this respect when we were children so we tend not to help children or do not know how to help. With special effort and by struggling to come to terms with questions about death ourselves, it is possible to overcome our difficulty to some extent.

Roger W. Neal

When parents understand that their children's greatest need is continued physical and emotional care by the surviving parent, they usually compromise for the sake of the child and find that they benefit as well.

Children before age 5 or 6 are incapable of abstract thinking and therefore unable to grasp religious or philosophical explanations. They usually distort them into concrete and often frightening concepts that have little to do with religion.

Support for parents

Parents usually do not mind when teachers talk at school about death as it relates to insects, worms, or even animals. Some teachers have found it helpful to meet with parents to discuss how such incidents are handled. Parents, perhaps even more than teachers, find it very difficult to talk with children about death, fearing that sooner or later the child will say, "Will I die?" "Will you die?" We are frightened of the answers that we would rather not give. However, the eventual next step in children's understanding death is that of relating it to themselves and to those they love and need. A meeting with parents on this subject does sometimes help to bring such questions into the open and offers the teacher an opportunity to help the parents. Whether a teacher wishes to arrange such meetings depends on the teacher's relationship with the parent group and the extent to which both sides are ready to grapple with the subject of death.

When a child asks, "Can this happen to me or to my mommy?" the answer should take into account the child's sense of time. A parent is hesitant to say, "No, I won't die," because he or she eventually will die. Yet should the parent say, "Yes, I will die," the child understands this to mean tomorrow or next week. We find that a young child can best understand when the parent says, "No, I do not expect to die for a long, long time," stressing the *no,* and adding that he or she expects to enjoy the child as a grown-up and have many years of being a grandparent.

Parents usually also raise the question of spiritual answers to the question of death. Children before age 5 or 6 are incapable of abstract thinking and therefore unable to grasp religious or philosophical explanations. They usually distort them into concrete and often frightening concepts that have little to do with religion. I know some very religious parents who chose not to introduce religious explanations to their children under the age of five precisely because they knew these concepts would be distorted and might later interfere with the children's attitudes about religion. By contrast, doubting or unbelieving parents quite often use explanations that involve *heaven* and *God.* This happens because they have not thought matters through themselves and want to shield the child from something frightening. In shielding the child they only shield themselves and create confusion in the child. Something that is not really believed by the adult cannot come across as true or reassuring to the child.

In our experience the most understanding parents have given concrete explanations of death and burial. When, in response to what they had heard from others, the children asked, "What about heaven?" or "Does God take people away?" the parents replied, "Many people believe that. Many people believe other things too and as you get older you will learn about them and will understand them better. Right now it is important that you understand how we all know when someone is dead."

Mourning . . . is a process that is not always visible from the outside. . . . Sometimes there are no overt signs of upset and yet the feelings may be there.

The concrete facts of death are usually much less frightening to children than to adults. An anecdote about one of Barnes's (1964) patients illustrates this point. A father had struggled very hard to help his young children understand what *dead* meant and what being in a coffin meant because their mother had died. Some months later their grandfather died. As the father tried to tell his little girl that they would choose a nice box with a soft blanket inside so that grandfather would be very comfortable, the little girl interrupted him and said, "But Daddy, if he is really dead then it doesn't matter about his being comfortable in the coffin." For that moment the child certainly had a better grasp than the father.

Bearing unpleasant feelings

Another factor which facilitates a child's mastery of bereavement is the ability to bear unpleasant feelings, particularly sadness and anger. Obviously, there is no way to anticipate the kind of feelings that come with a bereavement. Separations are very different from a loss through death, but there are some similarities. Separations, to a small extent, involve the same feelings of longing, sadness, and anger that we find in much greater intensity at a time of bereavement. Young children are able to bear these feelings to an incredible extent if they have been given appropriate help in developing this strength.

How does one help a child achieve such mastery? Basically there are two ways. One is to expose children only to bearable separations. When separations are too long they become unbearable and therefore not conducive to experiencing feelings. A very few hours of separation are bearable for a baby, perhaps half a day for a toddler, and at most a couple of days for a nursery school child. But it takes more than adjusting the lengths of separation. The second important step is the adults' willingness to help children recognize their feelings, express them appropriately, and cope with them. Before and after the separation this is the parents' task; during the separation the caregiving person can help.

It is often thought that children who do not react, do not make a fuss, or even enjoy the parents' absence, are well-adjusted, good children. To me, these children have not built appropriate mental muscles to bear unpleasant feelings. They shut themselves off from such feelings and therefore have no control of them. For nursery school teachers an excellent time to practice with children in building up the mental muscles for knowing and bearing unpleasant feelings is, of course, during entry to nursery school. At that time one can help parents understand that children who have no feelings, who react as though nothing has happened, or who immediately "love" the school, are children who are shut off from their feelings and in danger of stunting their emotional growth. Many mothers who do not welcome the child's unhappy or angry response to separation at the start of school would be very concerned if the child did not react feelingly to the loss of a loved person or readily preferred someone else in that person's stead. Yet how could a child acknowledge very intense feelings without previous help to cope with them in less threatening situations?

Coping with bereavement

So far we have considered how difficult it is to talk about death even in terms of animals and insects, and how hard to bear loneliness, sadness, and anger in terms of brief separations. We know, of course, how much greater the hardship is when we have to think about and feel fully the total loss of a loved person. There is no easy way to cope with bereavement. There is no shortcut, either for the bereaved or for those who help them. The goal of assisting bereaved persons is not to foreshorten their or our own pain and anguish but to strive toward inner mastery. Even if we achieve it, it does not mean that we have come to terms with death once and for all. In order to be able to help we too have to empathize anew with each bereavement and struggle through it again.

I would like to turn now to what teachers can do, and often have done, when a child in the nursery school suffers the death of a parent, sibling, or close relative. I do not have any easy remedies to offer, and my suggestions are much more easily said than done because pain and anxiety are an essential part of the task.

The teacher's first question often is, "Should I mention the loss to the child?" I have heard time and again about the fear of causing a child hardship by referring to his or her loss. Some years ago I met a boy whose father had died. His teacher had reported that the boy had no feelings about, or reaction to, the death of the father. When I saw this boy, said "Hello," and expressed my natural sympathy, he broke into tears at once. He cried for an hour and I had to see him a second time before he could begin to talk. I asked him later why he had never shown his feelings at school. The boy replied, "You know, that teacher was so mean! He never even bothered to come to me and say 'I am sorry your father died.' I would never show my feelings to that kind of guy." I suspect that this was not a mean teacher but that his reaction of silence built a barrier between the child and himself.

This and similar experiences have convinced me that the teacher has to take the first step by mentioning the loss and expressing sympathy in a way that implies, "This will be with us a long time. I hope you will feel free to come to me, talk with me, or feel with me about it." In practice, some children will come to the teacher much more than others. However often they do or do not come, the teacher needs to empathize with each and every feeling that may arise and help children tolerate them. This means not to falsify feelings, not to hold them back, not even to pour them out in order to be rid of them, but to recognize and contain them.

At opportune times the teacher can also help by talking with the child about the factual aspects of the bereavement —how the loved one died, where he or she is buried, and changes in the family setting and routine. I think it is equally important for the teacher to report to the parent what the child shows, thinks, or feels about this experience so that the parent can further help the child and perhaps be alerted to some aspect which has not yet been expressed at home.

In addition to work with the child, a second area in which the teacher can be helpful is with the parents or surviving parent. Hopefully, before a loss occurs, the teacher will have built the kind of relationship with the parent which will make it possible for him or her to inform the teacher as a friend, a special professional friend who has the parent's and child's welfare at heart. The parent will welcome talking with this teacher and perhaps accept some suggestions—how to tell the child about the death, how to talk it over with the child, whether to take the child to the funeral, what plans to make for the immediate future.

Assisting parents

Let me now share with you some of the things we have found helpful to parents at such a time. Adults with young children do not die uncomplicated deaths; the deaths are always untimely. This is also true about the death of siblings. It is important that the child

Steve Takatsuno

It is most important that the children understand not only that the parent or sibling is dead, but also what the cause of death was.

understand not only that the parent or sibling is dead, but also what the cause of death was. When these two things are not understood, when they are distorted or denied, it is impossible for the child even to begin mourning. I do not mean overwhelming the child with frightening details. Hopefully a teacher can help a parent to tell the child enough and in such a manner that the child can achieve a considerable amount of understanding.

Parents always want to know whether they should take the child to the funeral, and what they should say about it. We can only give an answer after we learn more about the specific situation. The child's attendance at the funeral will depend on the type of service, how the parent feels about it, how comfortable the parent is with the rites the

family observes, and how able the parent is to extend himself or herself emotionally to the child during the funeral.

Many families are willing to adapt the services to the needs of all the family. Children often find an open casket difficult. They find long services difficult. If the funeral rites are not suitable for a young child or if the parent is unable to care effectively for the child during the services, it is better that the child remain at home with a familiar person and with the full verbal knowledge of what is happening during that time. I had a patient who was sent to the zoo on the day of her father's funeral in the hope that she would not have to be sad. This hope was not fulfilled, and the arrangement produced an almost insurmountable barrier within the child and between child and surviving parent. Mourning has to happen together. Pain and anguish have to be shared. It is not fair to shut out the child.

When it comes to immediate plans for the future, the teacher can sometimes impress upon parents how very important it is for the child to keep the home and remaining family together. Adults often find it much easier to leave the place of distress, to throw away the things that remind them of the deceased. For children the opposite holds true. They need the concrete continuation and help of their surroundings in order to come to terms with what is missing. Sometimes people have asked how parents and children can ever be of support to one another when they have such different needs. When parents understand that their children's greatest need is continued physical and emotional care by the surviving parent, they usually compromise for the sake of the child and find that they benefit as well. Being a good parent brings a measure of self-esteem that cannot be gained in any other way and is especially helpful at a time of bereavement when so many other things seem not worthwhile.

Helping others in the group

Along with assisting the bereaved child and parent, the teacher has to extend help to the other children in the nursery school. This usually starts by discussing with the bereaved parent what to tell the other children and their families. Hopefully the bereaved parent is able to share the truth in simple realistic terms with his or her own child and is willing to have this information passed on. Then the teacher needs to take a few painful hours to call every parent in the nursery group. Each call is long and difficult and should, if possible, include several items: a brief account of what happened to their child's peer, which terms or phrases will be used in the nursery school to discuss the sad event, how the parents can tell their own child and how helpful it would be if the child learned the news first from them, and how to cope with some of the child's questions.

If a bereaved parent is initially unable to allow discussion of the cause of death, the teacher may have to say, for example, "Chris's father died. It is still too hard for Chris's mommy to talk about it, but she will tell us what happened later and I will share it with you." Hopefully, the teacher's relationship with the parent will help to make this delay brief.

The next morning all children will have been told of the death, even if not its cause, by their parents, and the teacher can sit down with them and initiate the first discussion of facts and feelings. The most important point to cover is, "This talk is only a beginning. We will talk about it and feel about it often and for a long time. It will be with us because it is a sad and scary thing."

There are usually three main questions that arise sooner or later. "What is *dead?*" "Can it happen to me?" and "Can it happen to you?" Until these questions are accepted and coped with, it is generally not possible for the peers or for their parents to extend genuine sympathy to the bereaved. When we are able to assist children in gaining gradual mastery, many months of painful struggle seem indeed worthwhile.

The mourning process

If the death is understood, if its cause is understood and the disposal of the body is understood, and if the bereaved child is reasonably sure of his or her own survival and of having bodily and emotional needs met to a sufficient extent, mourning will start of itself. It is a process that is not always visible from the outside because, contrary to what many people think, mourning does not consist of wailing, rages, crying, or complaining. Sometimes there are no overt signs of upset and yet the feelings may be there.

I worked with a mother and child. The little boy lost his father two years previously and experienced some difficulty in the aftermath. The mother told me that she had never cried in front of the child, since she only cries when she is alone in bed. The boy, who supposedly had not reacted at all to his father's death and had certainly never cried or raged, told me in his separate interview that he was not a person who ever cried in front of people. He only cried when he was alone in bed and no-

body knew that he cried. He cried night after night but his mother never cried. Although mother and child expressed feelings in the same form, they did not know that the other even had feelings. It was sad to see how hard they had made if for themselves and for each other. However, even if they had not cried at all they might have been able to mourn because mourning is a mental process that consists primarily of two parts: on one hand, a very gradual and painful detachment from the memories of the deceased, and on the other hand almost the opposite, a taking into oneself some traits or qualities of the deceased. How much there is of each part and whether the proportion leads to a healthy adaptive outcome depend on many factors, including the age of the bereaved person, the nature of the bereavement, the preceding relationship, and the personality of the deceased. With young children it is particularly important that they take into themselves the healthy rather than the sick attributes of the dead parent and that they detach themselves sufficiently, so that, in time, they will be free to form a parental bond with a new person.

Sometimes parents intuitively understand the ways in which their child's long inner mourning proceeds and sense when the child encounters difficulties. Sometimes it is much harder. It certainly is not a mark of failure to seek professional assistance at such a time. That is yet another area where the teacher can support the surviving parent. The sooner help is given, the better the chances of preventing possible damage to the child's growing personality.

References

Barnes, M. J. "Reactions to the Death of a Mother." *The Psychoanalytic Study of the Child* 19 (1964): 334–357.

Furman, E. *A Child's Parent Dies.* New Haven, Conn.: Yale University Press, 1974.

Hoffman, Y. "Learning about Death in Preschool." *Review, Spring 1974.* Cleveland: Cleveland Association for the Education of Young Children, 1974, pp. 15–17.

McDonald, M. "Helping Children to Understand Death: An Experience with Death in a Nursery School." *Journal of Nursery Education* 19, no. 1 (1963): 19–25.

Using Crisis-Oriented Books with Young Children

Mary Renck Jalongo

Teachers often turn to children's books as one resource in helping individuals or groups resolve a crisis. This article suggests guidelines for selecting and using picture books designed to facilitate a child's emotional health.

A 4-year-old child enrolled in preschool was relating the day's event to his interested mother during the ride home. "How's the new gerbil doing?" she asked. "Well," came the boy's cheerful reply, "I'll look at him tomorrow—he's dead for now." When conversations between adults and young children turn to sensitive topics like death, adults are understandably unsure of the best way to proceed. The adult's ability to interpret the intent of a child's comment, to formulate appropriate responses, and to apply knowledge of child development are easily put to the test by a young child's unique perspective on reality. Perhaps the most unnerving thought is that the explanations provided by adults might be confusing or even damaging to an impressionable young child.

We know, for example, that a euphemism about death like "Grandma has gone to sleep" can make a child fearful of bedtime, or that an anatomical inaccuracy such as "The baby is inside mommy's stomach" can lead a child to believe that food intake and childbearing are somehow synonymous. Dealing with children's candor and inquisitiveness in ways that are psychologically sound often places extraordinary demands on even the most com-

petent, poised, and experienced caregivers. Some adults react by giving a flustered reply that conveys uncertainty or annoyance. Others seek out reference materials or resource persons with the "right" answers in hopes that they will be better prepared the next time. Many simply avoid the subject entirely. And the realization that every one of these responses might result in diminished opportunities for learning leaves us to ponder how we might become more skilled in guiding young children's social and affective development.

New trends in literature for young children

The practice of using books as one way to foster emotional growth and stability has a long history. Initially, the term bibliotherapy referred to the therapeutic use of books with patients by specially trained librarians, usually in a hospital setting. Over the years, this definition has become increasingly general and now extends to the early childhood educator's use of picture books with young children (Moody and Limper 1971; Reid 1972; Rudman 1976). Recently, there has been a growing interest in literature that openly explores emotionally charged issues (Bernstein 1977; Bracken and Wigutoff 1979; DeHaven 1980). These books have gained popularity among practitioners because convincingly true-to-life situations are portrayed honestly, sensitively, and in consideration of the child's cognitive development level.

Reviews of children's picture books now regularly include themes like the search for identity, handling powerful emotions, coping with illness and hospitalization, sibling rivalry, dealing with divorce and separation, understanding handicapping conditions, and accepting individual differences (Braun and Lasher 1978). Obviously, the content of literature for the young child is undergoing some important changes and the same topics that were once viewed as inappropriate for young children are now the focus of numerous books. Before educators run the risk of going to extremes in endorsing all crisis-oriented children's literature, the following four questions must be thoroughly investigated:

1. How can this trend toward sensitive issues in picture books best be defined and described?

2. How might these books contribute to curricula for the preschool/primary child?

3. What criteria can be implemented to ensure that standards of quality in children's literature are not being compromised in the search for relevance?

4. What is a recommended procedure for the use of books that deal with difficult issues?

The combined efforts of psychologists, educators, librarians, authors, illustrators, and publishers have begun to successfully fill an obvious gap in literature for young children. Funda-

Mary Renck Jalongo, *Ph.D., is Associate Professor of Elementary Education at Indiana University of Pennsylvania, Indiana, Pennsylvania.*

*Although caregivers and children derive mutual benefit when literature is used to foster an emotionally enriching classroom experience, educators should keep in mind that books based on sensitive issues are not necessarily good literature. Ideally, these stories ought to reflect **both** quality and timeliness.*

mental to this goal have been the beliefs that books for the young child can function as a vehicle for adult-child discussion of difficult life issues, aid the child in sensing a common bond with others who have experienced a particular problem, and can prepare the child to cope more confidently with a personal crisis (Sutherland and Arbuthnot 1977).

Defining bibliotherapy

Using literature for the purpose of promoting mental health or the use of books in a therapeutic sense is referred to as bibliotherapy (Overstad 1981). With this as a working definition, it is entirely possible that even caregivers who are unfamiliar with the terminology are actively involved in using bibliotherapy. Some books like *The Dead Bird* (Brown 1979) are familiar stories that have been used in classrooms for years and are only now receiving the attention they merit. Others have made more recent contributions to literature depicting loss and grief such as *Let's Remember Corky* (Fine 1981) or *Pop's Secret* (Townsend and Stern 1980).

Although caregivers and children derive mutual benefit when literature is used to foster an emotionally enriching classroom experience, educators should keep in mind that books based on sensitive issues are not necessarily good literature. Ideally, these stories ought to reflect *both* quality and timeliness.

Evaluating crisis-oriented literature

There are at least three potential advantages of literature that addresses difficult life issues:

1. *Information*—it stimulates the adult-child exchange of ideas on significant topics.

2. *Relevance*—it encourages the child to make meaningful connections between school experiences and daily life.

Carolyn A. McKeone

3. *Acceptance*—it legitimizes the child's emotional responses to crisis situations.

Many of the general selection criteria for picture books offered by Maxim (1980) apply here: clarity of writing style, interesting characters, suitable illustrations, relationship to the child's experiential background, freedom from stereotypes, brevity, and teacher appeal. Due to the affective nature of bibliotherapy topics, however, some supplemental guidelines are warranted. Figure 1 summarizes the additional evaluation questions and offers children's book titles that successfully meet each criterion.

Implementing bibliotherapy

After caregivers have selected, evaluated, and procured books that treat emotionally charged topics, important decisions about the audience, timing, and method of presentation remain. Books intended to facilitate a child's emotional health must be *shared with* children as carefully as they are *chosen for* them.

Identifying the audience

Obviously, there is a considerable range of topics that could be listed under a broad category like bibliotherapy. One person's devastating emotional crisis can be another's exciting opportunity. Frequently the genuine anxieties and stresses experienced during childhood lessen in importance as they are surveyed from a more mature vantage point. It also seems, however, that the nearer a child's crisis comes to qualifying as an adult source of stress, the more likely it is to be embroiled in controversy. Books that describe the need for peer group acceptance like *Will I Have a Friend?* (Cohen 1967) are long-standing choices that are unlikely to offend anyone's sensibilities. On the other hand, a book like *Show Me!* (McBride and Fleischauer-Hardt 1976) has created quite a stir, and is no longer published in the United States. There is an inescapable element of censorship when literature ventures into highly controversial areas (Flood and Lapp 1981), and teachers must take care that their discussions with children are not being used to impose personal values that may be in direct conflict with those of the parents and community.

To the extent that children need adult guidance in understanding complex issues like sex or death, the use of some children's books ought to be closely supervised by caring adults. Certain books that deal with value-laden social issues do not belong on a shelf alongside children's pleasure reading picture books, partly because they are not written at the young child's reading level and partly because, in the absence of questions and answers directed by an adult, these books may lack effectiveness. Teachers should also be aware that some picture books, such as *Hiroshima No Pika* (Maruki 1982), may appear to be intended for children, but the subject matter or treatment is

---

Figure 1. Additional evaluation guidelines for crisis-oriented children's literature

Selection criteria	Examples	
A. Can children identify with the plot, setting, dialogue, and characters?	*Ira Sleeps Over* *Stevie*	*Goodbye, Hello* *A Baby Sister for Frances*
B. Does the book use correct terminology, psychologically sound explanations, and portray events accurately? Does the book have professional endorsements?	*Eric Needs Stitches* *What Is a Girl? What Is a Boy?*	*Where's Daddy?* *I Wish I Was Sick, Too!*
C. Are the origins of emotional reactions revealed and inspected?	*Grownups Cry Too* *Moving Day*	*David and Dog* *The Temper Tantrum Book*
D. Does the book reflect an appreciation for individual differences?	*Straight Hair, Curly Hair* *The Balancing Girl*	*Your Family, My Family* *Darlene*
E. Are good coping strategies modeled for the child?	*The Tenth Good Thing About Barney* *There's a Nightmare in My Closet*	*Silas and the Mad-Sad People* *Home Alone*
F. Does the book present crises in an optimistic, surmountable fashion?	*Nobody Asked Me If I Wanted a Baby Sister* *Frog Goes to Dinner*	*Howie Helps Himself* *Harry and the Terrible Whatzit*

too intense for young children; these books should be used in carefully supervised situations.

Before sharing a controversial book with children, obtain opinions from supervisory personnel and other caregivers in your program. If a book raises some serious reservations, leave it as a choice for parents and/or therapists. *Something Happened to Me* (Sweet 1981) is an example of a book that deals with the intense emotional crisis of sexual abuse and is more appropriate for use by an adult with specialized skills and an individual child who has been the unfortunate victim of this serious social problem. Another instance of a limited audience is the parent who is seeking information written at the child's level on a particular topic. Books from a series such as *Talking About Divorce and Separation* (Grollman 1969) or the Open Family books (Stein 1974) can then be used as family discussion guides.

Books that depict fairly universal experiences in novel contexts or with unusual characters often appeal to a wider child audience. Animals who serve as imaginary playmates (Hazen 1974) or suffer peer rejection (Sharmat 1977) can be interesting to a child who is currently experiencing the situation because a successful resolution to the problem is offered. Those listeners who have not yet encountered the difficulty are provided with a vicarious experience that might prove useful in developing personal coping strategies or in generating an empathic response to the plight of someone else.

When to use bibliotherapy

For people of all ages, there is tremendous satisfaction in locating information that applies to our special circumstances. Teachers who are attuned to their students' needs and interests can make informed book choices and thereby contribute significantly to the impact of literature used in a therapeutic sense. Events affecting one or more children can and should prompt schedule revisions that will permit time for the pursuit of pertinent issues. The birth of a sibling is an example of an event that might send the teacher searching to find a copy of Mercer and Marianna Mayer's wordless picture book, *One Frog Too Many* (1975). By composing and dictating a narrative to accompany the illustrations, children can collectively express feelings of resentment, jealousy, and hostility that are often associated with having to share parental affection with a baby brother or sister. Along the same lines, a holiday like Halloween might be an opportune time to discuss fears using the book *Don't Be Scared* (Vogel 1964). An aggressive incident among children might serve as a stimulus for reading and conversing about *The Hating Book* (Zolotow 1969) and *Let's Be Enemies* (Udry 1961). Both of these storytime choices offer children insight on misunderstanding as a primary source of conflict and model the use of verbal communication as a means for resolving disputes.

Presenting the book

After the book, audience, and time have been chosen, caregivers must give careful consideration to teaching methods. An overview of the teacher's role in bibliotherapy is included in Figure 2.

First and foremost, the reader should be thoroughly familiar with the book content. Emphasis is placed upon this step when reading any book to children, but it is doubly important when literature treats feelings, attitudes, beliefs, and values. The next responsibility of the teacher is the preparation of an introduction/motivation for the story. These comments should be brief and make reference to any naturally occurring situations which have prompted the teacher to use the book at this particular time. A third and crucial aspect of bibliotherapy is the advance preparation of specific questions that can be interspersed throughout the story to focus attention on major points (see Warren 1977 for ways in which adults can talk with young children about sensitive topics). Questions that encourage children to analyze the behavior of story characters, make inferences about emotional reactions, apply information to their own experience, and synthesize techniques for coping with

---

Figure 2. Steps for the teacher in using bibliotherapy

1 Plan	2 Motivate	3 Present	4 Follow up
Select book by studying content and format *Prepare questions* based upon: ■ children's background ■ story sequence ■ concept development ■ different levels of questioning	*Design introductory remarks* that: ■ focus attention ■ set discussion purposes ■ relate the story to children's direct experience ■ help the children to identify with story characters	*Read book/interject prepared questions* *Respond* to children's comments and concerns	*Conclude discussion* as needed ■ clarify any information presented ■ review concepts ■ answer children's questions ■ recognize children's contributions ■ communicate an acceptance of emotional responses ■ evaluate the story/ discussion

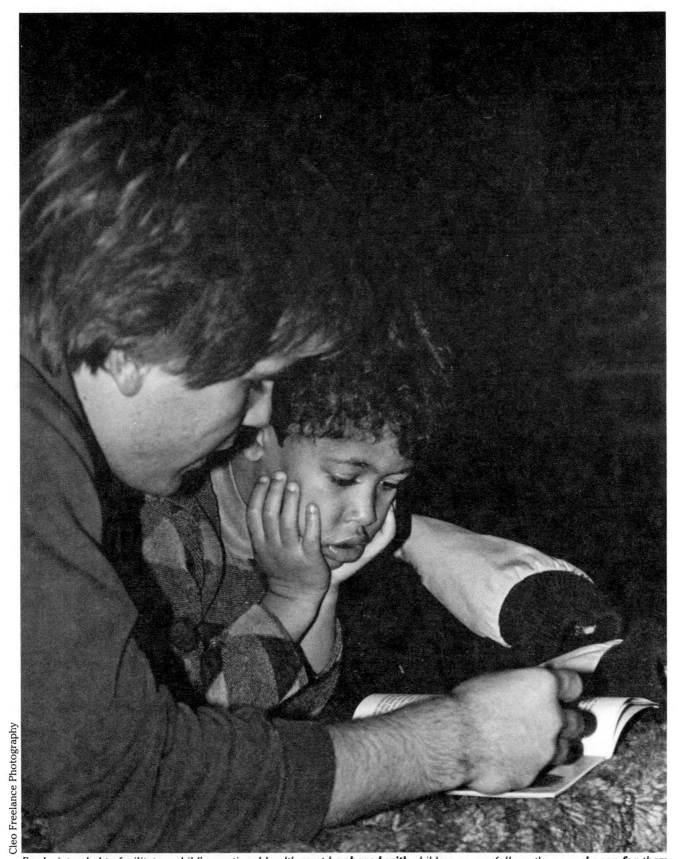

*Books intended to facilitate a child's emotional health must be **shared with** children as carefully as they are **chosen for** them.*

crises are all appropriate. The fourth and final step is the summary and concluding remarks. By rephrasing basic story concepts and responding to children's questions and concerns, ideas and information are reinforced and clarified.

The teacher as a resource

When books are presented for the specific purpose of increasing children's awareness of and appreciation for the human condition, the authenticity of a teacher's attitude is paramount (Feeney and Christensen 1979). Caregivers who haphazardly select and hastily read a story prior to dismissal may be conveying the message that books are an inconsequential part of the curriculum. Similarly, when a teacher conducts discussions of books that treat critical issues during time periods that are certain to be interrupted, children may learn that schedules take precedence both over their personal feelings and those of the story characters with whom they have identified. Any treatment of sensitive and serious issues demands these very qualities from the teacher. Careful selection, thoughtful reading, and thorough preparation are all expressions of caring from educators which are fundamental to the effective use of crisis-oriented literature. Properly used, these books can function as a valuable resource for children who are seeking social knowledge and the educators who are responsible for transmitting it.

References

Resources for teachers

Bernstein, J. *Books to Help Children Cope with Separation and Loss.* New York: Bowker, 1977.

Bracken, J., and Wigutoff, S. *Books for Today's Children.* Old Westbury, N.Y.: The Feminist Press, 1979.

Braun, S., and Lasher, M. *Are You Ready To Mainstream?* Columbus, Ohio: Merrill, 1978.

DeHaven, E. P. *Teaching and Learning the Language Arts.* Boston: Little, Brown, 1979.

Feeney, S., and Christensen, D. *Who Am I in the Lives of Children?* Columbus, Ohio: Merrill, 1979.

Flood, J., and Lapp, D. *Language/Reading In-struction for the Young Child.* New York: Macmillan, 1981.

Maruki, T. *Hiroshima No Pika.* New York: Lothrop, Lee & Shepard, 1982.

Maxim, G. W. *The Very Young.* Belmont, Calif.: Wadsworth, 1980.

Moody, M. T., and Limper, H. K. *Bibliotherapy: Methods and Materials.* Chicago: American Library, 1971.

Overstad, B. *Bibliotherapy: Books To Help Young Children.* St. Paul, Minn.: Toys 'n Things Press, 1981.

Reid, V. M. *Reading Ladders for Human Communication.* Washington, D.C.: American Council on Education, 1972.

Rudman, M. K. *Children's Literature: An Issues Approach.* Boston: Heath, 1976.

Sutherland, Z., and Arbuthnot, M. H. *Children and Books,* 5th ed. Glenview, Ill.: Scott, Foresman, 1977.

Warren, R. M. *Caring: Supporting Children's Growth.* Washington, D.C.: National Association for the Education of Young Children, 1977.

Suggested children's books

Sibling rivalry

Alexander, M. *Nobody Asked Me If I Wanted a Baby Sister.* New York: Dial, 1971.

Hoban, R. *A Baby Sister for Frances.* New York: Harper & Row, 1964.

Hughes, S. *David and Dog.* Englewood Cliffs, N.J.: Prentice-Hall, 1977.

Stein, S. *That New Baby.* New York: Walker, 1974.

Steptoe, J. *Stevie.* New York: Harper & Row, 1969.

Illness

Bradenberg, F. *I Wish I Was Sick, Too!* New York: Penguin, 1978.

Marino, B. *Eric Needs Stitches.* Reading, Mass.: Addison-Wesley, 1979.

Stein, S. B. *A Hospital Story.* New York: Walker, 1974.

Death

Brown, M. W. *The Dead Bird.* New York: Dell, 1979.

Fine, P. D. *Let's Remember Corky.* Shaker Heights, Ohio: P. D. Fine, 1981.

Townsend, M., and Stern, R. *Pop's Secret.* Reading, Mass.: Addison-Wesley, 1980.

Viorst, J. *The Tenth Good Thing About Barney.* Bloomfield, Conn.: Atheneum, 1971.

Sex

Bruenberg, S. M. *The Wonderful Story of How You Were Born.* New York: Doubleday, 1970.

Faison, E. *Becoming.* Putney, Vt.: Eleanora Patterson Press, 1976.

McBride, J., and Fleischauer-Hardt, L. *Show Me!* New York: St. Martin, 1976. Out of print.

Sweet, E. *Something Happened to Me.* Racine, Wis.: Mother Courage Press, 1981.

School

Cohen, M. *Will I Have a Friend?* New York: Macmillan, 1967.

Welber, R. *Goodbye, Hello.* New York: Random House, 1974.

Search for identity

Drescher, J. *Your Family, My Family.* New York: Walker, 1981.

Green, M. *Is It Hard? Is It Easy?* Reading, Mass.: Addison-Wesley, 1960.

Sharmat, M. *I'm Terrific.* New York: Scholastic, 1977.

Simon, N. *All Kinds of Families.* Chicago: Whitman, 1975.

Handicapping conditions

Fassler, J. *Howie Helps Himself.* Chicago: Whitman, 1975.

Greenfield, E. *Darlene.* London: Methuen, 1981.

Rabe, B. *The Balancing Girl.* New York: Dutton, 1981.

Stein, S. *About Handicaps.* New York: Walker, 1974.

Powerful emotions

Gackenback, D. *Harry and the Terrible Whatzit.* New York: Scholastic, 1977.

Hazen, B. *The Gorilla Did It.* New York: Scholastic, 1974.

Hazen, N. *Grownups Cry Too.* Chapel Hill, N.C.: Lollipop Power, 1973.

Kraus, R. *Leo the Late Bloomer.* New York: Scholastic, 1981.

Mayer, M., and Mayer, M. *One Frog Too Many.* New York: Dial, 1975.

Power, P. *I Wish Laura's Mommy Was My Mommy.* Philadelphia: Lippincott, 1981.

Preston, E. M. *The Temper Tantrum Book.* New York: Scholastic, 1969.

Schick, E. *Home Alone.* New York: Dial, 1980.

Tobias, T. *Moving Day.* New York: Knopf, 1976.

Udry, J. *Let's Be Enemies.* New York: Scholastic, 1961.

Vogel, I. *The Don't Be Scared Book.* Bloomfield, Conn.: Atheneum, 1971.

Waber, B. *Ira Sleeps Over.* New York: Scholastic, 1972.

Zolotow, C. *The Quarreling Book.* New York: Harper & Row, 1963.

Zolotow, C. *The Hating Book.* New York: Scholastic, 1969.

Divorce

Goff, B. *Where's Daddy?* Boston: Beacon Press, 1969.

Grollman, E. A. *Talking About Divorce and Separation.* Boston: Beacon Press, 1975.

These books are available from the publisher listed or through your local bookstore.

Part 2.
Strengthening contemporary families

The role of children in the family and in society has shifted through the years. Rather than lament what might have been, we need to build upon the strengths that today's adults can offer young children.

Our changing family structures need not always be viewed as harmful to children. The first three chapters of this section offer constructive ways to include every generation in contemporary programs and families.

When parents separate and divorce, we sometimes become so engrossed in our own crises that we fail to give attention to the children, who also feel the pain. Two chapters deal with the healing process, first in how we can assist children as they come to accept the divorce, and then how we can help them contribute to building a new blended family.

Many other pressures on today's families—financial, career, or even the consequences of earlier abuse— can result in child abuse, either physical or emotional.

As professionals, we can offer support and referrals to help families prevent, or heal the wounds of, abuse. We also have the ethical responsibility to report these crimes against children.

A Sense of *Real* Accomplishment

Young Children As Productive Family Members

Charlotte R. Wallinga and Anne L. Sweaney

"The more he practiced the better he could do the task and in return, he felt better about himself."

"It surprised me how helpful small children can be. This project has made our entire family more aware of work that is involved in running a home. . . . Even my husband helps more now. My son asked one night, 'Why isn't Daddy helping?' What a difference it makes when everyone pitches in . . . ."

In all good early childhood programs, children are expected to take increasing responsibility for themselves and others. As a result, children develop greater self-confidence, become more self-reliant, and gain a sense of real involvement in their daily lives. How can teachers help parents see the many values of a similar approach at home? Parents' responses like those above were typical after we carried out a classroom project to involve children more in household tasks.

First, let us look at the various ways in which children have been viewed as productive members of society, and why it is appropriate for them to take a more active role within the family.

Changes in views of childhood

Until recently, children worked long and demanding hours in homes, farms, and factories, leaving little time for childhood. Several major events, including the unemployment brought about by the Great Depression, the introduction of child labor laws in the 1920s, the affluence of the post-World War II era, and recent technological advantages, contributed to changes in American work patterns (Ingolsby & Adams, 1977). Early childhood professionals and families began to emphasize the need for children to experience a childhood free from adult work, problems, and concerns (Braun & Edwards, 1972).

As the American population changed from rural and producer-oriented to urban and consumer-oriented, families began to bear children to satisfy emotional desires rather than for the additional labor resources (Cogle & Tasker, 1981). Many other more recent factors, such as rising divorce rates, decreases in family size, increases in dual-earner households, and complex work schedules, have further affected the functioning of families (Masnick & Bane, 1980). Both men and women face the challenges of juggling careers and families (Lobodzinska, 1977; Sanderson, 1983).

Why share household tasks?

Values for children

All parents must balance two responsibilities—to protect their children and to help children become independent and confident. Parents can encourage independence, self-reliance, and healthy self-concept by involving children in household tasks that are appropriate for their level of development (Cogle & Tasker, 1981).

Household tasks can be adapted to children's abilities and interests, and can be instrumental in helping children become cooperative and independent (Mitton & Harris, 1954). As they assist in the daily function of the household, children become more coordinated, learn to organize people and procedures, and develop a better understanding of interpersonal relations. Children also learn to carry tasks to completion and develop positive attitudes about the importance of sharing household responsibilities.

Children's active participation within the family helps them feel they are vital to the family's functioning. Clearly, children can benefit by sharing in household tasks.

***Charlotte R. Wallinga**, Ph.D., is Assistant Professor in the Department of Housing, Home Management, and Consumer Economics, and is Director of Children's Programs at McPhaul Child and Family Development Center, University of Georgia, Athens, Georgia.*

***Anne L. Sweaney**, Ph.D., is Assistant Professor in the Department of Housing, Home Management, and Consumer Economics, University of Georgia, Athens, Georgia.*

Lucy Fein

In addition to the sense of well-being that comes with distributing the work load more fairly, parents will come to better understand how children think and of what they are capable.

Values for parents

The responsibility of maintaining a household with young children, especially for single parents or two-career families, can be overwhelming. Families often find that time, their most valuable resource, becomes a challenge to manage (McCullough, 1983). Since household tasks are a daily part of family living, they can either increase family togetherness or cause family problems.

In addition to the sense of well-being that comes with distributing the work load more fairly, parents will also come to better understand how children think and of what they are capable. Many parents believe that children must be of elementary age before they are capable of performing basic household and personal care tasks (Walters, Stromberg, & Lonian, 1957; Sweaney & Wallinga, 1983). However, children as young as 18 to 30 months of age imitate their parents at household tasks and even initiate some of the tasks (Rheingold, 1982). Encouraging young children to take part in family household chores while they still think it is fun may be an effective way to ensure participation (Kelly & Parsons, 1975; McCullough, 1983).

Some parents are concerned that their children may reject them if they expect regular help with household tasks (McClelland, 1976). However, when parents warmly acknowledge children's household efforts, the children in turn develop a sense of importance with no damaging effects (Nye & Hoffman, 1974; Vanek, 1974). In fact, children and parents can develop a better relationship while helping one another with household tasks.

With the many values for young children, and less parental time and fewer people to perform household tasks, it certainly is logical that all family members become productive members of the household as they are able.

The "Homework" project

In an effort to encourage parents to more fully involve their children in household tasks and to foster independence in young children, we began a 6-week project called "Homework." The project involved twenty-three 4-year-old children and their families. We began by asking parents whether they believed their children could perform six tasks:

1. **set the table**
2. **vacuum**
3. **sort clothes**
4. **save energy**
5. **clean the bathroom after a bath**
6. **wake up to an alarm clock**

Only 9% of the parents strongly agreed that their young children could successfully complete these responsibilities. We were confident that these tasks were appropriate for the children, and planned classroom activities to introduce all six.

Each week after the preschool teachers demonstrated a "Homework" task for the children in the group, they divided into smaller groups to try out the task. For instance, the teacher demonstrated how to operate several vacuum cleaners safely. Then the children selected a vacuum cleaner that looked most like the one they had at home and practiced vacuuming under the teachers' supervision. This proce-

dure ensured that the children knew how to do the task before they were asked to do it at home.

We then gave a form to the parents which provided directions for carrying out the activity at home, offered helpful suggestions, and included a brief evaluation (Figure 1). We asked parents to place a colorful sticker on the form each day the task was completed and to return the form at the end of the week so we could evaluate the success of the "Homework" project.

Responses to "Homework"

Throughout the project, the "Homework" tasks were well received by the children. They eagerly anticipated each new task and requested more when the project was completed. Their enthusiasm was matched, if not surpassed, by that of the parents. Children encouraged their parents to return the evaluations, and we telephoned parents who forgot. The families were probably willing to return the forms because they were so pleased with the results, and we obtained an average response rate of 87% for the six tasks.

After completion of the "Homework" tasks, the parents' perceptions changed dramatically: 100% of the parents agreed that their children were capable of accomplishing the six tasks.

Many parents were surprised at their children's prowess and willingness to help. The parents also reported that helping their child complete the tasks initially took additional time, but was worth the effort! They indicated that their children showed pride in their accomplishments and were excited to show their new helping skills to grandparents and friends. These are typical examples of parent responses:

"The 'Homework' tasks made it fun for my child to help with the housework; it has been a great help to have the input from the school."

"I had no idea my 4-year-old could be so helpful."

"He liked the feeling of accomplishment and participation with the family."

"It was a nice experience for both of us."

Figure 1

Homework Project

Directions

Since children enjoy being productive members of the family, we have another activity for your family to try.

For this week's activity we are asking your cooperation in helping your child with floor care. Areas of floor care that children usually enjoy are vacuuming and sweeping.

1. Once again, allow plenty of time for your child to complete the vacuuming and/or sweeping.
2. Select the area to be vacuumed or swept.
3. Gather the tools in one location.
4. Demonstrate the proper and safe use of the equipment.
5. Let the child begin.
6. When finished, help the child return equipment to the place it is stored.

Helpful Suggestions

- Limit the size of the task. If the child views the task as overwhelming, she or he will feel defeated.
- Encourage your child's effort and be prepared to accept less than perfection. Remember your child's standards may not be the same as yours.
- Show your child that she or he needs to prepare for the task. For example, pick up all larger items that may cause problems with vacuuming or sweeping.
- Choose a room or an area where the success rate is likely to be high. Avoid rooms which contain your most precious possessions.
- Remember to thank the child for her or his help with the work of the family.

Evaluation

Child's name _____

Dates _____

Please place a colorful sticker on the days your child swept or vacuumed the floor.

Monday _____   Tuesday _____   Wednesday _____

Thursday _____   Friday _____   Saturday _____

Sunday _____   **Parent comments:**

How did the vacuuming or sweeping go?

_____

How did your child feel about vacuuming or sweeping?

_____

How did you feel about having your child vacuum or sweep? _____

_____

Drawing adapted from original photo by Elaine M. Ward.

Please return this form to class on _____ so your child can receive recognition of her or his accomplishment.

"He liked 'Homework.' We have been working on the bathtime routine for about a year, but his interest picked up when he knew it was 'Homework'."

"My daughter loves doing the 'Homework' and appreciates that I give her an opportunity to help."

"I enjoyed having the help, especially when he got upset when the room he vacuumed got messy. I really liked that reaction for a change."

Parents can encourage independence, self-reliance, and healthy self-concept by involving children in appropriate household tasks.

Several parents also indicated that this experience encouraged discussions about the distribution of household tasks within the family. Children questioned why some of their fathers were not involved in household tasks.

"My husband hesitates to use the excuse he doesn't know how to do housework since our 4-year-old is capable of doing it."

"This experience has encouraged all family members (including my husband) to share more in chores. I can use the help since I have gone back to work."

As can be expected, everything did not always go smoothly. While one mother was talking on the telephone, her daughter vacuumed up a pair of pantyhose. Another child broke two sweeper belts because he forgot to pick things up before using the vacuum. Several of the children were so enthusiastic about saving energy that they turned off lights, leaving their parents

to sit in the dark. Another child turned on all the lights in the home just so he could turn them off again.

One parent wrote, "The first night I forgot about the bathtime assignment. My child became so upset, he insisted on undressing and getting back into the tub so he could do the after bath cleanup all by himself."

The preschool teachers also noted that children were eager to volunteer their newly acquired expertise by setting tables, saving energy, and keeping the classroom in order. One teacher said cleanup time had improved and she appreciated the children's reminders to keep everything picked up. Another teacher commented that children frequently volunteered to do tasks. One group took the initiative to reorganize the housekeeping area so materials could be put away quickly and neatly.

Suggestions for parents and teachers

Young children can learn to be self-reliant and independent, share in household responsibilities, and in the process develop a healthy self-concept. By becoming involved in household tasks, children become active producers rather than consumers (Walters & Walters, 1980).

Of course, including children in the work of the family must be kept in careful perspective. The object is not to have them do all the housework, but to assist with tasks that are developmentally appropriate. Even though young children are eager helpers, we must remember they need a balance between household contributions and play.

Our experiences with the "Homework" project have led to several recommendations for parents and teachers to help children become more productive members of families and society.

1. Be alert to when children are developmentally ready to help with tasks. Watch for clues such as imitating adult helping behaviors and volunteering to assist with work. Children are often willing to help much earlier than adults expect.

When children have input into the decision-making process, they will feel they play an important role in the family or classroom.

2. Involve parents in helping their children become productive. Parents can guide the child's development and give needed encouragement that will lead to success. Learning is a lifetime process and patience is essential.

3. Include children in planning what, when, and how tasks are to be done. When children have input into the decision-making process, they will feel they play an important role in the family or classroom.

4. Plan the task so children can complete it with ease. For example, if children are going to set the table, select dishes that will not break and that are within their reach.

5. Help children learn how to do the task before they attempt it. Demonstrate how to perform the task and have the child practice it first with adult supervision. Gradually withdraw as you see the child can handle it independently.

6. Divide the task into manageable portions. If children view the task as overwhelming or too time consuming, they can become discouraged easily. Children might begin by sorting out all of their own clothes for the laundry.

7. Select tasks where the success rates are likely to be high, such as sweeping or turning off lights. Prevent mishaps, hurt feelings, and embarrassment by making sure valuable possessions are safe. All children need to experience success.

8. Make the tasks fun instead of drudgery. Turn tasks into games, exhibit enthusiasm when you present them, provide positive reinforcement, and ro-

tate preferred and disliked tasks among family members or children in the classroom to make it more enjoyable.

9. Encourage and reinforce children's efforts. Be prepared to accept less than perfection. Children's standards may not be the same as adults' standards, but find some aspect of the work to compliment. "You really worked hard to clean the fingerprints off the mirror!"

10. Keep your suggestions simple. To avoid confusion, limit the amount of information you present at one time. Children may be able to turn on the alarm at night and turn it off in the morning, but an adult may be needed to set the time.

11. Offer assistance only when a major problem seems to be developing. Ask children whether or not they need assistance, rather than taking over the task, unless safety is a concern.

12. Refrain from creating additional tasks when the initial one is completed. A sense of accomplishment is important, and all of us become discouraged

if there is no end in sight. Children need child-size tasks. A child might help put groceries away after shopping, but would not be expected to then help prepare the meal as well.

13. Resist redoing a task children have completed. We all become discouraged if someone nullifies our work. Just keep in mind how you might present the task more clearly the next time.

14. Remember to thank the children for their help. Adult appreciation helps children feel worthwhile about their accomplishments.

Summary

Our role as adults is to help children become increasingly mature: independent, self-reliant, and confident. At the same time, parents and teachers are faced with increasing demands on our time, energy, and money. We can work together to achieve our goals for young children if we encourage them to con-

tribute their efforts in developmentally appropriate tasks at home and in group programs. All our lives will be enriched as a result.

Bibliography

Braun, S., & Edwards, E. (1972). *History and theory of early childhood education.* Belmont, CA: Wadsworth.

Cogle, F., & Tasker, G. (1981). Children: An untapped resource for building family strengths. In N. Stinnet, J. DeFrain, P. Knaub, K. King, & G. Rowe. Lincoln, NE: University of Nebraska Press.

Cogle, F., & Tasker, G. (1982). Children and housework. *Family Relations, 31,* 395–399.

Ingoldsby, B., & Adams, G. (1977). Adolescence and work experiences: A brief note. *Adolescence, 12,* 339–343.

Kelly, M., & Parsons, E. (1975). *The mother's almanac.* Garden City, NY: Doubleday.

Lobodzinska, B. (1977). Married women's gainful employment and household work in contemporary Poland. *Journal of Marriage and the Family, 39,* 405–415.

Masnick, G., & Bane, M. J. (1980). *The nation's families: 1969–1990.* Cambridge, MA: Joint Center for Urban Studies of the Massachusetts Institute of Technology and Harvard University.

McClelland, D. (1976). *The achieving society.* New York: Halsted.

McCullough, B. (1983). *Bonnie's household organizer.* New York: St. Martin's Press.

Mitton, B., & Harris, D. (1954). The development of responsibility in children. *Elementary School Journal, 54,* 268–277.

Nye, F. I., & Hoffman, L. (1974). *Working mothers.* San Francisco: Jossey-Bass.

Rheingold, H. L. (1982). Little children's participation in the work of adults, a nascent prosocial behavior. *Child Development, 53,* 114–125.

Sanderson, J. (1983). *How to raise your kids to stand on their own two feet.* New York: Congdon & Weed.

Sweaney, A., & Wallinga, C. (1983, February). Helping parents and children to become active, productive members of the family system. *Proceedings of the Southeastern Regional Association of Family Economics–Home Management 12th Annual Conference, Denton, TX.*

Vanek, J. (1974). Time spent in housework. *Scientific American, 231,* 116–120.

Walters, J., Stromberg, F., & Lonian, G. (1957). Perceptions concerning development of responsibility in young children. *Elementary School Journal, 58,* 209–216.

Walters, J., & Walters, L. (1980). Trends affecting adolescent views of sexuality, employment, marriage and child rearing. *Family Relations, 29,* 191–198.

White, L., & Brinkerhoff, D. (1981). Children's work in the family: Its significance and meaning. *Journal of Marriage and the Family, 43,* 789–798.

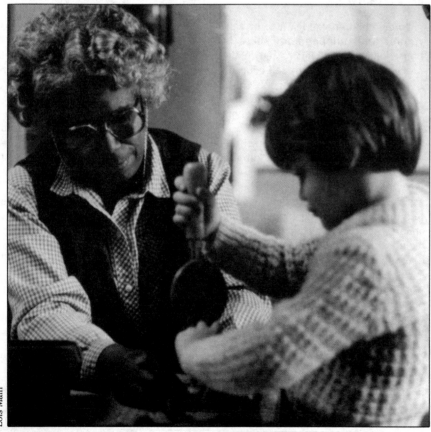

Lois Main

Ask children whether or not they need assistance, rather than taking over the task, unless safety is a concern.

"When will you be back?"

We Bring Generations Together!

Toni H. Liebman

While more people are living longer, healthier lives, there seems to be less interaction between grandparents and grandchildren than past generations have enjoyed. Those who lose the most are the grandchildren, since there is no substitute for grandparent love. Many grandparents would argue that their loss is easily as great. An exchange program between a school for young children and a nursing home can enrich the lives of the children and the elderly!

Our society seems to be increasingly segregated by age, either through geographic or emotional distances. Most modern households consist of small nuclear families with one or two parents and their children. Grandparents may reside nearby, sometimes in retirement communities. Some live and work in different states, while others live in nursing homes. Visits may be complicated by travel and time.

Many grandparents do not serve as nurturers and transmitters of family history and values because they or their grown children assume that emotional dependence is a sign of weakness (Kornhaber and Woodward 1981). Whatever the reason, the generations often fail to seek support from each other.

As early childhood educators, we know interactions between the young and the elderly are important. Our cooperative nursery school sponsors an exchange program between our children and residents in a nearby nursing home to encourage communication and understanding among generations. Children's fear of aging is often a result of inexperience, so we hoped that contact with some spry, alert, and loving older people might help dispel stereotypes and engender respect for the elderly. We enthusiastically support such exchanges, and hope our experiences will encourage others to start similar programs in their communities.

Building the foundation

The staff of Roslyn-Trinity Cooperative Day School made several fruitless contacts with senior citizen groups before we learned about an exchange program between a nursing home and a child care center in another Long Island community. We decided to try a similar arrangement, and began to work with Ellen Golann, the Activities Director of the Sunharbor Nursing Home, to design our program.

As a cooperative nonprofit school with 139 children, we are administered by a Parent Board, while educational concerns are handled by the teaching staff and myself as director. Our staff's first step to make our idea a reality was to obtain the Board's support. We believed that the Sunharbor residents would benefit, and that our expenditure of time and effort would be beneficial to the co-op children as well. We wanted to be certain that none of those involved were exploited in any way. How delighted we were that the Board received our recommendations with enthusiasm!

Bolstered by this support, we began to build the foundation for our program. We talked with people involved in the other exchange that was already operating to learn about their experiences. We discussed our plans among ourselves and with the co-op members. We decided that the children selected from those who were volunteered by their parents would be those who could most benefit from a non-judgmental, unhurried experience—just what many pressured parents find difficult to offer in this achievement-oriented society!

We agreed that eight children would be given the opportunity to participate because that number could be transported easily by two drivers and properly supervised at the nursing home. Three 4-year-olds, three 5-year-olds, and two mature 3-year-olds were selected from three classrooms in our school. Whom did we choose? One child came from a family embroiled in marital problems. One child spent most of her time with a housekeeper. Another's mother admitted she did not

Toni H. Liebman, M.S.Ed., is Director, Roslyn-Trinity Cooperative Day School, Roslyn, New York.

like her. Two had no contact with their grandparents. One had a handicapped brother who demanded most of the family's attention. Two were faced with inappropriately high expectations from their parents.

While we were selecting the child participants, Ellen and her assistant, Margaret Adams, were generating support from the administration of Sunharbor Manor and interviewing likely candidates. Criteria for participation included absence of severe senility or serious physical deformation, and the existence of a wholesome, loving, and accepting attitude toward children. Sonja Rath, a psychologist at the Adelphi Center on the Aging, which had generated the first program, graciously donated much of her time to screen patients using a questionnaire. A small one-time fee for the service was shared by our school and Sunharbor.

Preparing the participants

Parents of the eight children selected met with Sonja Rath, Ellen Golann, the teachers involved, and me. Attendance was mandatory because we felt that all expectations and concerns needed to be fully discussed. As we anticipated, the two major questions were "Will the children see any frightening sights?" and "What if somebody dies?"

Parents were reassured that participants were in the health-related program. The building's design was such that the children would not be subjected to some of the depressing sights of the nursing area. The section we would visit was spotless and cheerful.

How would we handle the situation if a participant died? We discussed the issue in terms of the value it might have for children in forming a more complete understanding of the life cycle.

After the parents felt comfortable enough to give their approval, we photographed the Sunharbor premises and the residents there. Our co-op president agreed to share driving with me in anticipation that other parents would volunteer to make the short trip too.

I brought photos and a brief personal history of each of the children to a meeting of the chosen Sunharbor residents. What a heartwarming reception they gave me! When the needs of the children were discussed, the adults' enthusiasm grew as they realized their knowledge and wisdom would be used for a good cause. "Give me the one who

Toni Liebman

Participants in the third year of the Sunharbor program (1982–83).

needs the most loving!" chimed Josie. They were so excited that we had to caution them not to expect instant loving from the children. The two men and six women decided what they wished to be called—Grandpa Frank, Carl, Aunt Peg, Granny—and agreed that they would be paired based on a drawing of names. For people who were used to having little control over their own lives, this opportunity to make decisions and feel useful was a welcome change!

The week before the first visit, photos of the elderly with their walkers and wheelchairs were posted in the classrooms with participating children. Everyone was told that these people lived in a special place where they received care and had constant companionship, but that they missed the enjoyment of seeing children. We explained who would visit every week and that they would discuss their experiences with the others.

On the day before the first visit I met with the three boys and five girls to show them pictures of Sunharbor Manor, including the elevators, activities room, bathroom with railing, the four activities room staff members, and the eight residents we would be meeting. Anticipation was building!

Our first visit

On January 15, one teacher, two parents, and I accompanied the children to Sunharbor Manor. One child pointed excitedly, "There's the elevator!" and, as we got off on the third floor, another volunteered "There's the number three and the clock!"

Ellen and her staff accompanied us to the sun-filled activities room where the eight elderly adults were waiting. The children recognized the adults from their photographs.

To break the ice, children sat on the floor and everyone sang favorite children's songs. We ended with an adapted version of "Where Is Thumbkin?" to match pairs of adults and children. The pairs moved cautiously to tables where clay invited flexibility and a focus on the activity rather than a product. The grandparents restrained themselves so

they wouldn't overwhelm the children! One staff person or parent stayed near each pair.

After about 15 minutes of talking and exploring with the clay, we gathered in a circle again, this time with children sitting on chairs next to their grandparents. We played a familiar record that necessitates play with beanbags. By the end of one side, most of the children had loosened up and the residents were thoroughly enjoying themselves! With the children pushing wheelchairs, the partners moved back to their tables for a snack.

We gave the group our traditional 5-minute warning before leaving. "So soon?" said Aunt Peg. "When will you be back?"

Immediately after this and every visit, Sonja and Ellen led a brief discussion with the grandparents about their feelings and concerns. Comments made included "Thursdays are the best days now. I get up at six so I can bathe and wash my hair." "This is better than any medicine." "I know Jane is very shy ... so I won't come on too strong. I used to be shy and my mother always told me to talk more." "I know that Suzy wants to know more about my walker. I'll let her touch it next time." "My child is the smartest ... Oh, I guess they're all smart."

Continuing the program

Notes were sent to children's parents after most of our visits, detailing many of the sessions and asking them to share with us any comments their children made about the program. We heard: "Now I have a grandma every Thursday," and "I like doing things with the grandmas and grandpas." "This is my friend, Carl," Jane said, showing a photo to her classmates.

Other indicators of success were behavioral changes we noted. Jane became less shy and entered the room with an increasingly large grin, in contrast to hiding briefly under a table the first day. She also became more outgoing at school. Mindy, who had previously rejected all physical contact with her teachers, became more hug-

gable. There were other subtle changes as well.

But all was not easy. As expected, a few of the residents became ill and two were replaced during the first year of our program. Carl, the youngest resident with no history of illness, died suddenly, shortly after the program began. A retired seaman with no family, he had never left the premises in his 5 years there until 2 weeks after our first visit when he went bowling! His whole demeanor had changed, and perhaps the excitement had been too much. Everyone agreed, however, that Carl had been very happy just before his death.

We were shocked and saddened, and discussed how to approach the children with the news. On Tuesday, Jane was told that Carl was very sick and might not be with us on Thursday. On Wednesday we met with all the children in the group and told them that Carl had died. Their reactions were evident for several weeks. "Yes, that means he may never come back to life again." "When you get very old, you die." "Are they gonna take his skin off and put his bones in a museum?" "You can't drive when you're dead. You lose your license." "I know a friend of mine who died. His name was Poppy." Some children were obviously more affected than others.

We explained to parents and the Sunharbor participants the importance of being honest with the children about Carl's death, rather than offering a false explanation. When we indicated that we would not replace Carl immediately, that we needed time to feel sad and to miss him, Jane said she would "miss him forever." After a few weeks, Jane was paired with a vibrant woman with whom she developed a very comfortable relationship.

The format of our visits remained the same with variations in the music and art projects. We celebrated birthdays and Easter. The children and their parents were invited to attend Sunharbor's Seder. Books, games, and puzzles were available for those who were interested. Occasionally we played group games. Once in a while 88-year-old Grandma Emily would treat us to a jig, a tune on her harmonica, or

Toni Liebman

Grandma Aida and Aylissa connect with the stethoscope.

a paper airplane flight. Although communication and personal interaction were the main goals, our activities were the vehicle for achieving them.

Relationships were built in other ways, too. Entire classrooms sent cards to ailing residents who acknowledged their receipt. Six of the grandparents spent a morning at our school, including Emily, who had always resisted leaving the nursing home. Co-op parents took their individual children to Sunharbor during spring vacation and the summer. All three classes that had participating children visited Sunharbor in the spring.

The first Sunharbor program ended on June 4 with a lot of sadness. Children and the grandparents were grouchy and ill-at-ease. The staff wondered if the separation experience would cause more grief than the program warranted, but we agreed that the positive values far outweighed the negative. The children were resilient, and the grandparents, accustomed to separations during their long lifetimes, had next year to anticipate.

The Sunharbor program is now in its fourth year. Fortunately, we have experienced no more deaths and only one serious illness. We now encourage parents of participating children to accompany us if possible, adding another dimension to the intergenerational relationships. Several parents have become involved and visited nursing home residents during school holidays! Others have provided home baked goods for our visits, a welcome change from institutional food!

We have learned that after the first three or four visits, parents and activity room staff offer sufficient assistance, so that we need not take teachers from their classrooms. Other changes have also enriched the program. Children visit residents' rooms and try out wheelchairs, walkers, and blood pressure equipment. Partners enjoy folk dancing and blow bubbles on the lawn.

Aside from the purchase of additional children's books about grandparents, expenses have been minimal, thanks to the willingness of our co-op parents to provide transportation.

The most critical factor for the program's success, however, is the close working relationship between staff of the school and nursing home. All of us care intensely about the people with whom we work, and we diligently ensure that visits go smoothly. We all agree that the program has tremendous benefits for both the young and elders, and urge groups to establish similar bridges between generations in other communities.

Reference

Kornhaber, A., and Woodward, K. *Grandparents, Grandchildren: The Vital Connection.* New York: Doubleday, 1981.

When Young Children *Move*

Mary Renck Jalongo

After Tracy's parents separated, he and his mother moved from their home into an apartment with a strict no-pets policy. Bingo, Tracy's beloved puppy, was adopted by his uncle in the country. One day while his kindergarten group was singing, a child requested "Bingo." Tracy's story came pouring out. The group decided to sing it as a tribute to Tracy's former pet and their voices had a wistful quality as they sang.

Every day, all over the country, families are relocating. One in five American families moves each year (Employee Relocation Council, 1983). Sometimes they move great distances, but more often they move to a neighboring state or within the same community. The incidents which precipitate a move can be both positive and negative—job promotions or unemployment, births and deaths, marriages or divorces. Whatever the reasons, moving away from one's home can be a stressful situation for people at any age, but relocation may be especially difficult during early childhood.

The concept of home

In her classic work on infancy, Kaplan (1978) describes one view of how children begin to acquire a sense of home.

> The origins of our attachment to home are to be found in the infant's earliest attachment to his [or her] mother—the mother he begins to use as a home base from which to explore the world . . . into ever-widening circles of the unknown. From then on, though he may roam but a few feet, . . . his body-mind is anchored by an image of home base. (p. 38)

If the early concept of home is personified in the primary caregiver as Kaplan suggests, then infants are not likely to be

Mary Renck Jalongo, *Ph.D., is Professor of Elementary and Early Childhood Education at Indiana University of Pennsylvania, Indiana, Pennsylvania.*

deeply affected by environmental changes when the people remain consistent. However, during the toddler and preschool years, children's familiarity with environments beyond home rapidly expands. Predictability, both in children's physical world and in the human beings who populate it, is important.

Moving has been regarded by many child development specialists as a disruptive or even adverse influence on children's lives. Relocation is often considered stressful because it places unusual demands upon children's adaptive responses (Adler, 1927; Sullivan, 1953; Packard, 1972). In Elkind's (1981) child stress scale, for example, school readjustment, moving to another place, changing schools, and changing friends are identified as important stressors.

According to Ames (1972), altering young children's concept of home through relocation can be traumatic. She suggests that 3- and 4-year-olds especially need stability in their lives. Tooley (1970) contends that 5- and 6-year-olds are most likely to suffer the negative consequences of their family's geographic mobility because of the additional stress of leaving home to enter school for the first time. However, now that the initial school experience of many children takes place earlier, preschoolers could well be the age group for whom moving will require the greatest adjustment.

Although early childhood is a time when the recognizable and routine are reassuring to children, the child's early years typically coincide with a period when families are highly mobile (Packard, 1983). Most of the research on the topic has examined demographic or ecological factors rather than individual human responses. When people's reactions have been studied, the subjects are generally groups of adults such as military personnel, migrant workers, or business executives.

The majority of the information on children moving is found in newspaper articles or pamphlets published by van lines. Research on moving is both sparse and difficult to locate because it is often embedded in a more general topic like social knowledge (Ziller & Long, 1967) or peer relationships (Feldbaum, Christensen, & O'Neal, 1980). Much of the research on children's reactions to relocation relies on parents to supply information about the child (Weimer, 1981).

Despite this lack of quality studies about the effects of moving on young children, we can answer these questions based on related child development research.

- What is the young child's perspective on moving?
- How do preschoolers typically react to relocation?
- How can parents and teachers ease the young child's transition into a new environment?

Perspective on moving

According to conventional wisdom, young children adapt to new situations more easily than older people. Since breaking peer ties is often cited as a major reason for adjustment problems following a move, it has been suggested that preschoolers, who are assumed to have more transitory friend-

ships (Selman, 1980), are less troubled by moving. Is it true, for example, that today's young children take a change of residence in stride while teenagers are often devastated by the dissolution of peer relationships (Sullivan, 1953)? Can preschoolers adjust rapidly to the stress of relocation although adults reportedly need an average of 16 months to adapt (Employee Relocation Council, 1983)?

Some psychologists contend that preschoolers have the same basic feelings as more mature individuals, but lack the linguistic sophistication to express abstract concepts like homesickness or loneliness (Raymond & Eliot, 1980). Hendrick (1984) describes children's emotional responses to loss by observing:

Sometimes teachers underestimate what it means to a child when a friend moves away, or makes a new friend and rejects the former one, or is transferred to another room in nursery school. But children often feel quite depleted and adrift when this occurs.... As in working through any kind of separation, the leaver's and the left-behind's feelings of grief, apprehension, and sometimes anger need to be recognized and honored. (p. 224)

Young children cope with emotional, social, and environmental changes in fairly predictable ways, as the following four cases illustrate.

Sheree's new room. When 3-year-old Sheree was taken on a tour of her new house, she was unusually subdued and apparently unimpressed. Her parents, who had made tremendous sacrifices to move from a highrise apartment into a house, were perplexed by Sheree's unenthusiastic reaction. It was later learned that she thought her new home was to be exactly what she had seen—barren rooms stripped of personal belongings.

Young children's limited experiences make it extraordinarily difficult for them to anticipate the extent or the nature of the changes that moving entails. Misconceptions like Sheree's can obviously be very disturbing to a child, especially if these inner conflicts go unsuspected by adults and remain unresolved.

Young children have many sentiments and questions which are hard to express. Parents who are preoccupied with all the details of moving tend to engage in fewer relaxed discussions which might allow children's concerns to surface. Two of Sheree's questions, "Where do I sleep?" and "Can't we have toys?" alerted her perceptive parents to Sheree's need for further clarification.

When a child is disappointed, confused, or frightened, becoming reticent and withdrawn like Sheree is one possible reaction. Lashing out with aggressive behavior is another.

Manolo's new country. A recent immigrant to the United States, 4-year-old Manolo was immediately enrolled in a cooperative nursery school. Fortunately, his teacher spoke some Spanish and they were able to communicate. But Manolo, who had previously been popular with peers, suddenly felt excluded. When he proudly wore a pair of red leather sandals to school and was taunted on the playground about wearing "girl's shoes," Manolo responded by pelting his tormentors with sand. To make matters worse, this rejection

Hildegarde Adler

Young children's limited experiences make it extraordinarily difficult for them to anticipate the extent or the nature of the changes that moving entails.

often a major variable by which adults gauge the disruptiveness of a move, but distance is largely irrelevant to young children. Barman (1981) astutely concludes that:

> Moving a few blocks away or across the continent—it doesn't seem to matter very much.... To preschool children, a small move can be every bit as upsetting as a major one. Their geographic horizons are limited: If you're not allowed to cross the street alone, being told the new house is only a mile from the old one doesn't help.... Moving diminishes a child's sense of being able to cope and homesickness for the old environment may result. (p. 20)

Environmental changes may be disruptive, but the upheavals in family relationships created by relocation can be equally, if not more, stressful.

Kimmie, Allison, and Brian's separation. Taking three children aged 9 months, 2½ years, and 5 years on a flight from Pittsburgh to Los Angeles to look for a new house was simply not feasible for one young married couple, economically or otherwise. So all three children were left with close friends who lived just two blocks away.

When their parents returned after a successful week of house-hunting, kindergartner Kimmie gave them a joyful reception, and the baby, Brian, who was initially rather aloof, soon warmed to the situation. But Allison's reaction was distressing. The toddler turned away when her parents arrived and struggled from her mother's lap to rejoin her neighbor.

When parents leave for long periods to search for a new residence, the separation raises the potential of young children's worst fear—abandonment by primary caregivers. If children feel deserted, they often respond in much the same way as adults who have been deeply hurt by someone whom they love. Mature individuals typically say they "don't want to get involved again."

Why should preschoolers be expected to adjust rapidly to the stress of relocation if adults need an average of 16 months to adapt?

Children use the same basic strategy to protect themselves from further emotional suffering, but instead of expressing their resentment verbally, they enact it, like Allison, by refusing to make eye contact and pushing the offender away. Negative reactions to familiar people who have caused the child anguish frequently accompany a move. Not only can preschoolers be distressed by changes in their home environment or in family life, they can be upset by new social situations, such as a change in schools (Ziegler, 1985).

Jessica's new school. Jessica had just adjusted to a small private playschool when her father accepted a transfer to another state. In her new location, Jessica was eligible for enrollment in a public school kindergarten. Suddenly the pre-

was followed by the disapproval of his admired teacher.

Rubin (1980) explains aggressive responses like Manolo's as a type of mourning.

> Severe reactions to moving may be understood in part as grief reactions to the loss of particularly close friends, people whom one comes to depend upon for companionship and support. Feelings of loneliness, depression, irritability and anger are all common responses to such loss. (p. 81)

Children like Manolo, who must learn a new language and customs, have an increased need for sensitive adult guidance (Jalongo, 1983). But a child does not need to have traveled thousands of miles to feel disoriented by a move. Distance is schooler who had walked with her mother two blocks to school, chosen her own play activities with friends there, and returned home at lunch, was expected to ride on a school bus with older children and function in a highly structured classroom all day.

By translating Jessica's situation into similar adult changes, one can appreciate why she developed a stomachache that seemed to improve shortly after the school bus engine could no longer be heard. If an adult took a new position that required twice as many hours of work, a less pleasant commute, lack of autonomy, and the dissolution of many peer relationships, the job might well be refused! Yet the magnitude of adjustments for Jessica is comparable. She felt frightened and attempted to cope the best way she could, by avoiding the stressful situation.

It is not unusual for children to temporarily feel ill or revert to less mature forms of behavior when they are apprehensive. Children who have quit sucking their thumbs, no longer speak with a lisp, or were successfully toilet trained will sometimes alarm caregivers by regressing in these developmental achievements during times of stress.

The positive side

Of course, not all of the effects of moving are negative. Geographic mobility can result in a fresh beginning or increased opportunity. But any appreciation of these presumed advantages requires some basis for making comparisons. Young children are often not sufficiently experienced to assess whether a new neighborhood or school is better or worse than before.

Preschoolers recognize that differences exist between the situations, but any opportunities created by the move would have to be fairly tangible and immediate for young children to take notice. Replacing an insensitive teacher with a caring, competent one, saying good-bye forever to the neighborhood bully, owning a pet for the first time, or inheriting a swing set are likely to make an impression. Even so, children typically do not assess the relative merits of situations until later during the elementary school years.

One of the advantages of moving is that it helps people expand their knowledge, develop new skills, re-examine their goals, and modify their attitudes.

Moving is one type of adaptation, the process through which the individual becomes more effective in dealing with the environment (Jersild, Telford, & Sawrey, 1975). If learning is seen as a change in behavior, relocation can contribute to

learning because moving intensifies the need for behavioral change. In fact, one of the advantages of moving is that it helps people expand their knowledge, develop new skills, re-examine their goals, and modify their attitudes.

Preschoolers are greatly influenced, not only by the change in their environment, but also by the extent and nature of changes they see in the significant people around them. If parents perceive moving as a generally positive experience, young children are likely to respond similarly.

Strategies to help children adjust to moving

- Acknowledge that preschoolers *are* affected by moving. Keep them informed and involved. Be patient and understanding.
- Be flexible. Give children time to observe before they are expected to participate.
- Be alert and sensitive to verbal and nonverbal expressions of feelings. Treat newcomers warmly and courteously.
- Provide continuity. Emphasize similarities between the new and old environments.
- Promote peer interaction. Have the new child arrive a few minutes early so others join the newcomer.
- Use children's literature to show how others cope with moving.

Although most young children eventually flourish in their new surroundings, relocation still involves a period of transition. In a survey by Jones (1973), mothers stated that their children needed more emotional support for 2 weeks before and 2 weeks after the move. Contrasted to this is the 16-month adult transition period in the same situation (Employee Relocation Council, 1983). Either children are considerably more adaptable than adults, or the adult interpretations of children's transition periods are inaccurate. Regardless of the length of the adjustment period, there are ways parents and teachers can smooth children's transitions.

Strategies to smooth transitions

Initially, young children often feel overwhelmed and intimidated by new people and surroundings. In response, they may withdraw, react negatively, avoid frightening situations, and backslide developmentally. Fortunately there are strategies that adults can use to make moving less traumatic and less likely to cause children to use these defense mechanisms.

The anxieties which escalate before and after a move are basically aggravated versions of common childhood fears. These apprehensions typically fall into two categories, fear of natural events and social anxieties (Miller, Barrett, & Hampe, 1974). Rational, irrational, and entirely imaginary fears are often associated with an environmental change.

Preschoolers' expectations regarding normal occurrences can sometimes surprise adults. A Southeast Asian child, for example, was fearful of moving to this country because she had the impression from *The Three Bears* that fending off hungry bears was a daily part of American life.

Anxieties prompted by social relationships are also common (Beem & Prah, 1984). Children may worry about being separated from loved ones, doing something for the first time, failing to establish friendships, unknowingly violating accepted rules and customs, or performing poorly in school (Wolman, 1978).

Early childhood educators who strive to help young children adjust under stressful circumstances may find the following six recommendations valuable.

Maintain empathy

The first step in helping young children cope with relocation is to acknowledge the idea that preschoolers *are* affected by moving. Although children may not manifest fear of the unknown in the same way adults do, they are concerned. Parents can talk with children about their new surroundings, and point out specifics regarding children's rooms, the kitchen, or any other area that has been especially important to them. "A playground is just down the street from the apartment. We will try to go there the first day after we move."

Some children may want to help pack and label boxes. This enables them to feel more in control of the move, rather than just an observer. Packing together is an excellent time to talk about where the items will go in the new home and other aspects of the move. Be sure that children's favorite items remain readily available throughout the transition to add to their sense of continuity and security. Movers suggest that the child's bed be the last item in the truck and the first to be unpacked.

Children need to know what to expect during the move. Explaining arrangements that affect them will help them prepare for the changes and feel less like they have been abandoned. A parent involved in a long-distance move might say, "On the day the giant moving van comes to load our furniture, the movers will need lots of space to lift the heavy pieces. You and your brother will stay at your friend Kendra's house that day. Before dinner, Mommy and I will pick you up."

Children may not demonstrate their best behavior in the midst of moving's upheaval. They will undoubtedly have an increased need for patience and understanding. Adults who are well-organized and enthusiastic about the move are more likely to offer this extra attention.

Communication among teachers, parents, and children is essential (Light & Hass, 1983). In the familiar school, teachers can help children plan for their leaving in a variety of ways (Ziegler, 1985). Teachers and parents should arrange a conference and a visit for the child prior to entry into school. Plan to have an interpreter if necessary. Children may worry about how to find the bathroom or where to hang their coats, so be sure to point out these and other familiar areas during the visit.

Be flexible

Parents and teachers often wonder how insistent they should be when new children are reluctant to conform to classroom procedures. New children at school have misgivings similar to those of adults who reluctantly join a party in progress and do not see a single familiar face. Most children need time to observe their teacher and peers before they dare to join in.

By far the best way to encourage participation is to allow children to proceed at their own pace. If a child chooses to remain on the sidelines, teachers can offer words of encouragement or make suggestions that will gradually incorporate the newcomer into classroom experiences.

It may be advisable as a first step, for instance, to take a piece of modeling clay to the child, rather than expecting her or him to sit down with a group of exuberant peers. At other times, an intermediary, such as a puppet, toy telephone, classroom pet, or children's book will promote a child's response more readily than direct interaction with an unfamiliar adult (Smardo, 1981).

Be observant and courteous

Parents and teachers should be particularly alert to nonverbal cues from children who may not use language to express their feelings. I once observed some insensitive teachers complain to each other about the shortage of cots while a frightened 3-year-old newcomer uncomfortably stood by. The child's obvious distress was overlooked until it was suggested they look at the child's facial expression. These adults would no doubt consider it inexcusable to raise concerns about not having enough food in front of dinner guests, yet the child was subjected to much more inhospitable behavior.

It is so easy to forget a quiet onlooker can be just as affected by a conversation or incident as an active participant. Teachers who are as alert to and courteous with young children as they would be with adults help preschoolers feel more secure, accepted, and truly welcome.

Provide continuity

Activities children know and enjoy should be continued at home and at school. Teachers can encourage a new child to bring a favorite book to share, respond to requests from the new child for songs and games, or prepare a preferred snack—all help reassure preschoolers that the changes in their lives may not be as drastic or perplexing as they first appeared.

By emphasizing similarities between the new and old environments, young children gain a better sense of control over their situation. It is equally important to supply children with precise, understandable information about their new surroundings. Many things that are viewed as common knowledge, such as milk in a carton instead of a cup, clean-up routines, or the rules for outdoor play, all need to be explained and/or demonstrated.

If possible, orient children to their new surroundings when other children are not present. In this way, children can become acquainted with the physical aspects of the situation first and concentrate on the social dimensions later when the other preschoolers are there.

Promote peer interaction

Generally speaking, people feel more comfortable sharing their feelings and ideas with others their own age. Teachers can structure brief contacts between the new child and peers with statements like, "Let's go over and show Elena your baby, Heather" or "Jason, Chan would like to paint at the easel. Please show him how you get ready to paint." One method to encourage participation is to have the new child arrive a few minutes early to begin an activity so that other children join the newcomer, rather than vice versa (Feldbaum, Christensen, & O'Neal, 1980).

Use children's literature

Picture books are a wonderful vehicle to help young children deal with difficult situations (Jalongo, 1983). Story characters who model successful coping strategies are an excellent resource for children faced with similar relocation situations. Good literature about moving also gives teachers an opportunity to sensitize other children to the new child's feelings and to prepare the group to be more accepting of newcomers. *New Faces, New Spaces* (Toys 'n Things Press, 1984) contains a unit on moving for teachers and resources for parents.

Children's Books About Moving

Alexander, S. (1984). *Dear Phoebe.* Boston: Little, Brown.

Aliki (1984). *We are best friends.* West Caldwell, NJ: Greenwillow.

Bourke, L. (1981). *It's your move: Picking up, packing up and settling in.* Reading, MA: Addison-Wesley.

Conrad, P. (1984). *I don't live here!* New York: Dutton.

Hickman, M. W. (1974). *I'm moving.* Nashville: Abingdon.

Hickman, M. W. (1979). *My friend William moved away.* Nashville: Abingdon.

Hughes, S. (1979). *Moving Molly.* Englewood Cliffs, NJ: Prentice-Hall.

Jones, P. (1980). *I'm not moving!* Scarsdale, NY: Bradbury.

Milord, S., & Milord, J. (1979). *Maggie and the goodbye gift.* West Caldwell, NJ: Lothrop.

Moncure, J. B. (1976). *A new boy in kindergarten.* Chicago, IL: Child's World.

Sharmat, M. W. (1978). *Mitchell is moving.* New York: Macmillan.

Smith, J. L. (1981). *The monster in the third dresser drawer and other stories about Adam Joshua.* New York: Harper & Row.

Tobias, T. (1976). *Moving day.* Westminster, MD: Knopf.

Watson, W. (1978). *Moving.* New York: Harper & Row.

Facilitating children's adjustment to moving is one way for them to reestablish their credentials. It is also a critical dimension of parenting and caregiving in our mobile society.

Ellen Levine Ebert

Conclusions

What are the immediate and long-term consequences of geographic mobility on young children? Levin (1983) foresees an impact on both the number and intensity of interpersonal relationships as one ramification of a highly mobile society.

Teachers, friends and others move in and out of children's lives today in rapid procession. With frequent home changes and the accompanying shifts in school and neighborhood, long relations with people outside the family have become rarer. (p. 434)

In Packard's (1983) view, "at all ages, [children] lose their credentials every time they move" (p. 56). Adults tend to discount the impact of moving on children's lives, yet recollections about how relocation affected them as children are unusually vivid. Anxieties about being the new child at school, the sense of powerlessness at being moved against their wishes, or the trauma of having emotional ties severed by distance are prevalent themes.

Facilitating children's adjustment to moving is one way for them to reestablish their credentials. It is also a critical dimension of parenting and caregiving in our mobile society.

References

Adler, A. (1927). *Understanding human nature.* New York: Fawcett.

Ames, L. B. (1972). Quoted by V. Packard in *A nation of strangers* (p. 237). New York: McKay.

Barman, A. (1981). *Helping children face crisis.* (Report No. 541). New York: Public Affairs Committee.

Beem, M., & Prah, W. (1984). When I move away, will I still be me? *Childhood Education, 60* (5), 310–314.

Elkind, D. (1981). *The hurried child.* Reading, MA: Addison-Wesley.

Employee Relocation Council. (1983, January 26). Close-up: When career moves uproot families. *USA Today,* p. 3D.

Feldbaum, C. L., Christensen, T. E., & O'Neal, E. C. (1980). An observational study of the assimilation of the newcomer to the preschool. *Child Development, 51* (2), 297–507.

Hendrick, J. (1984). *The whole child: Early education for the eighties* (3rd ed.). St. Louis: Mosby.

Jalongo, M. R. (1983, July). Using crisis-oriented books with young children. *Young Children, 38* (5), 29–36.

Jalongo, M. R. (1983, November/December). Promoting peer acceptance of the newly immigrated child. *Childhood Education, 60* (2), 117–124.

Jersild, A., Telford, C., & Sawrey, J. (1975). *Child psychology* (7th ed.). Englewood Cliffs, NJ: Prentice-Hall.

Jones, S. B. (1973, May). Geographic mobility as seen by the wife and mother. *Journal of Marriage and the Family, 35,* 210–218.

Kaplan, L. (1978). *Oneness and separateness: From infant to individual.* New York: Simon & Schuster.

Levin, R. (1983). *Child psychology.* Monterey, CA: Brooks/Cole.

Light, P., & Hass, E. (1983, June). Moving day. *Parent's Magazine, 58* (6), 124–131.

Miller, L. C., Barrett, C. L., & Hampe, E. (1974). Phobias of childhood in a prescientific era. In A. David (Ed.), *Child personality and psychopathology: Current topics.* New York: Wiley.

Packard, V. (1972). *A nation of strangers.* New York: McKay.

Packard, V. (1983). *Our endangered children: Growing up in a changing world.* Boston: Little, Brown.

Raymond, R., & Eliot, S. (1980). *Grow your roots anywhere, anytime.* New York: Scribners.

Rubin, Z. (1980). *Children's friendships.* Cambridge: Harvard University Press.

Selman, R. L. (1980). *The growth of interpersonal understanding.* New York: Academic Press.

Smardo, F. A. (1981, September/October). Books about moving. Geographic mobility: How do we help children cope? *Childhood Education, 58* (1), 37–45.

Sullivan, H. S. (1953). *The interpersonal theory of psychiatry.* New York: Norton.

Tooley, K. (1970). The role of geographic mobility in some adjustment problems of children and families. *Journal of the American Academy of Child Psychiatry, 9* (2), 366–378.

Toys 'n Things Press. (1984). *New faces, new spaces. Helping young children cope with change* (rev. ed.). St. Paul, MN: Author.

Weimer, G. D. (1981, September/October). Geographic mobility, family life cycle and marital adjustment of husbands and wives. *Dissertation Abstracts International, 42* (3), 1208-B. (University Microfilms No. 81-10, 530)

Wolman, B. (1978). *Children's fears.* New York: New American Library.

Ziegler, P. (1985, March). Saying good-bye to preschool. *Young Children, 40* (3), 11–15.

Ziller, R. C., & Long, B. (Eds.). (1967). Self-social constructs of children. (ERIC Document Reproduction Service No. ED 021 615)

The Teacher's Role in Facilitating a Child's Adjustment to Divorce

Patsy Skeen and Patrick C. McKenry

"At first it's so terrible you could really die, but then it gets better." (Andy—age 9)

"If I'd only kept my room clean [like Daddy asked], he wouldn't have left me." (Alice—age 4)

"Silence." (Becky—age 5)

These actual responses of children involved in divorce are typical of those observed by teachers. Such observations are increasing as the lives of an alarming number of children are being disrupted—at least temporarily—by divorce. The divorce rate has more than doubled in the past 10 years. Currently almost four out of ten marriages end in divorce (United States Bureau of the Census 1976). More than 60% of these divorcing couples have children at home. Because almost 50% of all divorces occur in the first 7 years of marriage, the children involved in divorce are usually quite young (Norton and Glick 1976). It is estimated that 20% of the children enrolled in elementary school have divorced parents. In some of the kindergarten and first grade classes, this figure is closer to the 40 to 50% level (Wilkinson and Beck 1977).

The period of disorganization following divorce is usually extended. The family living standard is likely to change and a nonworking mother often goes to work. One parent generally leaves the home and siblings can be lost as well (Derdeyn 1977). Because divorce is a crisis involving disruption of the family structure, the role of the school and the teacher are of particular importance. A child's sense of continuity and stability is likely to be dependent upon the availability of extrafamilial supports such as the school, as well as upon what protection and concern can be mobilized in the parent-child relationship during this time (Kelly and Wallerstein 1977).

The purpose of this article is to provide information that will enable the teacher to be a positive support to children and families during divorce. Research and theory concerning the effects of divorce on children, parenting through divorce, and the role of the school are summarized. Practical suggestions for the classroom teacher are presented.

Children and divorce

Without exception divorce is a significant event in the life of any child. For the child, divorce may represent a sense of loss, a sense of failure in interpersonal relationships, and the beginning of a difficult transition to new life patterns (Magrab 1978). It cannot be assumed, however, that children will all react to divorce in the same way. For the most part, they are healthy, normal children who are confronted with an extremely stressful situation (Wilkinson and Beck 1977). Research findings indicate that the experience of divorce itself is less harmful than the nature of the parents' personalities and relationships with their children (Despert 1962; McDermott 1968; Westman and Cline 1970). The child's reactions also depend upon such factors as the extent and nature of family disharmony prior to divorce, emotional availability of important people to the child during the divorce period, and the child's age, sex, and personality strengths (Anthony 1974; McDermott 1968).

Some evidence indicates that children of divorce may be better adjusted than children remaining in two-parent homes where there is ongoing tension, conflict, and stress (Nye 1957; Landis 1960; Hetherington, Cox, and Cox 1978). Hetherington et al. (1978) suggest that divorce is often the most positive solution to destructive family functioning. Divorce can have a positive influence. For example, some children of divorce exhibit more empathy for others, increased helping behavior, and greater independence than children from intact families. However, the ease and rapidity with which divorce may be obtained and the recent emphasis on "creative" and "positive" divorce may mask the pain, stress, and adjustment problems inherent in divorce.

Patsy Skeen, Ed.D., is Assistant Professor, Child and Family Development, University of Georgia, Athens, Georgia.

Patrick C. McKenry, Ph.D., is Assistant Professor, Family Relations and Human Development, School of Home Economics, Ohio State University, Columbus, Ohio.

Revision of a paper presented at the 1978 National Association for the Education of Young Children Annual Conference.

Available research findings on children of divorce tend to agree that divorce is to an extent a developmental crisis for children (Jones 1977; Magrab 1978; Wilkinson and Beck 1977). Wallerstein and Kelly (1977) comment that they drew heavily from crisis intervention theory in their research, and Hetherington, Cox, and Cox (1976) use the term *critical event* to describe divorce as it affects families. Cantor's (1977) review of the literature revealed that in a period of parental divorce, children often show marked changes in behavior, particularly in school, and the changes are likely to be in the direction of acting-out behaviors.

Kelly and Wallerstein (1976) and Wallerstein and Kelly (1975, 1976) have researched the impact of the divorce process on children. In their preschool sample, they found that the children's self-concept was particularly affected. The children's views of the dependability and predictability of relationships were threatened, and their sense of order regarding the world was disrupted. Some suffered feelings of responsibility for driving the father away. Older preschoolers were better able to experience family turbulence and divorce without breaking developmental stride. The older preschoolers were also better able to find gratification outside the home and to place some psychological and social distance between themselves and their parents. However, heightened anxiety and aggression were noted in this group. Almost half of the children in this preschool group were found to be in a significantly deteriorated psychological condition at the followup study one year later.

Kelly and Wallerstein (1976) reported that young schoolage children respond to divorce with pervasive sadness, fear, feelings of deprivation, and some anger. At the end of 1 year, many still struggled with the task of integrating divorce-related changes in their lives. For older schoolage children, Wallerstein and Kelly (1976) found that divorce affected the freedom of children to keep major attention focused outside the family, particularly on school-related tasks. These children displayed conscious and intense anger, fears and phobias, and a shaken sense of identity and loneliness. At the end of 1 year, the anger and hostility lingered, and half the children evidenced troubled, conflictual, and depressed behavior patterns.

Hetherington et al. (1976) characterized behaviors of children of divorce as more dependent, aggressive, whiny, demanding, unaffectionate, and disobedient than behavior of children from intact families. Hetherington et al. (1976) noted three areas of anxiety: fear of abandonment, loss of love, and bodily harm. Anthony (1974) noted other behaviors of low vitality, restlessness, guilt, shame, anxiety, depression, low self-esteem, failure to develop as a separate person, a preoccupation with death and disease, inability to be alone, regression to immature behavior, separation and phobia anxiety, and an intense attachment to one parent. With certain groups of children—i.e., handicapped, adopted, and chronic illness cases such as asthmatics, epileptics, and diabetics—the divorce process might precipitate a psychosomatic crisis requiring hospitalization. Jacobson (1978) found the more the amount of time spent with the father was reduced during a 12-month period following divorce, the more a child was likely to show signs of maladjustment. Anthony (1974) concluded that the major reaction *during* divorce is grief associated with guilt, while the major reaction *after* divorce is shame coupled with strong resentment.

Hozman and Froiland (1977) suggested that the experience of losing a parent through divorce is similar to that of losing a parent through death. They adopted the Kubler-Ross model for dealing with loss. In this model, children go through five stages as they learn to accept loss of a parent. Initially, children deny the reality of the divorce. Denial is followed by anger and then bargaining in which children try to get parents back together. When they realize that their efforts cannot persuade parents to live together again, they become depressed. The final stage is acceptance of the divorce situation.

Anthony (1974) and Hetherington et al. (1978) cautioned against expecting all children and parents to react the same way in divorce. Each individual's behavior depends upon his or her unique personality, experiences, and the support system available.

Parenting during divorce

For parents, divorce is a time of marked stress in everyday living and emotional as well as interpersonal adjustment. Feelings of loneliness, lowered self-esteem, depression, and helplessness interfere with parenting abilities (Hetherington et al. 1978). Several studies have noted a serious deterioration in the quality of the mother-child relationship in divorced families because of the mother's emotional neediness and her ambivalence about her new role as single parent (McDermott 1968; Hetherington et al. 1976; Wallerstein and Kelly 1976). After divorce, some fathers may become freer and less authoritarian. However, other fathers who are absent from the household may become less nurturant and more detached from their children with time (Hetherington et al. 1976; Weiss 1975).

During divorce, specific developmental needs of children are often unmet because of parental preoccupation with their own needs and parental role conflicts. When compared to parents in intact families, Hetherington et al. (1976) found, divorced parents of preschoolers were less consistent and effective in discipline, less nurturant, and generally less appropriately behaved with their children because of the preoccupation with the divorce process. When compared to parents in intact families, divorced parents communicated less well and made fewer demands for mature behavior of their children (Hetherington et al. 1976).

In summary, parent-child relationships are altered as a result of divorce. Parenting becomes difficult as the structure of the family breaks down and parents must make interpersonal adjustments such as dealing with stress, loneliness, and lowered self-esteem. However, there are many unanswered

Marlene Getz

Some children of divorce exhibit more empathy for others, increased helping behavior, and greater independence than do children from intact families.

questions concerning parenting capabilities and behaviors during divorce. A great deal more research needs to be done before we can draw definitive conclusions in this area.

Schools and divorce

The important role that schools can play in facilitating children's adjustment has not been clearly addressed in the divorce literature. Because children spend a great number of hours in school, as compared to time with parents, it is reasonable to assume that schools may be providing emotional support and continuity to a large number of children from divorcing parents. In other words, schools as a major socializing institution for children may play a more vital role in offsetting some of the negative impact of family disruption that accompanies divorce than previously thought (Jones 1977).

Key relationships in the family are often disrupted in part because of the geographic inaccessibility of the noncustodial parent. In addition, the custodial parent may be emotionally unavailable in the usual role to the child. Therefore, it has been argued that the school has an obligation to intervene with children of divorce to prevent re-

actions from being repressed and thus to prevent future disorders. Because parents are often involved in conflicts over financial support, visitation rights, and a battle for the children's loyalties, the teacher may be forcibly thrust into the role of an interim parent substitute (McDermott 1968).

Many children find some support within the school setting because their attitudes and performance in school provide gratification which is sustaining to them in the face of divorce stress. Kelly and Wallerstein (1977) found that the attention, sympathy, and tolerance demonstrated by teachers who had been informed about the divorce were supportive to a number of children who were feeling emotionally undernourished at home. In their study, teachers became a central stable figure in the lives of several children in the months following the separation, in some cases the only stable figure in these children's lives.

School personnel should be interested and involved in providing developmental assistance to individuals faced with critical life situations such as divorce. To date, few strategies have been published concerning ways that teachers can provide specific assistance to the child involved in divorce (Wilkinson and Beck 1977). Existing strategies that have been developed have been directed primarily to the school psychologist and guidance counselor. The following specific techniques are suggested for the classroom teacher who perhaps first notices behavioral changes and is in a position to help the child on a long-term basis. The teacher's role is discussed in three sections: working in the classroom, working with parents, and working with counselors.

What can the teacher do?

In the classroom

Team teachers Harriet Sykes and George Brown have just discovered that more than one-half of the families of their kindergarten children have been involved in divorce. They decide that they want to help the children in their classroom grow through the divorce experience. What can they do?

Be a careful observer

1. Look for behavioral cues that help you understand how a child is feeling and what problems and strengths the child might have. Free play, art activities, puppet shows, and individual talks with the child are particularly good opportunities for observation.

2. Observe the child frequently, over a period of time, and in several types of situations such as at quiet time, in group work, alone, in active play, in free play, and at home. Such varied observations allow the teacher to construct a more complete picture of the total child and reduce the likelihood that judgments will be made on the basis of a "bad day."

3. Be a good listener to both verbalization and body language.

Make a plan

1. When teachers are attempting to understand, predict, and intervene with behavior, it is important to determine first the child's physical, social, emotional, and cognitive developmental levels. A plan can then be developed to meet the child's individual needs. Direct observation, parents, counselors, and relevant literature are good sources of information to use when planning.

Provide opportunities for working through feelings

1. Help the child recognize and acceptably express feelings and resolve conflict through the use of curriculum activities such as painting, flannel board, clay, drawing pictures, writing experience stories about the child's family, dramatic play, doll play, books about alternate family styles, free play, woodworking, music, and movement.

2. If the child appears to be going through the Kubler-Ross stages, prepare to help the child deal with the feelings in each stage. Give the child time for a resolution in each stage.

3. Allow children the solitude and privacy they sometimes need.

4. Support the establishment of divorce discussion and/or therapy groups for children led by trained leaders or counselors.

Help the child understand cognitively

1. Help the child understand cognitively what his or her situation is, how and why he or she feels, how feelings can be expressed, and the consequences of such expression. Many discussions over an extended period of time will be necessary before such cognitive understanding is established.

2. Provide opportunities for the child to be successful in controlling his or her life. For example, make sure equipment and learning materials are matched to the child's abilities. Tell the child about the sequence of the day's events and notify the child about changes in schedule well ahead of time. Give the child opportunities to make as many choices as he or she can handle.

3. Books and discussions can be used to give information about divorce in general and promote peer acceptance and support for a child from a divorced family. (See Relevant Books.)

Maintain a stable environment

1. Remain consistent in expectations for the child. This may be the only area of consistency in a rapidly changing and difficult period of the child's life.

2. Although children must be dealt with patiently and might regress to immature forms of behavior at times, avoid overprotecting the child.

3. Even though the child might have problems, he or she should not be allowed to "run wild." Because parents may be having difficulty setting limits for the child, it is extremely important for the classroom teacher to lovingly, but firmly, set reasonable limits for the child's behavior.

4. Make a special effort to love the child. Let the child know that he or she is important and worthwhile through smiles, hugs, praise, and attention to appropriate behaviors. However, avoid "being a mother or father" or allowing the child to become overly dependent upon you since you and the child will separate at the end of the year.

5. Prepare the child for separation from you at the end of the year (or an extended absence from you during the year) by telling the child ahead of time about the separation, why it will occur,

and what will happen to the child. A visit to the new teacher and room can be very helpful. The child must be reassured that you are not leaving because he or she is "bad" or because you have stopped loving the child.

6. Encourage the child to work through stressful situations (e.g., a move to a new house) by talking about and role playing the situation in advance.

Examine your attitude

1. Avoid expecting a child to manifest certain kinds of problems simply because parents are divorcing. Children are skillful in "reading" adult expectations and often will behave accordingly. Adults might also assume that divorce is the reason for a behavior problem when in actuality other factors are the causes. Children have different reactions to divorce just as they do to all other aspects of life.

2. Examine personal feelings and values about divorce. Feelings and values consciously and unconsciously affect the way teachers interact with children and parents.

3. Try to help each child grow through divorce. Remember that divorce can have the positive effects of ending a highly dysfunctional family and providing growth opportunities for family members.

Working with parents

Andy Robinson's mother has just told Andy's teacher, Mr. Wang, that she and her husband are going to get a divorce. She is worried about how this will affect Andy and wants to do whatever she can to assist her son. How can Mr. Wang help?

1. Realize that since divorce is a stressful time, teacher-parent communications should be especially supportive and positive.

2. Understand that parents are in a crisis situation and may not be able to attend to parenting as well as you or they would like.

3. Support the parent as an important person about whom you are concerned.

4. Provide books written for both children and adults for the parent to read concerning divorce (See Relevant

Jim Cronk

Young children may respond to divorce with pervasive sadness, fear, feelings of deprivation, and anger.

13. Correctly address notes to parents. "Dear Parent" can be used when you are not sure if the child's parents are divorced or if the mother might have remarried and have a different name from the child.

Working with counselors

Becky's teacher, Ms. Jones, has been patiently listening for 2 hours to Becky's father talk about the pain he feels and how hard it is to cope with life as a single man after 15 years of marriage. Ms. Jones wants to help but is at her wits' end. What can she do?

1. Refer children and parents to competent counselors in the community instead of trying to assume the role of counselor. A great deal of harm can be done by well-meaning listeners who "get in over their heads" and do not know how to handle a situation.

2. The American Association of Marriage and Family Therapists (225 Yale Ave., Claremont, CA 91711) and the American Psychological Association (1200 17th St., N.W., Washington, DC 20036) maintain lists of qualified counselors. Counselors belonging to these organizations also generally indicate such membership in yellow page phonebook listings. However, the teacher should find out firsthand about the effectiveness of a counselor before referrals are made. Former clients, other teachers, and a personal visit to the counselor are good sources of information.

3. Work with the counselor when appropriate. The teacher can provide a great deal of information as a result of daily observation and interaction with the child. The teacher might also help carry out treatment strategies in the classroom.

In summary, divorce is a time of crisis for parents and children. The role of the school becomes particularly important during divorce since the family support system is under stress. Teachers are especially significant to the family since they probably spend as much or more time with the child than any other adult outside the family. When teachers are skilled and concerned, they can help parents and children grow through divorce.

Books on page 69.)

5. Encourage parents to be as open and honest as possible with the child about the divorce and their related feelings.

6. Urge parents to assure their children that divorce occurs because of problems the parents have. The children did not cause the divorce and cannot bring the parents back together.

7. Encourage parents to elicit their children's feelings.

8. Assure parents that children will need time to adjust to divorce and that difficulties in the child's behavior do not mean that the child has become permanently psychologically disturbed.

9. Encourage parents to work together as much as possible in their parenting roles even though they are dissolving their couple role. The attitudes that parents display toward each other and their divorce are vital factors in the child's adjustment. The use of the child as a messenger or a "pawn" in the couple relationship is particularly harmful to the child.

10. Help alleviate parental guilt by telling parents that their child is not alone. Indicate to parents that there is also evidence that children from stable one-parent families are better off emotionally than children in unstable, conflictual two-parent families.

11. Encourage parents to take time to establish a meaningful personal life both as a parent and as an important person apart from the child. This can be their best gift to their children.

12. Provide an informal atmosphere in which parents can share their problems and solutions.

References

Anthony, E. J. "Children at Risk from Divorce: A Review." In *The Child in His Family,* ed. E. T. Anthony and C. Koupernils. New York: Wiley, 1974.

Cantor, D. W. "School-Based Groups for Children of Divorce." *Journal of Divorce* 1 (1977): 183–187.

Derdeyn, A. P. "Children in Divorce: Intervention in the Phase of Separation." *Pediatrics* 60 (1977): 20–27.

Despert, L. *Children of Divorce.* Garden City, N.Y.: Dolphin Books, 1962.

Hetherington, E. M.; Cox, M.; and Cox, R. "The Aftermath of Divorce." In *Mother/Child, Father/Child Relationships,* ed. J. H. Stevens and M. Mathews. Washington, D.C.: National Association for the Education of Young Children, 1978.

Hetherington, E. M.; Cox, M.; and Cox, R. "Divorced Fathers." *The Family Coordinator* (1976): 417–429.

Hozman, T. L., and Froiland, D. J. "Children: Forgotten in Divorce." *Personnel and Guidance Journal* 5 (1977): 530–533.

Jacobson, D. S. "The Impact of Marital Separation/Divorce on Children: Parent-Child Separation and Child Adjustment." *Journal of Divorce* 1 (1978): 341–360.

Jones, F. N. "The Impact of Divorce on Children." *Conciliation Courts Review* 15 (1977): 25–29.

Kelly, J. B., and Wallerstein, J. S. "Brief Interventions with Children in Divorcing Families." *American Journal of Orthopsychiatry* 47 (1977): 23–39.

Kelly, J. B., and Wallerstein, J. S. "The Effects of Parental Divorce: Experiences of the Child in Early Latency." *American Journal of Orthopsychiatry* 46 (1976): 20–32.

Landis, J. "The Trauma of Children when Parents Divorce." *Marriage and Family Living* 22 (1960): 7–13.

Magrab, P. R. "For the Sake of the Children: A Review of the Psychological Effects of Divorce." *Journal of Divorce* 1 (1978): 233–245.

McDermott, J. F. "Parental Divorce in Early Childhood." *American Journal of Psychiatry* 124 (1968): 1424–1432.

Norton, A. J., and Glick, P. C. "Marital Instability: Past, Present and Future." *Journal of Social Issues* 32 (1976): 5–20.

Nye, F. I. "Child Adjustment in Broken and in Unhappy Unbroken Homes." *Marriage and Family Living* 19 (1957): 356–361.

United States Bureau of the Census. *Current Population Reports,* Series P-20, No. 297. Washington, D.C.: U.S. Government Printing Office, 1976.

Wallerstein, J. S., and Kelly, J. B. "Divorce Counseling: A Community Service for Families in the Midst of Divorce." *American Journal of Orthopsychiatry* 47 (1977): 4–22.

Wallerstein, J. S., and Kelly, J. B. "The Effects of Parental Divorce: Experience of the Child in Later Latency." *American Journal of Orthopsychiatry* 46 (1976): 256–269.

Wallerstein, J. S., and Kelly, J. B. "The Effects of Parental Divorce: Experience of the Preschool Child." *Journal of Child Psychiatry* 14 (1975): 600–616.

Weiss, R. *Marital Separation.* New York: Basic Books, 1975.

Westman, J. C., and Cline, D. W. "Role of Child Psychiatry in Divorce." *Archives of General Psychiatry* 23 (1970): 416–420.

Wilkinson, G. S., and Beck, R. T. "Children's Divorce Groups." *Elementary School Guidance and Counseling* 26 (1977): 204–213.

Relevant books for children

Picture books
Adams, F. *Mushy Eggs.* New York: C. P. Putnam's Sons, 1973.

Caines, J. *Daddy.* New York: Harper & Row, 1977.

Kindred, W. *Lucky Wilma.* New York: Dial Press, 1973.

Lexau, J. *Emily and the Klunky Baby and the Next-Door Dog.* New York: Dial Press, 1972.

Lexau, J. *Me Day.* New York: Dial Press, 1971.

Perry, P., and Lynch, M. *Mommy and Daddy Are Divorced.* New York: Dial Press, 1978.

Stein, S. B. *On Divorce.* New York: Walker & Co., 1979.

Elementary and middle school
Alexander, A. *To Live a Lie.* West Hanover, Mass.: McClelland & Stewart, 1975.

Bach, A. *A Father Every Few Years.* New York: Harper & Row, 1977.

Blue, R. *A Month of Sundays.* New York: Franklin Watts, 1972.

Blume, J. *It's Not the End of the World.* New York: Bradbury Press, 1972.

Corcoran, B. *Hey, That's My Soul You're Stomping On.* New York: Atheneum, 1978.

Donovan, J. *I'll Get There. It Better Be Worth the Trip.* New York: Harper & Row, 1969.

Duncan, L. *A Gift of Magic.* Boston: Little, Brown & Co., 1971.

Fox, P. *Blowfish Live in the Sea.* Scarsdale, N.Y.: Bradbury Press, 1970.

Gardner, R. *The Boys and Girls Book about Divorce.* New York: Bantam Books, 1977.

Goff, B. *Where is Daddy?* Boston: Beacon Press, 1969.

Greene, C. *A Girl Called Al.* New York: Viking Press, 1969.

Hoban, L. *I Met a Traveller.* New York: Harper & Row, 1977.

Johnson, A., and Johnson, E. *The Grizzly.* New York: Harper & Row, 1964.

Klein, N. *Taking Sides.* New York: Pantheon Books, 1974.

LeShan, E. *What's Going to Happen to Me? When Parents Separate or Divorce.* New York: Four Winds Press, 1978.

Mazer, H. *Guy Lenny.* New York: Delacorte Press, 1971.

Mazer, N. *I, Trissy.* New York: Dell Publishing Co., 1971.

Nahn, P. *My Dad Lives in a Downtown Motel.* Garden City, N.Y.: Doubleday, 1973.

Newfield, M. *A Book for Jodan.* New York: Atheneum, 1975.

Rogers, H. *Morris and His Brave Lion.* New York: McGraw-Hill, 1975.

Simon, N. *All Kinds of Families.* Chicago: Whitman, 1976.

Steptoe, J. *My Special Best Words.* New York: Viking Press, 1974.

Stolz, M. *Leap Before You Look.* New York: Harper & Row, 1972.

Talbot, C. *The Great Rat Island Adventure.* New York: Atheneum, 1977.

Walker, M. *A Piece of the World.* New York: Atheneum, 1972.

Relevant books for teachers and parents
Gardner, R. *The Parents Book about Divorce.* Garden City, N.Y.: Doubleday, 1977.

Grollman, E. *Explaining Divorce to Children.* Boston: Beacon Press, 1969.

Hunt, M., and Hunt, B. *The Divorce Experience.* New York: McGraw-Hill, 1977.

Kessler, S. *The American Way of Divorce: Prescriptions for Change.* Chicago: Nelson-Hall, 1975.

Krantzler, M. *Creative Divorce.* New York: M. Evans & Co., 1974.

Salk, L. *What Every Child Would Like Parents to Know About Divorce.* New York: Harper & Row, 1978.

Sinberg, J. *Divorce is a Grown Up Problem: A Book about Divorce for Young Children and Their Parents.* New York: Avon, 1978.

Stein, S. B. *On Divorce.* New York: Walker & Co., 1979.

Stevens, J., and Mathews, M., eds. *Mother/Child, Father/Child Relationships.* Washington, D.C.: National Association for the Education of Young Children, 1978.

Turow, R. *Daddy Doesn't Live Here Anymore.* Garden City, N.J.: Anchor Books, 1978.

Weiss, R. *Marital Separation.* New York: Basic Books, 1975.

Journals
Journal of Divorce. Editor: Esther O. Fisher. Haworth Press, 174 Fifth Ave., New York, NY 10010.

The Single Parent: The Journal of Parents Without Partners, Inc. Editor: Barbara Chase. Parents Without Partners, Inc., International Headquarters, 7910 Woodmont Ave., Bethesda, MD 20014.

Blended Families

Overcoming the Cinderella Myth

Patsy Skeen, Bryan E. Robinson, and Carol Flake-Hobson

Young children are familiar with stories of wicked stepmothers—Cinderella's stepmother gave her the vilest household tasks and competed with her for the prince's attention. Hansel and Gretel were abandoned in the woods by their stepmother. Snow White's jealous stepmother tried to poison her. Today's stepfamily relationships are quite different from these portrayals, but they do also differ from intact family relationships. Teachers of young children can be a positive support to children and their stepfamilies if we are better informed.

Demographic information

The high incidence of stepfamilies in this country is *not* a myth. There are an estimated 25 million stepparents (Visher and Visher 1979), and 6.5 million children live in stepfamilies (Francke and Reese 1980; Jacobson 1980). Sometimes called reconstituted, recoupled, or blended families, such families may be a widow with one child marrying a bachelor, or as complex as four divorced individuals, all with joint custody of their children trying to form two new households. Children may visit rather than live with stepparents (Visher and Visher 1978b). Most blended families are formed through divorce and remarriage (Jacobson 1980), a phenomenon which is expected to continue.

Stepfamily research

Empirical research on stepfamilies is limited. Duberman (1973) studied remarried parents using a Parent-Child Relationship Rating Scale. Her results showed that 64% of the blended families had "excellent" relationships, although steprelations were more successful when previous marriages ended in death rather than divorce. Furthermore, stepparent-child relationships were better among families of higher social classes, and among Protestants as compared to Catholics.

Findings from a study of junior and senior high school students contrasted with Duberman's positive report on blended family relationships. Bowerman and Irish (1962) contrasted adjustments of children residing in three family conditions—with natural parents, with a mother and stepfather, and with a father and stepmother. They reported that homes involving steprelations were more characterized by stress, ambivalence, and low cohesiveness than natural parent homes. Stepparents also had more trouble establishing the same degree of affection and closeness with the children than did biological parents. Children in stepfamilies said they felt more rejected than those in nonstepfamilies. In contrast to Duberman's findings, Bowerman and Irish found that children adjusted better toward stepparents when previous marriages were broken by divorce rather than death.

One explanation for these conflicting reports is the differences in research methodology. Duberman surveyed only the husbands and wives involved in stepfamilies, asking spouses to evaluate their own children's relationship with the stepparent. In contrast, Bowerman and Irish's data are based on questionnaires completed by stepchildren, who might evaluate relationships differently from their parents. Changing social attitudes about divorce may also account for some differences.

Touliatos and Lindholm (1980) asked teachers to rate the behavior of children of kindergarten age through eighth grade. Compared to children in intact homes, children in homes with stepparents were rated as having more conduct problems (e.g., negativism, aggression), and children living with a mother and stepfather also had socialized delinquency (e.g., bad companions, cooperative stealing).

Bohannan and Erickson (1978)

Patsy Skeen, Ed.D., is Assistant Professor of Child and Family Development at the University of Georgia, Athens, Georgia.

Bryan E. Robinson, Ph.D., is Associate Professor of Human Development and Learning at the University of North Carolina, Charlotte, North Carolina.

Carol Flake-Hobson, Ph.D., is Associate Professor of Education at the University of South Carolina, Columbia, South Carolina.

studied stepchildren and children raised by natural parents. Ratings of stepfathers made by both stepchildren and mothers were as positive as those of biological fathers made by their natural children and by the children's mothers. Lending additional support to this view, two national surveys found no social-psychological differences between high school students brought up in stepfather families and those raised in natural-parent families (Wilson et al. 1975). In addition, Burchinal (1964) assessed the questionnaire responses of adolescents and parents from unbroken, broken, and reconstituted families. He found no significant differences in the personality and social relationships among the three groups. Santrock et al. (1982) also observed unbroken, broken, and stepfamilies. They concluded that the social behavior of children in stepfamilies is not necessarily less competent than that of children in intact or broken families. Nye (1957) did find more adjustment problems in stepfamilies than in unbroken families, but he noted that the greatest adjustment difficulties exist in unhappy intact families. Other reports (Bernard 1956; Bohannan 1970; Goode 1956; Landis 1962; Stinnett and Walters 1977) indicate that stepfamilies had no more difficulty than nonstepfamilies. Instead, children from stepfamilies could have mostly positive, mostly negative, or mixed experiences—the same as children from unbroken families (Wilson et al. 1975).

Stepfathers

I was really turned on by her—then I met her kids.... I began to look at them in a very different way after I got serious.... Everybody warned me not to marry a woman with children. They said there'd be problems: There were. But the youngest goes off to college next month and I think we've won. (Bohannan and Erickson 1978, p. 53)

More than one-half of families formed by divorce and remarriage include stepfathers (Rallings 1976), but we know very little about stepfatherhood. What we do know is that stepfathers face a real challenge trying to fit into a new family.

Stepfathers tend to be either inattentive and disengaged, giving the mother little childrearing support, or very actively involved. The highly active stepfathers are often restrictive, especially to sons. However, if the stepfather is able to set consistent limits and communicate warmly and well with the children and if the mother welcomes the stepfather's support, the stepchildren, especially boys, generally function better than children in single-parent families or conflicted nondivorced families (Hetherington, Cox, and Cox 1981). Oshman and Manosevitz (1976) also found that stepfathers have a positive effect on stepsons. However, children aged 9 to 15 are less likely to accept an effective stepparent than are younger or older children (Hetherington, Cox, and Cox 1981). Stern (1978) suggests that fathers are likely to be more successful disciplinarians when they adopt a slow, gentle, flexible approach built on friendship which includes the child's participation rather than authoritarian controls over the child.

As mentioned earlier, mothers and children thought stepfathers were just as good parents as biological fathers (Bohannan and Erickson 1978), but stepfathers had lower opinions of their own performance. Some stepfathers whose children lived with their mothers felt pain and regretted the time spent with stepchildren, when they could spend so little time with their own children (Brooks 1981). Stepfathers viewed their stepchildren as less happy and they felt less effective in the fathering role than natural fathers. Stepfathers, wanting to do a good job, seemed more self-conscious about their effectiveness and more self-critical, so they set their standards high—measuring themselves against what they thought an ideal father should be (Bohannan and Erickson 1978).

Lending additional support to these findings, Duberman (1973) found that stepfathers had better relationships with stepchildren than did stepmothers. Moreover, better parent-child steprelations existed among never-before-married stepfathers. Although stepfathers may not believe it, other stepfamily members view them to be just as competent in their role as biological fathers are with their children.

Stepmothers

At the beginning you would find my husband's four children off playing in one corner and my two playing in another corner. But now they don't do that. There's no open hostility, and we handle it by trying hard to be fair. Time and adjustment have brought an improvement in the relationships among them all. (Duberman 1975, p. 69)

Stepmothers have been portrayed as wicked or evil in folklore and literature, much more than stepfathers. There is evidence that stepmothers do have a harder time adjusting to stepparenting than stepfathers (Bowerman and Irish 1962; Jones 1978). Perhaps the Cinderella myth of the cruel stepmother lingers, causing more problems for stepmothers and children. Also, society is more apt to give assistance and social support to stepfathers (Bowerman and Irish 1962).

Duberman (1973) reported that younger mothers had better steprelations with children than older mothers, and that stepmothers had better steprelations with children younger than 13 than with teenage children. Draughton (1975) suggested that stepmothers can expect better success by being the child's friend than by trying to become a second mother.

Stepchildren

Fifteen-year-old child: The main change is getting used to the new parent. Our family has become more closely knit, even though we are separated because my stepfather is a student at a university and I am also. I find him to be a good man and a fine parent. (Bernard 1956, p. 323).

The plight of children in blended families is not as dismal as it is often portrayed. Generally, research shows that stepchildren are just as happy and just as socially and academically successful as children in unbroken families (Bohannan and Erickson 1978), although one study indicated that children from unbroken families reached a higher level of education than children from stepfamilies (Wilson et al. 1975).

One of the problems that usually arises in blended families is the question of "turf." For example, "Why do I have to share my toys with you?" or "He's *my* dad, not yours" (Johnson 1980). Duberman (1973) found that positive stepsibling relationships are crucial to the success of stepfamilies. The better the relations between stepsiblings, the better the total family integration. When remarried couples had a child together, their children from former marriages were more likely to have harmonious relations. On the other hand, sometimes children from the former marriages feel left out or not as important as the new child which belongs to both the natural parent and the stepparent (Brooks 1981).

Complexities of blended families

The twins and my stepdaughter hate each other.... They always pull this bit about "your mommie" and "my daddy" jazz.

There's lots of jealousy among them. The kids drive us crazy with fighting. (Duberman 1975, p. 68)

Living in a blended family is different from simply moving from one primary family into another! There are clear structural differences in how intact nuclear families and stepfamilies interact (Draughton 1975; Nelson and Nelson 1982; Perkins and Kahan 1979; Sager et al. 1981; Schulman 1972; Visher and Visher 1979).

Stepfamilies face a special dilemma because of the difficulty in acquiring stepparenting skills (Fast and Cain 1966; Kompara 1980). Most adults have not had previous experience having a stepchild or living in a stepfamily. Kompara (1980) further points out that "in a remarriage ... the children have been partially socialized by the first parents" (p. 69). Stepfamily members have separate histories, memories, and habits. These factors pose difficulties in the socialization process of stepfamilies. Solidarity must be reestablished, and status, duties, and privileges must be redefined in the context of the new family system (Duberman 1973).

The challenge of the blended family involves dealing with the past as well as the present and future. The loss of the initial family must be mourned (Thies 1977). Parents must work through their relationships with the former spouse as well as help their children deal successfully with the divorce (Kleinman, Rosenberg, and Whiteside 1979). Former spouses and their relatives may be part of the new stepfamily's interactions. These interactions can be destructive if former spouses use the children to continue the battle which was not ended with divorce (Brooks 1981).

Children in blended families are faced with adjusting to more complex family interaction than before:

The child has to adjust to one and sometimes two stepparents (one of whom is visited) and still retain relationships with the biological parent out of the home, biological siblings in and/or out of the home and develop a relationship with stepsiblings who may be in and/or out of the home. (Jacobson 1980, p. 2)

As a result of such complex interaction children may experience divided loyalties (Visher and Visher 1979). Stepchildren may feel twice as defeated—first for not preventing the divorce and second for not preventing the remarriage. They may direct anger for the absent parent toward the new stepparent (Francke and Reese 1980). These situations are compounded when relationships are recast in such a way that stepparents and children are thrown into instant, intimate relationships with strangers for which they are not ready (Kompara 1980). Belief in the myth that blended families should instantly love each other because they are now a family sets families up for failure (Visher and Visher 1978a).

Messinger (1976) identified the stepfamily as a high-risk group for which there are no societal norms. Lack of clear role expectations or guidelines for acceptable stepfamily behavior causes role uncertainty and stress in stepfamily relationships (Fast and Cain 1966; Messinger 1967; Rallings 1976). Some stepparents spend too much time and energy trying to work out their stepparent roles at the expense of working on the couple relationship (Hetherington, Cox, and Cox 1981). The higher divorce rate in second marriages—40% compared to 33% in first marriages—attests to the difficulty of working out the complex problems typical of stepfamilies (Francke and Reese 1980).

Summary of research findings

Research findings on the effects of children living in blended families are mixed. Some studies indicate the presence of more difficulty for children in stepfamilies than children living with both biological parents, while others suggest no major differences in difficulties in either family type. The nature of the blended family network, however, is strikingly different from the unbroken family network, so stepfamilies experience some complications which unbroken families do not.

Despite the potential difficulties in blended family relationships, there are positive outlooks. Messinger (1976) suggests that stepfamily stress can be

Faith Bowlus

The transition from unbroken to blended families is not an easy one, but when blended families have realistic expectations and support, it is possible for most to manage their lives with reasonable success.

prevented or reduced through remarriage preparation courses. Before embarking upon remarriage, Jacobson (1980) recommends "a rehearsal for reality" in which soon-to-be blended family members express their feelings and anticipate potential problems which might arise after the marriage.

Family counselors can help the couple work out their inevitable differences in values, develop faith in their parent-child relationships, and accept rejection by stepchildren (Visher and Visher 1978b). Counselors can also help family members mourn the loss of the initial family and develop productive methods of communication. Stepchildren, having observed the break of adult relationships through death or divorce, are given a renewed opportunity to see a couple work together in a posi-

tive way (Visher and Visher 1979). The transition from unbroken to blended families is not an easy one, but when blended families have realistic expectations and support, it is possible for most to manage their lives with reasonable success (Schulman 1972). In the next section we will discuss the teacher's unique role in facilitating a stepchild's adjustment after a parent's remarriage.

What can the teacher do?

Because adjustment to divorce and to being a member of a blended family both involve considerable change and stress, some of the techniques teachers can use in facilitating a child's adjustment to divorce are also appropriate for use with children in stepfamilies. Some

of the suggestions in this section are modified from those developed by Skeen and McKenry (1982, pp. 232–237) for use with children of divorce.

In the classroom

You and your colleagues know that several children in your groups are members of blended families. You want to help the children grow through this experience. What can you do?

Observe carefully

1. Look for behavioral cues that help you understand how a child is feeling and what problems and strengths the child might have. Free play, art activities, puppet shows, and individual talks with the child are particularly good opportunities for observation.

2. Observe the child frequently, over a period of time, and in several types of situations such as at quiet time, in group work, alone, in active play, in free play, and at home. Such varied observations allow the teacher to construct a more complete picture of the total child and reduce the likelihood that judgments will be made on the basis of a "bad day."

3. Be a good listener to both verbal and body language.

Make a plan

1. When teachers are attempting to understand, predict, and intervene with behavior, it is important to first determine the child's physical, social, emotional, and cognitive developmental levels. A plan can then be developed to meet the child's individual needs. Direct observation, parents, counselors, and relevant literature are good sources of information to use when planning.

Provide opportunities for working through feelings

1. Help the child recognize and acceptably express feelings and resolve conflict through the use of curriculum activities such as painting, flannel board, clay, drawing pictures, writing experience stories about the child's family, dramatic play, doll play, books about alternate family styles, free play, woodworking, music, and movement.

2. Allow children the solitude and privacy they sometimes need.

3. Support the establishment of blended family discussion and/or therapy groups for children led by counselors.

Help children understand

1. Help children understand what their situation is, how and why they feel, how feelings can be expressed, and the consequences of such expression. Many discussions over an extended period of time will be necessary before such understanding is established.

2. Provide opportunities for the children to be successful in controlling their lives. For example, make sure equipment and learning materials are matched to the children's abilities. Tell them about the sequence of the day's events and notify children about changes in schedule well ahead of time. Give children opportunities to make as many choices as they can handle.

3. Books and discussions can be used to give information about blended family relationships and to promote peer acceptance and support for a child in such a family. (See the additional resources at the end of the article.)

Maintain a stable environment

1. Remain consistent in expectations for the child. This may be the only area of consistency in a rapidly changing and difficult period of the child's life.

2. Although children must be dealt with patiently and may regress to immature forms of behavior at times, avoid overprotecting the child.

3. Even though children may have problems, they should not be allowed to "run wild." Because parents may be having difficulty setting limits for the child, it is extremely important for the classroom teacher to lovingly, but firmly, set reasonable limits for the child's behavior at school.

4. Make a special effort to love children in blended families. Let them know that they are important and worthwhile through smiles, hugs, praise, and attention to appropriate behaviors. However, avoid taking on the role of a mother or father or allowing children to become overly dependent upon you since you will separate at the end of the year.

5. Prepare children for separation from you at the end of the year (or an extended absence from you during the year) by telling them ahead of time about the separation, why it will occur, and what will happen to the children. A visit to the next teacher and room can be very helpful. Children must be reassured that you are not leaving because they are bad or because you have stopped loving them.

6. Encourage children to work through stressful situations (e.g., a move to a new house) by talking about and role playing the situation in advance.

Examine your attitude

1. Avoid expecting children to manifest certain kinds of problems simply because they are members of blended families. Children are skillful in "reading" adult expectations and often will behave accordingly. Adults might also assume that the stepfamily is the reason for a behavior problem when in actuality other factors may be the causes. Children have different reactions to life in a blended family, just as they do to all other aspects of life.

2. Examine your personal feelings and values about blended families. Feelings and values consciously and unconsciously affect the way teachers interact with children and parents.

3. Remember that blended families must deal with issues that do not come up in natural families. Although life can be stressful, especially at first, family members can grow through the experience and benefit from membership in a family situation that has struggled and made it.

Working with parents

Gillian Price's father has just told her teacher that he is marrying a woman who has two children. He is concerned about how this will affect 4-year-old Gillian and wants to do whatever he can to assist his new family. How can a teacher help?

1. Realize that since the establishment of a stepfamily is a stressful time, teacher-parent and teacher-stepparent communication should be especially supportive.

2. Understand that parents and stepparents are involved in a difficult situation requiring adjustments different from those in a natural family. They may not yet feel comfortable in their new stepparenting role.

3. Support parents and stepparents as important persons apart from their parenting role about which you are concerned.

4. Provide information for parents and stepparents. For example, lend the school's copies of books for parents and children suggested at the end of this article or ask the local library to order them. Use the films mentioned at the end of this article. Have parent meetings concerning child discipline and guidance.

5. Encourage stepparents and parents to prepare for their marriage by honestly sharing feelings, defining roles for all family members, discussing changes the new family arrangements will necessitate, and discussing finances.

6. Assure parents and stepparents that they and their children will need considerable time to adjust. Also, stepfamilies that have realistic expectations about typical problems are more likely to deal with them successfully than those who expect instant love and a happily-ever-after life following marriage of the stepparent and parent.

7. Encourage the parent and stepparent to work together in deciding how to parent and interact in their day-to-day relationships with their children. However, parents and stepparents should also be free to disagree as well as include children so that children do not feel it is "us against them."

8. Encourage stepparents to take time and use patience in building relationships with stepchildren. Anger, guilt, jealousy, testing, confusion, comparison with the natural parent, and rejection are typical stepchild responses, especially in the early stages, but can be overcome with time and understanding.

9. Urge parents and stepparents to keep open channels of communication and to involve their children in making family decisions, defining roles of family members, and working out living arrangements.

10. Help stepparents develop realistic expectations regarding their parenting roles. For example, they cannot replace the natural parent, but they can

be a vital friend and supporter of the stepchild.

11. Help stepparents to treat both their natural and stepchildren fairly and honestly.

12. Encourage the parent and stepparent to develop new projects and traditions in which the stepfamily can be involved. For example, during holidays new blended family traditions can be begun while previous traditional activities are maintained.

13. Encourage the stepparent and child to spend some time alone together. For example, sharing a hobby or walking might be enjoyable activities which can help build a relationship.

14. Encourage parents and stepparents to elicit their children's feelings.

15. Encourage stepparents to maintain as good a relationship as possible with their former spouses and to avoid making derogatory comments about the other parent which could anger children and force them to be defensive.

16. Encourage parents and stepparents to build a strong couple relationship apart from parenting by sharing feelings, listening to each other, and taking time for themselves as individuals and as a couple. A loving couple relationship which works can be the best gift to children.

17. Encourage parents to make special efforts to help the visiting stepchild feel comfortable and a part of the family by involving the child in planning activities, providing a permanent drawer or toys, or inviting the stepchild's friend along.

18. Correctly address notes to stepparents, remembering that parental surnames may be different from the child's.

19. Provide an informal atmosphere or help establish support groups in which stepparents can share their problems and solutions.

Working with counselors

John's teacher, Mr. Wilson, has been patiently listening to John's mother talk about the serious problems in her stepfamily for an hour. Mr. Wilson wants to help but feels lost. What can he do?

1. Refer stepfamilies to a competent counselor who works with whole families (Visher and Visher 1978b). Well-meaning listeners can do a great deal of harm.

A note of caution: Teachers' roles in working with parents vary. Teachers should be aware of legal restrictions and school policy concerning the degree and type of parental involvement considered appropriate for teachers.

2. Counselors belonging to professional organizations generally indicate their membership in the Yellow Pages telephone listings (see additional resources). The local Mental Health Association, Human Resources Department of local or state government, or pastoral counseling services may also be good sources of information. However, the teacher should find out about the counselor firsthand from former clients, other teachers, or a personal visit before referrals are made.

3. Work with the counselor when appropriate. Teachers can provide helpful information based on their daily interaction and observation of the child. The teacher might also help carry out treatment strategies in the classroom.

Life in a blended family is different from life in a natural family. Establishing a blended family is a particularly stressful time. Teachers are especially significant since they spend as much or more time with the child than any other adult outside the family. When teachers are skilled and concerned, they can help parents and children grow and create healthy blended families.

References

Bernard, J. *Remarriage: A Study of Marriage.* New York: Dryden, 1956.

Bohannan, P., ed. *Divorce and After.* New York: Doubleday, 1970.

Bohannan, P., and Erickson, R. "Stepping In." *Psychology Today* 11 (1978): 53–59.

Bowerman, C. E., and Irish, D. P. "Some Relationships of Stepchildren to Their Parents." *Marriage and Family Living* 24 (1962): 113–121.

Brooks, J. B. *The Process of Parenting.* Palo Alto, Calif.: Mayfield, 1981.

Burchinal, G. "Characteristics of Adolescents from Unbroken, Broken, and Reconstituted Families." *Journal of Marriage and the Family* 26 (1964): 44–50.

Draughton, M. "Step-Mother's Model of Identification in Relation to Mourning in the Child." *Psychological Reports* 36 (1975): 183–189.

Duberman, L. "Step-Kin Relationships." *Journal of Marriage and the Family* 35 (1973): 283–292.

Duberman, L. *The Reconstituted Family: A Study of Remarried Couples and Their Children.* Chicago: Nelson-Hall, 1975.

Fast, I., and Cain, A. C. "The Stepparent Role: Potential for Disturbances in Family Functioning," *American Journal of Orthopsychiatry* 36 (1966): 485–491.

Francke, L. B., and Reese, M. "After Remarriage." *Newsweek* 11, no. 6 (February 11, 1980): 66.

Goode, W. J. *Women in Divorce.* Glencoe, Ill.: Free Press, 1956.

Hetherington, M. E.; Cox, M.; and Cox, R. "Divorce and Remarriage." Paper presented at the annual meeting of the Society for Research in Child Development, Boston, Massachusetts, April 1981.

Jacobson, D. S. "Stepfamilies." *Children Today* 9 (1980): 2–6.

Johnson, H. C. "Working with Stepfamilies: Principles of Practice." *Social Work* 25 (1980): 304–308.

Jones, S. M. "Divorce and Remarriage: A New Beginning, a New Set of Problems." *Journal of Divorce* 2 (1978): 217–227.

Kleinman, J.; Rosenberg, E.; and Whiteside, M. "Common Developmental Tasks in Forming Reconstituted Families." *Journal of Marriage and Family Therapy* 5 (1979): 79–86.

Kompara, D. R. "Difficulties in the Socialization Process of Stepparenting." *Family Relations* 29 (1980): 69–73.

Landis, J. T. "A Comparison of Children from Divorced and Non-Divorced Unhappy Marriages." *Family Life Coordinator* 11 (1962): 61–65.

Messinger, L. "Remarriage Between Divorced People with Children from Previous Marriages: A Proposal for Preparation for Remarriage." *Journal of Marriage and Family Counseling* 2 (1976): 193–200.

Nelson, M., and Nelson, G. "Problems of Equity in Reconstituted Family: A Social Exchange Analysis." *Family Relations* 31 (1982): 223–231.

Nye, F. I. "Child Adjustment in Broken and in Unhappy Unbroken Homes." *Marriage and Family Living* 19 (1957): 356–361.

Oshman, H. P., and Manosevitz, M. "Father Absence: Effects of Stepfathers on Psychosocial Development in Males." *Developmental Psychology* 12 (1976): 479–480.

Perkins, T. F., and Kahan, J. P. "An Empirical Comparison of Natural-Father and Stepfather Family Systems." *Family Process* 18 (1979): 175–183.

Rallings, E. M. "The Special Role of Stepfather." *The Family Coordinator* 25 (1976): 445–449.

Sager, C. J.; Walker, E.; Brown, H. S.; Crohn, H. M.; and Rodstein, E. "Improving Functioning of the Remarried Family System." *Journal of Marital and Family Therapy* 1 (1981): 3–13.

Santrock, J.; Warshak, R.; Lindbergh, C.; and Meadows, L. "Children's and Parents' Observed Social Behavior in Stepfather Families." *Child Development* 53 (1982): 472–480.

Schulman, G. L. "Myths That Intrude on the Adaption of the Stepfamily." *Social Casework* 53 (1972): 131–139.

Skeen, P., and McKenry, P. C. "The Teacher's Role in Facilitating a Child's Adjustment to Divorce." In *Curriculum Planning for Young Children,* ed. J. F. Brown. Washington, D.C.: National Association for the Education of Young Children, 1982.

Stern, P. N. "Stepfather Families: Integration Around Child Discipline." *Issues in Mental Health Nursing* 1 (1978): 326–332.

Stinnett, N., and Walters, J. *Relationships in Marriage and Family.* New York: Macmillan, 1977.

Thies, J. M. "Beyond Divorce: The Impact of Remarriage on Children." *Journal of Clinical Child Psychology* 5 (Summer 1977): 59–61.

Touliatos, J., and Lindholm, B. W. "Teachers' Perceptions of Behavior Problems in Children from Intact, Single-Parent and Stepparent Families." *Psychology in the Schools* 17 (1980): 264–269.

Visher, E. B., and Visher, J. S. "Common Problems of Stepparents and Their Spouses." *American Journal of Orthopsychiatry* 48 (1978a): 252–262.

Visher, E. B., and Visher, J. S. "Major Areas of Difficulty for Stepparent Couples." *International Journal of Family Counseling* 6 (1978b): 70–80.

Visher, E. B., and Visher, J. S. *Stepfamilies: A Guide to Working with Stepparents and Stepchildren.* New York: Brunner/Mazel, 1979.

Wilson, K. L.; Zurcher, L. A.; McAdams, D. C.; and Curtis, R. L. "Stepfathers and Stepchildren: An Exploratory Analysis from Two National Surveys." *Journal of Marriage and the Family* 37 (1975): 526–536.

Additional resources

Books for children

Picture books

Drescher, J. *Your Family My Family.* New York: Walker, 1980.

Green, P. *A New Mother for Martha.* New York: Human Sciences Press, 1978.

Lewis, H. *All about Families the Second Time Around.* Atlanta: Peachtree, 1980.

Stenson, J. *Now I Have a Stepparent and It's Kind of Confusing.* New York: Avon, 1979.

Books for young readers

Burt, M., and Burt, R. *What's Special About Our Stepfamily?* Garden City, N.Y.: Doubleday, 1983.

Byars, B. *The Animal, The Vegetable and John D. Jones.* New York: Delacorte, 1982.

Clifton, L. *Everett Anderson's Nine Months Long.* New York: Holt, Rinehart & Winston, 1978.

Gardner, R. *The Boys and Girls Book about Stepfamilies.* New York: Bantam, 1982.

Phillips, C. *Our Family Got a Stepparent.* Ventura, Calif.: Regal Books, 1981.

Sobol, H. *My Other Mother, My Other Father.* New York: Macmillan, 1979.

Books for teachers, parents, and stepparents

Atkin, E., and Rubin, E. *Part-Time Father.* New York: Signet, 1977.

Berman, C. *Making It As a Stepparent.* Garden City, N.Y.: Doubleday, 1980.

Capaldi, F., and McRae, B. *Stepfamilies.* New York: New Viewpoints/Vision Books, 1979.

Duberman, L. *The Reconstituted Family.* Chicago: Nelson-Hall, 1975.

Duffin, S. *Yours, Mine, and Ours: Tips for Stepparents.* DHEW Pub. No. (ADM) 78-676, 1978. National Institute of Mental Health, Public Inquiries, 5600 Fishers Ln., Rockville, MD 20857.

Einstein, E. *The Stepfamily: Living, Loving, and Learning.* New York: Macmillan, 1982.

Espinoza, R., and Newman, Y. *Step-Parenting.* DHEW Pub. No. (ADM) 78-579, 1979. National Institute of Mental Health, Public Inquiries, 5600 Fishers Ln., Rockville, MD 20857.

Gardner, R. *The Parents Book About Divorce.* Garden City, N.Y.: Doubleday, 1977.

Jensen, L., and Jensen, J. *Stepping into Stepparenting: A Practical Guide.* Palo Alto, Calif.: R & E Research Asso., 1981.

Maddox, B. *The Half-Parent: Living with Other People's Children.* New York: Evans, 1975.

Noble, J., and Noble, W. *How to Live with Other People's Children.* New York: Hawthorn, 1977.

Ricci, I. *Mom's House, Dad's House: Making Shared Custody Work.* New York: Macmillan, 1980.

Roosevelt, R., and Lofas, J. *Living in Step.* New York: Stein & Day, 1976.

Rosenbaum, J., and Rosenbaum, V. *Stepparenting.* Corte Madera, Calif.: Chandler & Share, 1977.

Simon, A. W. *Stepchild in the Family: A View of Children in Remarriage.* New York: Odyssey, 1964.

Thayer, N. *Stepping.* New York: Playbook Paperbooks, 1980.

Troyer, W. *Divorced Kids.* New York: Harcourt Brace Jovanovich, 1979.

Visher, E. B., and Visher, J. S. *Stepfamilies.* New York: Brunner/Mazel, 1979.

Visher, E. B., and Visher, J. S. *How to Win As a Stepfamily.* New York: Dembner Books, 1982.

Newsletter

Stepparent News. Newsletter for parents and professionals. $9–$15 yearly. Listening Inc., 8716 Pine Ave., Gary, IN 46403.

Filmstrip and film for adults

"Daddy Doesn't Live Here Anymore": The Single-Parent Family. Written by Robert Weiss. Four parts of the filmstrip include The Changing Family, When Parents Divorce, One Day at a Time, The Stepparent Family. Sound filmstrip, 52 min., color. Rental: unavailable. Purchase: $145. Human Relations Media, 175 Tompkins Ave., Pleasantville, NY 10570.

Stepparenting: New Families, Old Ties. Film, 25 min., color. Rental: $35. Purchase: $345. Polymorph Films, 118 South St., Boston, MA 02111.

Organizations

American Association of Marriage and Family Therapists. 225 Yale Ave., Claremont, CA 91711.

American Psychological Association. 1200 17th St., N.W., Washington, DC 20036.

National Registry of Clinical Social Workers. 7981 Eastern Ave., Silver Spring, MD 20910.

The Stepfamily Foundation. 333 West End Ave., New York, NY 10023.

Self Care

John Merrow

Terms like *self care* and *survival skills* are linguistic cop-outs that obscure a serious and widespread evasion of social responsibility.

Sometimes we use language to avoid responsibility for our actions. Computer freaks who steal other people's software call themselves *pirates;* and politicians speak of *revenue enhancement* because they are afraid to say *tax increase.*

I have another candidate for the list, *self care.* It's a kind of day care, like home care or center care. *Self care* sounds strong and independent. . . . Who could be against that?

Well, I am—because self care means no adult supervision for young children, and that's dangerous. Basically, the child looks after himself or herself after school until the adults get home. Now, maybe self care is OK when the child is 15 or 16, but most of the kids in self care are still in elementary school or junior high. We've got lots of 6-, 7-, and 8-year-olds responsible for themselves for several hours a day, 5 days a week.

Come to think of it, the day care field is developing other misleading terms, like "survival skills." That's what kids left on their own are taught, courtesy of women's magazines and supermarket handouts. They learn how to dial 911 in emergencies, or how to lie and say "Mom's in the shower right now and can't come to the phone," when a stranger calls. That's not enough. Death and serious injury by accidental home fires are increasing rapidly among children left to themselves, and lately I've heard of increases in "sibling injury"—brothers and sisters hurting each other because no adult was around to keep the normal give-and-take from getting out of hand.

Terms like *self care* and *survival skills* may make working parents feel better about having to work, but they are linguistic cop-outs that obscure a serious and widespread evasion of social responsibility that threatens many of our children.

I said "social responsibility," not parental, because I look at the situation this way: Back when only a few people had cars, society wasn't responsible for roads, drivers' licenses, and so forth. Today, nearly everybody drives, and society must be responsible for traffic control. Today, the vast majority of adults have to work outside the home, and most children are in some form of child care. That makes child care a social responsibility. *Self care* and *survival skills* are verbal smoke screens. It's time for community action, for all our children.

John Merrow, *a Washington, D.C. journalist, is creator of the renowned television program* "Your Children, Our Children" *for the Public Broadcasting System, and producer of the radio program* "Options in Education" *for National Public Radio.*

Child Abuse and Neglect

Cleo Freelance Photo

Prevention and Reporting

Barbara J. Meddin
Anita L. Rosen

Each year nearly 1.2 million children in the United States are reported to be abused or neglected. Even more alarming is the possibility that more than 2 million other cases are not reported to the agencies whose responsibility it is to protect children from further abuse (U.S. Department of Health and Human Services, 1981).

Most of these situations are treatable, however, and a great deal of harm to children is preventable (Kempe & Helfer, 1972). Because teachers are often the only adults who regularly see the child outside of the immediate family, teachers are often the first to observe children who have been or are at risk for abuse and/or neglect (McCaffrey & Tewey, 1978).

Teachers of young children are an essential part of the professional team that can prevent abuse and neglect. What steps can you as a teacher take to be alert to potential abuse or neglect? If indeed you believe a child has been harmed or is at risk of harm, how should it be reported?

What is child abuse and/or neglect?

Child abuse and/or neglect is any action or inaction that results in the harm or potential risk of harm to a child. Includes

- physical abuse (cuts, welts, bruises, burns);
- sexual abuse (molestation, exploitation, intercourse);
- physical neglect (medical or educational neglect, and inadequate supervision, food, clothing, or shelter);
- emotional abuse (actions that result in significant harm to the child's intellectual, emotional, or social development or functioning); and
- emotional neglect (inaction by the adult to meet the child's needs for nurture and support).

Barbara J. Meddin, Ph.D., is a child protection specialist and human services consultant in Carbondale, Illinois.

Anita L. Rosen, Ph.D., is a private consultant in Silver Spring, Maryland.

Reducing Stress

Every state mandates that *suspected* cases of child abuse be reported by professionals such as teachers (Education Commission of the States, 1976). In Illinois, for example, professionals who do not report are subject to loss of their license to practice the profession. Those who report suspected cases are protected by law from any personal or civil liability growing out of that report (Illinois Public Law, 1979).

Teachers are not expected to know for sure whether a child has been harmed as a result of abuse and/or neglect. It is up to the child welfare or child protection agency to confirm the existence of abuse or neglect. Neither is the teacher expected to take custody of the child. The child protection agency or the police decide what action needs to be taken to protect the child.

Only about 13% of all child abuse reports are made by teachers or other school personnel (The American Humane Association, 1983). It appears that teachers are reluctant to report suspected cases, especially when physical neglect or emotional abuse and neglect are involved. Some teachers may feel they should not interfere with family relationships or childrearing techniques, and thus do not report cases where children are at risk (Underhill, 1974). However, it is both a legal and ethical responsibility for teachers to combine their knowledge of child development and their observation skills to identify children in need of protection.

Indicators of abuse and neglect

Physical manifestations, child or adult behaviors, and environmental situations may indicate a child has or may be at risk of abuse or neglect. The factors that most often can be observed by teachers will be discussed here.

Child characteristics

Many of the characteristics described here occur in contexts other than abusive situations. Rarely does the presence or absence of a single factor signal child abuse. A pattern of these factors and behaviors will more likely indicate harm or risk to the child.

Teachers of young children often observe bruises or wounds on children that are in various stages of healing. This indicates the injuries occurred at different times, and may have been inflicted on a regular basis. Physical abuse can be suspected, for example, if injuries appear a day or so after a holiday or long weekend (bruises take a day to show up). Injuries that occur on multiple planes of the body or that leave a mark that looks like a hand or tool should also be considered nonaccidental.

Children naturally use their hands to protect themselves. Usually when a child falls, the hands go out to stop the fall and protect the face. Children's hands, knees, or foreheads are usually injured when they attempt to break their fall. If children report their injuries were caused by a fall, but the injuries do not include these areas, you should be suspicious.

When children fall, they also are most likely to fall on one side or plane of the body. Therefore, multiple injuries, such as a head injury coupled with a bruise to the ribs or buttocks, should be considered suspicious because more than one plane of the body is involved.

For example, a first grade teacher noticed that a child in her class returned from the Christmas holiday with bruises on the right side of her face and on the back of her left arm. Although the child said she had fallen, the teacher contacted the state child welfare agency. The child's mother initially contended the girl had been roughhousing with her brothers. Further investigation revealed that she had been hit twice by her grandfather who had been visiting and allegedly could not tolerate the girl's loud noises.

Burns often leave clues as to their origin. Oval burns may be caused by a cigarette. Stocking or doughnut-shaped burns may indicate that the child was put into a hot substance. Any burn that leaves an imprint of an item, such as an electric stove burner on a child's hand, may indicate that the injury was not accidental. The natural response of children is to withdraw when a body part comes in contact with a hot object; thus only a small section of skin is usually burned if the burn is accidental.

School-age children who come to school early and leave late may be indicating they have a reason not to go home. Likewise, young children who say they have been harmed should be believed. Rarely do children make up reports of abuse.

Older children may also discuss harmful events with classmates. Help children feel comfortable enough to confide in you because of your shared concern for a child. Susan, age 8, told a friend she had been molested by her father. The classmate confided in the teacher, who made a report. Susan had indeed been molested. Through counseling for the family, the molestation was stopped.

Children who take food from others may be suffering from neglect. One agency investigated a case where a preschool child constantly took food from other children's lunches. The child was receiving one-half of a peanut butter sandwich a day at home and needed the additional food for survival.

Another common sign of neglect is children who come to school inappropriately dressed for the weather. The child who wears sandals in the winter or who doesn't wear a coat on a cold snowy day meets the definition of neglect and can be seen as at risk of harm.

Young children cannot be expected to sit still for long periods. However, some children who have trouble sitting may be experiencing discomfort in their genital areas as a result of sexual abuse. Children whose knowledge of the sexual act is much more sophisticated than that of peers or for their level of development may also be indicating they have been sexually abused. For example, a child might engage in inappropriate sex play with dolls or with other children in the dramatic play area or at recess.

Radical behavior changes in children, or regressive behavior, should be viewed as a possible indicator of abuse or neglect. For example, children who suddenly become extremely hostile or withdrawn should be considered to be possible victims of abuse or neglect. Regression often indicates that children are attempting to protect themselves or to cope with the situation. Typical of such a behavior change might be the 5-year-old child who develops toileting problems. Likewise, the child who strives to do everything exactly right, or fears doing anything wrong, may be trying to avoid incurring the anger of adults.

Another behavior that is a possible clue to abuse or neglect is the child who always stays in the background of activities. This child usually watches intently to see what adults are doing—possibly to keep out of the way of adults in order to prevent being harmed.

Children who are abused frequently expect such abuse from all adults. Do you know children who cower when you lift your hand in the air? Are there children in your group who hide broken crayons rather than asking for tape to repair them? Discussion, stories written by the children, drawings, or sharing time may also reveal episodes of abuse and neglect.

It is important to stress that teachers should be alert to a *pattern* of characteristics and behaviors that indicate child abuse or neglect.

Indicators of child abuse

Child

- bruises or wounds in various stages of healing
- injuries on two or more planes of the body
- injuries reported to be caused by falling but which do not include hands, knees, or forehead
- oval, immersion, doughnut-shaped, or imprint burns
- reluctance to leave school
- inappropriate dress for the weather
- discomfort when sitting
- sophisticated sexual knowledge or play
- radical behavior changes or regressive behavior
- child withdraws or watches adults
- child seems to expect abuse
- revealing discussion, stories, or drawings

Adult

- unrealistic expectations for child
- reliance on child to meet social or emotional needs
- lack of basic childrearing knowledge or skills
- substance abuse

Stress

- positive or negative changes—moving, new baby, unemployment, divorce

Watch for a *pattern* of characteristics and behaviors that indicate child abuse or neglect.

Adult characteristics

Parent (or other prime caregiver) behavior may also give clues that children are at risk of harm. Most preschool program staff see parents twice a day, and occasionally during parent conferences or home visits as well. Teachers of primary-age children have fewer occasions to observe parents, but can still be aware of parent behaviors through responses to notes, questionnaires, or phone calls.

There are a number of indicators of an adult's inability or unwillingness to care for and protect children. The parent who has unrealistic expectations for the child can be seen as placing the child at risk. For example, a parent may believe a 6-month-old child can be toilet trained, or that a 5-year-old should be able to read, or that an 8-year-old should always act like a lady.

Adults who look to their children to meet some of their own social or emotional needs can also be seen as a high-risk parent. The teenager who keeps her baby to have someone to love her is likely to be very disappointed!

Whenever possible, observe the parent and child interacting with one another. Parents who lack basic childrearing knowledge or skills place children at risk. For instance, a parent who doesn't know about nutrition or health care, or who has a serious physical illness, may be unable to adequately care for a child. Parents who are substance abusers—either drugs or alcohol—place their children at risk. Because most parents don't deliberately harm their children, all the parents with these types of problems need support to help them function in healthier ways with their children.

At the same time, when teachers observe parenting styles, they must be aware of and sensitive to social and cultural differences. Child protection services are not designed to impose middle-class parenting standards on everyone, but are aimed at insuring a *minimum* standard of care for all children so they are free from harm.

While none of the above factors automatically indicate child abuse, the presence of any of them, along with other clues or patterns of suspected abuse, may indicate harm or potential harm for children.

Stress in the environment

Adult stress can often be the cause of one-time or chronic harm to children. Therefore, whenever a family is under stress, the likelihood that abuse or neglect may occur is increased. The source of stress can be either positive or negative—a move, the birth of a new baby, unemployment, death, inadequate housing, divorce. Any stressor can affect parents' ability to care for their children and to maintain their own self-control.

Once again, however, stress should be considered as just one indicator that may produce a potentially dangerous situation for children.

Preventing abuse and neglect

Teachers of young children have many opportunities to aid in the prevention of child abuse and neglect. Certainly each teacher is a role model for parents. Many of your actions, such as your way of greeting children when they return from an illness or vacation, your methods for handling misbehavior, and your expectations for children, can help parents see positive ways to guide children.

For teachers who are not in contact with children's parents every day, it is more difficult to serve as a role model. However, you can talk with parents often by phone, hold discussion groups about common concerns such as discipline or early reading, and encourage parents to visit your classroom.

Once you are familiar with the clues that indicate children and families may be at risk, you can spot potential problems early. If a family is going to move, for example, you can talk with them about how to make a more comfortable transition for their children into their new school (Jalongo, 1985).

If you sense a potential danger to the child, you can help the family link up with appropriate supports, such as counseling services or material assistance, before their need becomes overwhelming and children are harmed.

What happens when a report is made?

In most states, one child welfare agency receives and investigates reports of suspected child abuse or neglect. The main purpose of the agency is to protect children from harm or from further harm, not to punish parents. These agencies work on the assumption that the best context for childrearing is in the child's own home (Kadushin, 1978).

When abuse or neglect is a reality, children will not necessarily be removed from their parents. The agency will strive to take the appropriate action to protect the child at home in the short run, while working with the parents to solve the problem for the future. All services are aimed at enhancing the parents' ability to care for and protect their children.

Before calling your local child protection agency, review the policy and procedures established for your program or school. These policies may help you determine when it is best to report, may support you in making the report, and may stipulate channels for reporting. The report should always be made in accordance with those policies and procedures, and should be done factually and without emotion.

Teachers are role models for parents.

Depending upon the state, a report is made either to a central or a local field office of the child welfare agency. That agency must begin its investigation by contact with the child, the child's family, and the alleged perpetrator of the harm. This contact is usually initiated within 24 hours, but can begin immediately if it appears the child is currently in danger.

While the family will not be told who initiated action, the agency may ask for your name, address, and phone number when you make the report. This identification is necessary in case the agency needs to get back to you for further information.

Program directors and principals should offer in-service training to teachers to keep them abreast of the state's reporting law, the specific practices of the state child welfare agency, and the school's policy and procedures. Familiarity with the procedure, and the implicit support for reporting suspected abuse, can help teachers to follow through with their responsibility.

All services are aimed at enhancing the parents' ability to care for and protect their children.

Copy, fill in with local numbers and place near your program's phone.

Filing a report of suspected child abuse begins a process through which the child welfare agency determines whether or not the child has actually been harmed or is at risk of harm from abuse or neglect. When harm has occurred, then the agency works to protect the child and help the family protect the child. The emphasis is always on treatment, not punishment. Teachers are an important part of a multidisciplinary team to help prevent and treat victims of abuse and neglect.

While teachers may hesitate to report suspected cases of abuse or neglect for fear of straining the parent-teacher relationship, that fear is often unfounded (Jirsa, 1981). Most parents love their children and are concerned about their welfare. Abuse and neglect rarely occur as a result of delib-

erate intent to harm a child. Rather, it occurs when a parent temporarily lacks control or judgment, or lacks the knowledge or resources to adequately care for the child. After their initial and appropriate anger at the intervention of the agency, most parents feel a sense of relief that the problem has been identified, and they are usually very willing to work toward a solution.

In cases where only the potential for abuse or neglect exists, the link with the child welfare agency can provide parents with the resources or referrals needed to create a more effective home environment.

Like teachers, child welfare professionals' first allegiance is to the child. Teachers of young children are in a unique position to both report and help prevent child abuse and neglect through their daily contact with children and families.

When in doubt, report. Only then can we all work together to intervene on behalf of the child, work toward solutions, and enhance the quality of life for children and families.

References

American Humane Association. (1983). *Highlights of official child neglect and abuse reporting*. Denver, CO: Author.

Education Commission of the States. (1976, March). *A comparison of the states' child abuse statutes* (Report No. 84). Denver, CO: Author.

Kempe, H., & Helfer, R. (Eds.). (1972). *Helping the battered child and his family*. Philadelphia: Lippincott.

Jalongo, M. R. (1985, September). When young children move. *Young Children, 40*(6), 51–57.

Jirsa, J. (1981). Planning a child abuse referral system. *Social Work in Education, 3*(2), p. 10.

Kadushin, A. (1978). *Child welfare strategy in the coming years*. Washington, DC: National Association of Social Workers.

Illinois Public Law. (1979, November). *The abused and neglected child reporting act* (Public Act 81-1077).

McCaffrey, M., & Tewey, S. (1978, October). Preparing educators to participate in the community response to child abuse and neglect. *Exceptional Children, 45*(2), p. 115.

Underhill, E. (1974). The strange silence of teachers, doctors, and social workers in the face of cruelty to children. *International Child Welfare Review*, (21), 16–21.

U.S. Department of Health and Human Services. (1981). *Study findings: National study of the incidence and severity of child abuse and neglect*. Washington, DC: Superintendent of Documents.

The authors wish to thank Leigh Bartlett of the Department of Community Services in Perth, Australia for her help in developing case examples provided here.

Part 3.
Making sure we don't contribute to children's stress

Often unwittingly, parents, teachers, or other well-meaning people create undue stress for children. It may not be intentional, but some adults tend to make life more difficult for children than it should be. What do we often do? We may say one thing and mean another . . . rob children of precious time to play . . . expect perfect behavior . . . offer children wrong choices or no choice at all . . . ask children to perform like much older children . . . fail to help them learn to get along with each other . . . lack respect for their heritage . . . or frighten them with reports of and plans for war. Sometimes our own stress is contagious.

Once again, knowledge about how children grow and learn will help us select more appropriate ways to live with children. We also need a good measure of respect, common sense, and self-control. And compassion. Each of the articles in this section will add to the skills and sensitivities we all need as parents and teachers of young children.

Teaching Children Non-Sense—*Charles A. Smith and Duane E. Davis* ● Reaffirmations: Speaking Out for Children. A Child's Right To Play—*Millie Almy* ● View-point. There Is More to Early Childhood Education Than Cognitive Development—*Peter E. Haiman* ● Viewpoint. Obedience Is Not Enough—*Constance Kamii* ● Choice With Responsibility—*Davia M. Veach* ● Research Report. Circle Time: Getting Past "Two Little Pumpkins"—*Oralie D. McAfee* ● "But what about sharing?" Children's Literature and Moral Development—*Suzanne L. Krogh and Linda L. Lamme* ● Ideas That Work With Young Children. Why Not Holiday Performances? ● Research in Review. The Unpopular Child—*Jaipaul L. Roopnaire and Alice S. Honig* ● Dealing With Difficult Young Children: Strategies for Teachers and Parents—*Anne K. Soderman* ● Research in Review. Black Children: Their Roots, Culture, and Learning Styles—*Janice Hale-Benson* ● Reaffirmations: Speaking Out for Children. A Child's Right to the Valuing of Diversity—*Mary Lane* ● *The Butter Battle Book:* Uses and Abuses With Young Children—*Nancy Carlsson-Paige and Diane E. Levin* ● "It'll be a challenge!" Managing Emotional Stress in Teaching Disabled Children—*Barbara P. White with Michael A. Phair*

Teaching Children Non-Sense

Charles A. Smith and Duane E. Davis

Crazymaking (Bach and Wyden 1968; Bach and Goldberg 1974; Wahlroos 1974) refers to a variety of communication styles utilized by one individual to inhibit another person's rational understanding of reality. The victims of crazymaking become confused and uncertain of their own experiences because of distorted feedback; they begin to doubt and mistrust their own perception of what the world is like and eventually develop non-*sense, the inability to recognize and deal with personal and interpersonal reality.*

Crazymaking and reality construction

Rather than being born with an understanding of how the world operates, children must experience and construct reality as they interact with their environment. One aspect of mastering reality involves learning about the nature of **things** ("What is that?"). For example, children learn that certain animals at certain times are dangerous, and that some objects will break when dropped.

Another important aspect of reality construction involves learning about **people** ("Who are they? How are we going to relate to each other?"). For example, children learn that people have different values and generally prefer to be treated with gentleness. This particular process of growth involves a movement from egocentric to sociocentric thinking (Piaget 1965).

A third important goal involves getting in touch with **personal** reality ("Who and what am I?"). For example, children learn that they have emotions,

that they experience pain, that their blood will not "leak" out if they have a cut, that they have a name and belong to a family, etc.

Learning about reality depends on feedback from **things** (e.g., the child observes a glass breaking) and **people** (e.g., the child hears another say, "*I do not* like to be hit!"). This feedback can be either supportive or distortive. **Supportive** feedback is a clear, accurate,

Charles A. Smith, *Ph.D., is Assistant Professor and Director of the Child Development Center, Texas Tech University, Lubbock, Texas, and a former teacher of 4-year-olds.*

Duane E. Davis, *M.A., is an elementary teacher in the Northern St. Paul-Maplewood, Minnesota, Public Schools and a former elementary counselor.*

This article is based on a keynote address by Charles A. Smith at the Minnesota AEYC Conference, October 1975, in Minneapolis.

Michele Cody

Adults may exploit a child's natural dependence and need to be wanted and accepted; they may also deny a child the opportunity to confront the irrational behavior.

ation within the controlling person who is generally unaware of his or her unreasonable behavior.

Each of these factors is especially relevant and lethal in parent-child and teacher-child relationships. Adults may exploit a child's natural dependence and need to be wanted and accepted; they may also deny a child the opportunity to confront the irrational behavior. In moments of thoughtlessness, though, most of us can be guilty of crazymaking in various forms and degrees toward children whose lives we touch. Nevertheless, if crazymaking communication is a pervasive norm in their lives, some children will withdraw from or distort a confusing reality and develop severe emotional problems.

Children depend on adults to help clarify and reaffirm their experiences with the world. Unfortunately, this sensitive awareness of self and others is easily sabotaged by adults who frequently seem determined to peddle a phony image of reality to willing and receptive young minds. We must stop this destructive response by becoming more aware of our own crazymaking habits and by investing the time and effort to help children develop a more rational understanding of reality.

Types of crazymakers

The following list identifies the types of responses that prevent children from constructing an accurate understanding of reality. Although some of these forms of communication may resemble each other, each type of crazymaker illuminates a different aspect of irrational communication. Also, the amount of confusion experienced by victims may vary somewhat from one crazymaker to another.

Disconfirming (discounting). Confirmation is a process through which individuals are recognized, acknowledged, or "endorsed" by others. A response to another that is relevant to the other's needs "confirms" the other and supports that person's feeling of being OK (Laing 1961). Disconfirming, however, ignores the needs and wishes of others by "putting down" or dis-

rational representation of reality. **Distortive** feedback, however, is a confusing, inaccurate, and irrational misrepresentation of what is real. **Crazymakers** are distortive forms of feedback from people.

The basic and necessary ingredients in a crazymaking relationship (Bach and Goldberg 1974) include:

1. An emotional dependency and vulnerability of at least one person in the relationship;
2. An unequal power balance;
3. A socially traditional role relationship which provides the opportunity for crazymaking to be masked by "good" intentions;
4. Resentment, hostility, and/or alien-

counting their feelings or thoughts. Disconfirming also includes *conditional* acceptance: "I will like, love, or accept you only if you...."

Example: An excited preschooler runs to his teacher to show her a worm he has found.

Boy: "Teacher, look at this fat worm I found!"

Teacher: "It's time for a snack and you're dirty. Go wash your hands."

Example: After a rather hectic ordeal to get the children seated for music time, the teacher positions himself near a record player and holds up two records he was planning to play.

Teacher: "Would you like to hear these records during rest today?"

Children: (Most do not respond, but a few say "No.")

Teacher: (With a broad smile on his face) "Okay, I think you'll like them." (Proceeds to play the records.)

One of the most frightening experiences a child can have is to be threatened with bizarre, senseless consequences by an adult.

Steve Herzog

Mind threatening. One of the most frightening experiences a child can have is to be threatened with bizarre, senseless consequences by an adult. Unreal threats are especially mystifying because of the child's limited understanding of reality and readiness to believe everything a controlling adult says.

Example: A young girl who had been rather troublesome at bedtime was told by her parents that if she didn't behave "... the boogeyman is going to come and get you during the night." The child responded by quieting down and going to her room without protest. Recently, however, she has been troubled by nightmares and bedwetting.

Example: The father of a 4-year-old boy recently responded to his son's fighting with a younger brother with the statement: "If you don't stop hitting your brother, I'm going to beat your head in!" Although the fighting stopped, the little boy developed a fear of his father, expressed both by nightmares of being hurt and an actual withdrawal from him.

Young children do not disregard what the adult says as exaggerations. "What *is* this 'boogeyman'? What is he going to do to me? Would father really beat my head in? Will he hurt me in other ways too?" Although adults readily understand the real intent behind these statements, mind threats are no laughing matter to children.

Strategic failing. This crazymaker involves two necessary features or strategies: The controlling adult de-

mands that the child do something he or she is not capable of doing and then *punishes* the child for failing to successfully complete the task. The child is in a total "no win" situation.

Example: After reading "How to potty-train your child in five days" in a popular magazine, a mother initiated a rather structured toilet training schedule for her 10-month-old. The child is confused about her mother's intentions and expectations and is biologically unable to gain necessary control over the muscles involved. Recently the mother has been scolding her daughter for having wet diapers.

Example: Four-year-old Billy is attending his sister's wedding ceremony. He has experienced a structured morning and, feeling both anxious and excited about the event, he begins to fidget. Father demands that ". . . he behave himself." After a brief period of nonactivity, the little boy begins to squirm again. The father gives him a sharp slap.

Masking. Masking (Lidz et al. 1958) is an attempt by a controlling person to conceal some disturbing situation within the group by acting as though a problem did not exist. The individual who resorts to this crazymaker relies on intimidation and uncertainty to enlist the cooperation of group members in ignoring or masking the obvious. Out of an ill-conceived desire to be "protective" the masking adult will sometimes overlook the child's need to understand what is happening. As with the other crazymakers, children begin to doubt the trustworthiness of their own perceptions.

Example: One child in a preschool group has an obvious physical disfigurement. Several of the children seem curious, while others are somewhat frightened regarding the physical problem. The teacher firmly avoids discussing or dealing with the matter out of a misguided concern for ". . . hurting the poor child's feelings."

Example: Ann has returned to school after the recent death of her father.

Child: "Teacher, Ann is crying."

Teacher: "Don't worry. I'm sure everything is OK; go back and play now."

Mixing messages. A person who denies a feeling which others can clearly observe is communicating a mixed message. The victims are lured into a trap (Briggs 1970) involving two messages: one based on what the other *says* (e.g., "I'm *not* angry.") and another which contradicts the first in terms of *tone* or *body language* (e.g., loud voice, clenched fist). Mixing messages is a result of believing that an underlying feeling is unacceptable and that admitting or acknowledging the feeling will have dangerous consequences. Yet feelings are very difficult to hide from others. Children, for example, may be very aware of their teacher's anger despite any attempts to appear cool and calm.

If they accept the adult's false front as reality, children may distrust their own real experiences. Children may also substitute their own personal concerns to reduce their confusion. For example, they may conclude that their teacher is angry with them for something they did (which may not actually be the case). Mixing messages creates a climate of masks that teach distrust.

Example: A child approaches a teacher who is obviously very sad, almost to the point of crying.

Child: "Teacher, why are you so sad?"

Teacher: "What? Oh, I'm not sad. I feel fine."

Example: A 4-year-old boy has thrown his lunch on the floor during a heated conversation with another child. The teacher (who has had a bad day) removes the child from the table. As she carries him to the office, she smiles and says rather sweetly, "Now Chad, you know you're not supposed to do that." But the teacher's tight grip, abrupt handling, and clenched teeth convey something else. After being

seated, Chad asks, "Mrs. Brown, why do you hate me?" Mrs. Brown responds, "Why honey, you know that isn't so."

Double binding. This crazymaker subjects others to incongruent or conflicting demands. Victims are doomed to rejection because they are in a "no win" situation. If one command is obeyed, then another is disobeyed. Double binding differs from mixing messages in that the double bind involves conflicting *commands.* The necessary ingredients of a double bind (Watzlawick et al. 1967; Bateson et al. 1963) are:

1. Two or more persons are involved in an intense relationship with a high degree of physical and/or psychological value for one or more of them.
2. The less powerful individual is confronted with two incongruent directives. For example: "I order you to disobey me." Negative commands can be expressed through action or be implicit in the situation of interaction as well as being directly expressed through words. Punishment is expected regardless of the response.
3. A third injunction or demand is also present that prevents the victim from escaping the interaction.

The double bind is particularly disruptive if it occurs frequently with children.

Example: A child is feeling hostile toward the teacher. The teacher approaches and the following exchange occurs.

Teacher: "What's wrong? Tell me how you feel." (Command 1)

Child: "You are a bum teacher."

Teacher: "Now you shouldn't say things like that." (Incongruent command 2)

Faced with this type of bind, the child may escape the teacher's anger only by becoming skillful in hiding true feelings. But then again, the teacher might show disappointment in the child's unwillingness to reveal those feelings.

Example: It is late in the school year, and the teacher has just told the children he would like to have them take more responsibility in caring for things in the classroom, since they are now big enough to help him. Later that day, Ann sees an opportunity to be helpful by watering the plants. As she starts to water the first plant, the teacher rushes over and says, "Oh, no! I'll do that. It's too difficult for you." It becomes quickly apparent that the teacher is unwilling to allow any significant responsibilities for the children. Because the teacher was not specific about the things the children could help him with, Ann becomes very confused. She may feel she is in trouble if she helps and in trouble if she doesn't help.

Guiltmaking (scapegoating). In this crazymaker one person is blamed for the personal problems, concerns, or "hang-ups" of another. Individuals who scapegoat may select another person to be the recipient of their own negative dealings toward themselves. Instead of assuming responsibility for their own weaknesses, they may project their problem onto another, blaming others for their own destructive or ineffective behavior. The victim then develops an exaggerated and destructive sense of his or her impact on others, generating a fear of self-expression (Bach and Goldberg 1974). Scapegoaters thus create the illusion that they are actually the victims.

Example: A young child approaches the teacher and asks for some glue for an art project. The teacher, who has just finished a rather bitter fight with another teacher, ignores the request. The child continues to ask for the glue. Finally, the teacher explodes in a rather hostile outburst.

Teacher: "No glue! Stop bugging me!"

Child: (Cries)

Teacher: "See! Now you *made me* lose my temper!"

Example: A teacher is on a short walk through the neighborhood with a group of young children. One child has been particularly difficult for the teacher to handle.

Teacher: "All right, I guess we will all have to go back to the school. It seems as if some of us don't know how to behave ourselves on a walk."

Psyching-out (mind reading, jumping to conclusions). This crazymaker includes unrealistic and totally unfounded interpretations or predictions about the behavior of others. Psyching-out may also include accusing others of vicious or sinister motivations for their actions (Wahlroos 1974). Adults who are involved in psyching-out make the false assumption that they know what is going on in the other's mind.

Example

Child: "Dad, can we go to the fair this weekend?"

Father: "No, dear, it's so crowded you wouldn't like it."

Child: "I wouldn't? Oh, Dad, can we go anyway?"

Father: "No, *you know* the last time we went to the fair you just didn't like it!"

Child: "I didn't?"

Example: Child sadly walks into room.

Child: "Tommy (his older brother) got to go to grandma's. I didn't get to go."

Teacher: "I bet you're really angry with Tommy."

Example: Mother has repeatedly asked her toddler not to open a certain drawer. Despite her requests, the child continues to stand on her tiptoes to open the drawer.

Child: (Opens drawer)

Mother: (Frustrated) "Sally, why are you trying to get my goat?"

False harmonizing. False harmonizing describes group relationships which are based on facade or pretense. In false harmonizing the emphasis is on presenting an image of satisfaction at the expense of allowing true feelings and needs to emerge in the relationship (Wynne et al. 1958). In contrast, genuine harmony and mutuality provide an opportunity for persons in the group to develop a sense of their own meaningful identity, which is also acknowledged by the others in the group. As growth and change occur, the group helps its members affirm their own sense of well-being. There is a recognition, exploration, and negotiation of differences and disagreements. For example, teachers can give children the opportunity to discuss classroom problems and identify potential solutions. Disagreement is seen as an opportunity to get to know and reach out to others. In false harmonizing all disagreements with the adult controller's definition of a happy group are actively if not openly discouraged.

Example: A teacher talks about her class in glowing terms: "Oh, they're such a wonderful group. They don't give me any trouble." A visit to the class gives the initial impression that everyone is extremely well behaved. But everything is too right. There is an absence of spontaneity, novelty, humor, and zest as children move about. A weary sense of oppression hangs like a heavy blanket over the entire group. The classroom is physically enriched but emotionally stifled.

Example: A teacher approaches a child who is getting rather loud in his play and says, "Now Jamie, WE always use our quiet voices when WE are in school." The response is both confusing and oppressive. Is the statement an accurate reflection of the child's reality? Not really. Jamie has observed this teacher yelling many times in the classroom. The teacher also creates the illusion of togetherness and agreement by using the impersonal term "we."

Emotional blackmailing. This crazymaker is a form of benevolent violence where one person threatens another with the withdrawal of love, affection, or interest in order to manipulate the other's behavior. This tactic is especially threatening because it disrupts another's need for security in a relationship.

Example: A child is continually disrupting the activities of the other children, and the teacher is feeling frustrated with her inability to handle the problem. Suddenly the child deliberately knocks down another child's block tower. The teacher forcefully removes the child from the situation and says, "If you keep on being nasty, I don't want you to come to school. I will send you home."

Example: A child has been caught taking some candy from another child in the classroom.

Teacher: "I am very ashamed of you because you stole this candy. People don't like little children who steal."

Bugging (interrogating). This crazymaker (Egan 1970) refers to the use of the repeated and/or meaningless questioning of a person who is experiencing a problem. Questions are asked to show "interest": "How do you feel? When did it happen? What did you do?" This holds the victim as the center of attention and reduces the possibility of meaningful and potentially threatening conversation. Bugging or interrogating is often used in connection with preaching or lecturing and can be very irritating to others. Good questions can be very insightful and deeply supportive if they are sincere and lead to deeper involvement, but bugging ensures emotional distance and does not bring about a resolution of the problem.

Example: Ken was hiding in a makeshift tent during snack period. The teacher peeked inside and said, "Looks like you don't want to eat lunch today." Ken responded with a rather "put-on" sarcastic tone, "All the teachers come up to me and say, 'What's the matter, Kenneth, what's the matter?'" Ken had been sitting in his tent all day because he felt sad that some special packages had not yet arrived by mail at home. After discussing the problem for a minute, his spirits brightened and he joined the rest of the children. Ken was disgusted with the well-intentioned but interrogating student teachers who were more concerned with identifying his motives than dealing with his current feelings. They probably would have been more successful if they had just sat quietly next to him.

Example: Karen began crying as soon as she came into the classroom.

Teacher: "Karen, what's wrong?"

Karen: (No response)

Teacher: "What happened? Did you get hurt?"

Karen: "No."

Teacher: "Did someone take something from you?"

Karen: "No."

Teacher: "Did something bad happen at home?"

Karen: (No response)

The teacher and Karen continue to play this interrogating game until one of the two becomes tired and walks away.

Shunning (nonengagement, emotional withdrawal). A shunning response involves the "cold-shoulder" treatment of silence, ignoring, sulking, or pouting. Probably one of the greatest needs of all humankind is to have one's existence and significance acknowledged by another person (Wahlroos 1974). To have other people act as though we did not exist can be the cruelest of all experiences. Children have an obvious need for recognition, especially from parents and teachers. Unfortunately, many children discover that the only way they can get attention is to misbehave.

Example: A teacher has decided to ignore the disruptive behavior of a child. Regardless of what the child did, the teacher would turn away. Later in the day, the teacher finds color crayon marks all over the papers on his desk.

Example: A kindergarten teacher has been avoiding a certain child. Whenever she is in the child's presence, she feels uncomfortably "turned off," and talks to the child only when necessary. The child initially made overtures of friendship to the teacher but has now given up after the repeated rebuffs. Recently the child has been complaining about stomachaches.

Thinging (childism, racism, sexism). This crazymaker is present in a dehumanized interpersonal relationship characterized by treatment of victims as if they were objects, commodities, or status symbols rather than persons with unique needs and special backgrounds. Overcrowded classrooms and bureaucratic management techniques making "thinging" a common experience for those involved in many school situations.

Example: At the end of his first year in the public school, Paul was given an IQ test. Because of the low score, he was "held back." The new teacher was informed of the test results and later was overheard to remark that Paul was one of her "slow" children. Paul is confused when he learns that he will not be going to school with the rest of his friends.

Door slamming (sidetracking, derailing). Door slamming involves shifting the focus during a problematic confrontation to prevent the resolution of a conflict (Bach and Goldberg 1974). The natural flow of energy being channeled into the encounter is disrupted, and the victim becomes confused and frustrated. Door slamming can be the result if teachers try distraction at inappropriate moments.

Example: During outside play, a toddler makes an attempt to climb up a slide for older children, but her teacher picks her up and carries her to another more suitable piece of equipment. The child gets up, however, and begins to run to the slide. The teacher then carries her to the sandbox and tries to interest her in digging. After a brief involvement, the child makes another attempt to go to the slide. This time she begins to cry when the teacher intercepts her.

In this case it was important for the teacher to try to communicate to the child the motives for her intervention. Without some explanation ("I cannot let you climb up this slide. Climbing this is dangerous."), the distraction does not make any sense to the child. As far as she is concerned the adult's behavior is bizarre and unreasonable.

The prevention of crazymaking

Since crazymakers are more likely to occur in relationships characterized by a power imbalance, as in child-adult interactions, one strategy for reducing their occurrence is for adults to share as much control as possible with children. Sharing control means the adult must be ready to deal with conflict in an open and forthright manner. Adults can strive to enable children to become decision makers rather than dependent and conforming automatons. On the other hand, they must also acknowledge the exact nature of the power structure in the relationship, since some decisions cannot be left to children and some rules must be appropriately enforced.

Crazymaking is also a potential in relationships where power imbalances are hidden and disguised behind the facades of equality (Bach and Goldberg 1974) and when one person assumes a complete understanding of what is going on in the mind of another person. Adults should recognize that children are people, individuals worthy of the same type of respect and consideration granted to any adult. Finally, crazymaking is a potential in relationships where individuals have unrealistic expectations toward others and for themselves (Smith 1974). Unreasonable self-demands (e.g., "Good teachers do not get angry with children.") immediately create an artificial relationship which will ultimately have to be maintained by crazymakers (e.g., "No! I'm NOT ANGRY!").

The most productive response to the discovery of our own crazymaking habits involves gentle self-acceptance combined with self-determined change. Certainly irrationality is not something to be admired. But true self-renewal will occur only if we recognize our inevitable destiny to be imperfect. We must not forget that, like the children we serve, we too are involved in a continual process of growing up.

References

Bach, G. R., and Goldberg, H. *Creative Aggression: The Art of Assertive Living.* New York: Avon Books, 1974.

Bach, G. R., and Wyden, P. *The Intimate Enemy: How to Fight Fair in Love and Marriage.* New York: Avon Books, 1968.

Bateson, G.; Jackson, D.; Haley, J.; and Weakland, J. "A Note on the Double-Bind—1962." *Family Process* 2 (1963): 34–51.

Briggs, D. C. *Your Child and His Self-Esteem.* Garden City, N.Y.: Doubleday, 1970.

Egan, G. *Encounter: Group Processes for Interpersonal Growth.* Belmont, Calif.: Brooks/Cole, 1970.

Laing, R. D. *The Politics of Experience.* New York: Ballantine Books, 1967.

Lidz, T.; Cornelison, A.; Carlson, D. T.; and Fleck, S. "Intrafamilial Environment of the Schizophrenic Patient: The Transmission of Irrationality." *Archives of Neurology and Psychiatry* 74, no. 3 (1958): 305–316.

Piaget, J. *The Moral Judgment of the Child.* New York: Free Press, 1965.

Smith, C. A. "Peopleteaching: A Personalized Approach to Teacher Education." In *Teacher Education,* edited by B. Spodek, pp. 35–44. Washington, D.C.: National Association for the Education of Young Children, 1974.

Vogel, E. F., and Bell, N. W. "The Emotionally Disturbed Child as the Family Scapegoat." In *The Psychosocial Interior of the Family,* edited by G. Handel, pp. 424–442. Chicago: Aldine, 1967.

Wahlroos, S. *Family Communication.* New York: Macmillan, 1974.

Watzlawick, P.; Beavin, J. H.; and Jackson, D. D. *Pragmatics of Human Communication.* New York: W. W. Norton, 1967.

Wynne, L. C.; Ryckoff, I. M.; Day, J.; and Hirsch, S. I. "Pseudomutuality in the Family Relations of Schizophrenics." *Psychiatry* 21 (1958): 205–220.

A Child's Right To Play

Reaffirmations: *Speaking Out for Children*

Millie Almy

In response to today's retrogressive attitudes toward human needs, the U.S. National Committee for Early Childhood Education of the Organisation Mondiale pour L'Education Prescolaire (OMEP), the Association for Childhood Education International, and the National Association for the Education of Young Children urge child advocates to speak out about public responsibility for assuring children's basic rights. This series of statements, compiled by Monroe Cohen, Director of the Queens College Institute for Family and Community Life, is not copyrighted, and may be freely reproduced with credit to the authors.

Why play?

Children's play is often depreciated by adults who think of it as a mere time filler rather than an essential component of healthy development. Were these adults to follow the lead of an increasing number of researchers and teachers, examining closely what children do when they play, they might understand why play is so essential to the child's well-being and competence.

Play is a very special activity with distinctive features that set it apart from other behaviors.

When children play their interest is self-directed. They are intrinsically motivated to solve problems that stem from either the physical or the social world and are important to them.

When children play they are not as concerned with particular goals or ends as they are with the variety of ways a goal may be achieved. In play they ex-periment with possibilities and become more flexible in thinking and problem solving.

When children play their behavior is not literal. Much of what they do stands for something else. They represent their experiences symbolically. Their ability to conceive objects and situations as if they were something else is thought by researchers to contribute to later skill in hypothetical reasoning and the understanding of abstract symbols and logical transformations.

When children play they free themselves from external rules, from the restrictions imposed by adult regulations, and from the realities imposed by time and space. Paradoxically, however, children generate rules for their play situations and establish roles and plots. Close study of such play reveals that children's negotiations with one another are complex. They make longer utterances and use more varied vocabulary than in other situations.

When children play with objects they discover what they can do with them. Increasing their own repertoire of behaviors in this way contrasts with the exploration of objects in which they establish what properties the objects have. Both play and exploration, involving on the one hand the familiar, and on the other the novel, are essential to children's understanding of the world and of their own powers.

Finally, *when children play* they are actively engaged. Their attention is not easily distracted. Children who are unable to so involve themselves in play signal that something has gone seriously amiss in their development.

Adults who give serious consideration to these distinctive features of children's play will recognize that play is as essential to the child's all-around development as adequate food and rest. They will understand why those who wrote the United Nations' *Declarations of the Rights of the Child* set the right to play parallel to such rights as special protection, adequate nutrition, housing, health care, and education.

Children realize their right to play when the adults around them appreciate and respect their playfulness and provide ample time and space for them to play. Materials and equipment are also important, although they need not be elaborate. The crucial role that parents and teachers have in responding to and supporting children's play ideas, while not overwhelming them, becomes increasingly evident.

Play, the child's way of coming to terms with personal experience in and knowledge of the physical and social world, is never sufficient in itself. Adults must also provide ever-expanding opportunities for children to learn from their own actions and observations, as well as from being told, the nature of the people and of the things that surround them. But it is in play that children come to terms with those realities, comprehend them more, and more effectively create new possibilities for dealing with them.

Millie Almy is Professor Emerita at the University of California. She was 1952–53 President of NAEYC.

There Is More to Early Childhood Education Than Cognitive Development

Peter E. Haiman

NAEYC has a strong influence on early childhood education in the United States. Through its local, state, and national organizations, it has provided useful information to educators across the country. *Young Children* disseminates valuable ideas about educational topics and findings of child development research. Over the years early childhood educators and NAEYC have focused primarily on cognitive and educational issues.

I believe it is time to examine this focus. As the eminent German psychotherapist Dr. Alice Miller wrote in her recent book *For Your Own Good,* "reason constitutes only a small part of the human being, and not the dominant part at that" (1983, p. 144). I am concerned that by emphasizing cognition in early childhood education, NAEYC and teachers of young children are not presenting an accurate picture of children and their world. From the point of view of the child's developmental needs, the most important dynamics of life are emotional and social. Cognitive life is secondary, based upon and generated from the child's affective and interpersonal experiences. Would it not be helpful if NAEYC and other leaders in early childhood education focused more on presenting the emotional and social characteristics of young children and how these dynamics interact with cognition and learning? This would offer a more accurate and complete understanding of young children, put early childhood education in

Peter E. Haiman, Ph.D., is an Education Consultant in the San Francisco area, a former Associate Professor of Early Childhood Education, and past President of San Francisco AEYC.

developmental perspective, and shed a fuller and more revealing light on learning.

At stake here is how this focus on cognition and curriculum influences the way educators and parents perceive and interact with young children. By emphasizing curriculum and cognitive development in the child's early years, NAEYC and most leaders within the field disseminate an image of young children that is not in developmental focus. They set the stage for adult interactional patterns that can be harmful.

> By emphasizing cognition in early childhood education, [we] are not presenting an accurate picture of children.

This is an issue of comparative will and power. In their interactions with children, educators and parents have far more power and influence. Compared to adults, children are relatively helpless and emotionally vulnerable. As they attempt to help young children become independent and competent, it is easy even for good early childhood educators and parents to overlook these facts and to overpower the will of the child. When this happens most children do not protest. If it happens regularly, the child's creativity, vitality, and feelings are suppressed. This suppression has long lasting and deleterious effects. With the best of intentions parents and early childhood educators can harm young children when adult behavior does not reflect an awareness of and sensitivity to children's emotional and social strength and vulnerability. By adjusting the focus on their efforts, NAEYC and other leaders in the early childhood field can sensitize adults and help prevent this covert damage to children.

Obedience Is Not Enough

Viewpoint

Constance Kamii

Some adults are responsible and have initiative. They have the initiative not only to notice what needs to be done, but also to go ahead and do it. Others have to be told everything and often forget what they promised to do.

Some adults have integrity. In the Watergate coverup affair, for example, Elliott Richardson refused to lie to the public when President Nixon told him to do so. The rest of the men on Nixon's cabinet obeyed their superior and went along with what they knew to be wrong.

Why do such differences exist among adults? One answer can be found in the theory of Jean Piaget. This theory helps us understand why children can be expected to become responsible and have integrity if adults interact with them in certain ways. Let us look at a few examples of interactions.

Different ways of interacting with children

When a child spills milk or paint, an adult can scold by saying, "I told you to be careful!" An adult can also say, "Would you like me to help you clean it up?" or "What do you have to do?" The important thing in this situation is that the child become more careful in the future. Being asked to restore the original condition is far more conducive to being careful the next time than a scolding. The child who spilled something already feels bad about what has been done. Being scolded makes children resentful rather than more thoughtful.

Similarly, when children break, damage, or take something that belongs to somebody else, asking them to re-pair, replace, or return the object is much more conducive to thoughtfulness in the long run than a scolding or punishment. One day, in a kindergarten class, for example, a child came up to the teacher and was crying because his art project had been damaged. The teacher turned to the class and said that she wanted the person who broke the object to tell her privately so that she could help him repair the object. The child responsible for the breakage was helped to see the point of view of the victim, and was encouraged to make for himself the rule of reparation. When children are not afraid of being punished, they are willing to come forward and make restitution. The teacher helped him repair the broken object and told him that next time something similar happened, she wanted him to tell her so that she could help him fix the object again.

Reward and punishment

Many parents and teachers believe that the way to raise children to be moral is by punishing "bad" behaviors and rewarding "good" ones. Reward and punishment may be effective in the short run, but not in the long run.

Punishment leads to three possible outcomes. The most common one is calculation of risks. The child who is punished will repeat the same act but try to avoid being caught the next time. Sometimes, the child stoically decides ahead of time that even if caught, the price will be worth paying for the pleasure. The second possible outcome of punishment is the opposite of the first one, blind conformity. Some com-pliant children become perfect conformists because conformity assures them of security and respectability. When they become complete conformists, children do not have to make decisions any more, as all they have to do is obey. The third possible outcome is revolt. Some children are angels for years but decide at a certain point that they are tired of pleasing their parents and teachers all the time, and that the time has come for them to begin living for themselves. They may, thus, even begin to engage in various acts of delinquency.

While rewards are more pleasant than punishments, they too discourage children from judging for themselves what is right or wrong. Children who help parents only to get an allowance, or those who keep a promise only to get candy are governed by others, just like children who are "good" only to avoid being punished. Adults exercise power over children by using rewards and punishments, and it is these that keep them obedient and dependent on others to know what to do.

It is true that adults are influenced by rewards and punishments. But when we are influenced more by the reward system than by personal conviction about what is right, we get phenomena like the Watergate affair. The great ma-

Constance Kamii, *Ph.D., is Professor of Early Childhood Education, University of Alabama in Birmingham, Birmingham, Alabama.*

The author would like to express appreciation to Maureen Ellis for critically reading a draft of this article and for making many helpful suggestions.

Dutchie S. Riggsby

Being asked to restore the original condition is far more conducive to being careful the next time than a scolding.

jority of people in the Watergate affair obeyed their superior, who controlled them with rewards and punishments. A more recent example is Klaus Barbie, who disclaimed any responsibility for the murder of so many Jews by saying that he was only carrying out orders.

Two kinds of morality

The Watergate affair illustrates the difference between two kinds of morality distinguished by Piaget: the morality of autonomy and the morality of obedience. *Autonomy* means being governed by one-self. An example of the morality of autonomy is Elliott Richardson. As I said earlier, he was one of the few people under Nixon who refused to obey his superior and resigned from his position. The others are examples of

the morality of obedience.

When children tell a lie, adults can punish them by saying, "You will not have any dessert tonight" or "You will have to write 'I will not lie' 50 times." The adult could also refrain from punishing and, instead, look the child straight in the eye with great skepticism and affection and say, "I really can't believe what you are saying because ... (and give the facts that render the statement hard to believe)." The adult can also say that a relationship of trust is broken when a person says something that is not true. This is an example of an exchange of points of view that contributes to the development of autonomy in children. Children who can see that adults cannot believe or trust them can be motivated to think about the necessity of telling the truth. Chil-

dren who are raised with many similar opportunities can, over time, come to the conclusion for themselves that it is best in the long run for people to deal honestly with each other. As an adult faced with a superior like Mr. Nixon, this person is likely to insist on being honest because of a personal conviction about the value of honesty.

The importance of exchanging viewpoints with children and letting them make decisions

The most important elements for children's development of autonomy are opportunities to exchange viewpoints with other people and the possibility of making decisions. The morality

94

of autonomy is based on an individual's personal values, rather than the reward system. This means that children need many opportunities to construct personal values for themselves, and this is why the above two elements are essential.

As we saw in the example of children's lies, they can feel the value of being honest only if they have had many opportunities to see for themselves that people could not believe or trust them when they told lies.

Children learn to make wise decisions not by being obedient, but by making choices and decisions for themselves. The decisions they make are often unwise, and this is the hardest part for parents and teachers to watch.

Making decisions is important for children for two reasons. First, children cannot find out about the wisdom of one decision if they do not have opportunities to compare its consequence with the consequence of a bad decision. By deciding to wear new patent-leather shoes to school, for example, they can learn the wisdom of wearing tennis shoes that allow them to run freely and to climb on the Jungle Gym.

Second, children can become responsible only when they are truly responsible for the decisions *they* make. As long as decisions are made by somebody else, children are not responsible for them because all they have to do is obey.

Young children can make only small decisions at first, and gradually become able to make bigger ones. For example, making a schedule for the entire day in school is out of the question for young children, but choosing an activity during free play time and voting on a rule at clean-up time are perfectly manageable decisions for 4-year-olds.

Certain decisions are not open to discussion. Naptime and bedtime are examples of decisions that are made by adults. The important thing is that children be allowed *as much as possible* to make decisions for themselves. Even bedtime can be made more acceptable

to children by letting them know well in advance that after dinner, a television program, and a story, it will be time for bed.

Why start so early?

Many people believe that autonomy is for adults, and that what is appropriate for young children is obedience. But good judgment does not develop all of a sudden when the child is 16, 18, or 21 years old.

By age 5, children already vary a great deal in their ability to make decisions for themselves. Some 5-year-olds run to adults to say, "Johnny hit me," and expect adults to solve every problem of this kind. Others tell their teachers and parents to stay out of their conflicts because, "It is up to us to settle things between the two of us."

When the teacher leaves the room, some groups immediately explode in chaos. Others go on as if the teacher had never left the room. If children are used to making decisions for the good of the entire group, they can govern themselves without being controlled by an adult.

Some 5-year-olds even have the initiative to say to the entire class, "There is a problem here that we have to discuss." A teacher who believes in fostering the development of autonomy reacts by saying, "What do you think we should do?" and "Does everybody agree that that is a good idea?"

The autonomy of 5-year-olds does not happen by chance. It is the result of exchanging viewpoints with other children and adults day in and day out, and of being allowed to make decisions. The more autonomous children become, the greater the possibility for them to become even more autonomous. This is why it is important to start fostering autonomy early in life. Five-year-olds who can already govern themselves with respect to small decisions are more likely to become more autonomous in dealing with bigger issues.

Intellectual development

Exchanging of viewpoints and negotiations are important not only for children's moral development, but also for their intellectual development. For example, being told that another person cannot believe a lie motivates the child to reconsider the situation from the adult's perspective. This kind of coordination of viewpoints is essential for children's development of logic. I still remember wondering, with all the intellectual power I had as a child, how my mother could possibly know that I was lying!

Adults often repeatedly tell children to be quiet at the dinner table and in waiting rooms. This command is good neither for their moral development nor for their intellectual development. It is much better to negotiate a solution with them by asking what they think they can do to occupy themselves. They may think of going to another room, looking at a book, or drawing a picture. This negotiation requires inventiveness, if-then relationships, and the coordination of points of view. Children who thus negotiate mutually acceptable solutions day after day develop their ability to think logically because they have to make sense to others if they are to be convincing. This ability to think logically is an important foundation for learning to read, to do arithmetic, and to organize every other kind of knowledge in and out of school.

The principles discussed above may require more patience than you think you have. But if we want children to become able to act with personal conviction about what is right, independently of the reward system, we must reduce our adult power and avoid the use of rewards and punishments as much as possible. We must, instead, exchange points of view with children, negotiate solutions, and let them make decisions for themselves. Only then can they build for themselves their own personal feelings of necessity about what is fair and right for everybody concerned.

Choice with Responsibility

Davia M. Veach

Young children can be expected to show some evidence of independent thinking, following through with a task, dependability, self-confidence, and willingness to admit mistakes.

Marietta Lynch

Parents and teachers of young children generally agree that the stage should be set for children to make wise choices and accept responsibility during the early and middle childhood years. However, we often tell a child exactly what to do. If he does it "wrong" the first time, we tell him precisely where he "goofed," so that next time he will be able to make a wiser decision. As parents and teachers we need to ask ourselves, "Is this really the way to help a child grow toward making wise choices and behaving responsibly?"

Young children can be expected to show some evidence of independent thinking, following through with a task, dependability, self-confidence, and willingness to admit mistakes. Each of these characteristics is in some way related to making wise choices and behaving responsibly. Yet, these desirable outcomes do not just happen. They are learned. Furthermore, they are learned mostly from parents and teachers. Our crucial concern comes in how the goal is reached.

Choice with responsibility rightfully belongs to the child

Parent or teacher reactions can definitely determine the value of the learning experience inherent in the following incident.

Tim, Jamie, and John (ages 4, 5, and 6) were on their way to the ice cream stand when they stopped by the wishing well at the

Davia M. Veach, *Ph.D., is Assistant Professor of Early Childhood Education at Wichita State University, Wichita, Kansas. She has also taught and directed programs for young children.*

corner of the park. Jamie's family was new in town and he had never seen a wishing well before. He expressed his amazement at seeing nickels, dimes, and pennies on the bottom of the well. Tim, who had thrown many nickels and pennies into the well, said, "Yeah, you make a wish and throw in your money and your wish will come true." Jamie pondered for a moment, trying to sort out the new information. Then he asked, "If I throw my money in, can I get anything I want?" Tim nodded. However, John, who had also thrown pennies into the well, quickly added, "No, that's just pretend, your wish really won't come true."

Jamie stood there for a few seconds with his hand in his pocket fingering his only quarter which was just enough to buy one ice cream cone. Then he gripped the quarter tightly, withdrew his hand from his pocket, and said in a hesitating voice, "I wish for two ice cream cones," and threw his money into the water.

A child in Jamie's position is likely to be upset when he faces the consequences of his decision. But surely his perceptions will become sharper, and his thinking more logical if he is expected to accept the responsibility for his act. Adults often react with a feeling of pity in these situations. However, Jamie definitely will not learn to accept the responsibility for his behavior if someone always gives him another quarter or if, out of pity, he is promised a new toy or a special treat. If this happens continuously in Jamie's life, will he ever stop throwing his money into the wishing well?

Jamie does not need someone to say, "I told you so," "You should have known better," "I'm sorry," or "Next time you'll know." All he needs is someone to listen as he tells his story about losing his quarter and not getting an ice cream cone. One might say, "You must have been so mad at yourself when you realized you had thrown away your quarter and couldn't get any ice cream." A statement such as this encourages Jamie to talk about his upset feelings. It is nonpunitive and does not fault him for his unwise decision. It also lets him know that someone understands how he feels. As a result, Jamie's hurt can ease a great deal and he can take a giant step toward wiser decisions and more responsible behavior.

Marja Bergen

Five-year-olds can decide which clothes to wear.

There must be a gradual but continuous assumption of responsibility

Freedom of choice and the assumption of responsibility for choices must be gradually expanded in view of a child's physical, social, emotional, and intellectual growth. Two-year-old children can decide whether they want a chocolate cookie or a vanilla cookie. Five-year-olds can decide which clothes to wear or which toys to play with. Preteens can decide upon the time, food, decorations, and friends for a pajama party or an outing. Teenagers can decide whom to date, whether or not to cheat on an exam, cut class, or leave school. However, teenagers are not going to be equipped to make logical decisions if they have never had the chance to decide whether they wanted a chocolate cookie or a vanilla cookie. Neither are they equipped to analyze all available data if they were never allowed to accept the responsibility for their selection when they found out they did not like chocolate.

The age at which a child is allowed to make various choices and accept the consequences of those choices depends upon the child's developmental level. For example, 2-year-old children are not ready to accept complete freedom in deciding where to play. They may decide to play in the street and of course they are not yet capable of realizing the possible consequences of that decision.

A teacher once told me, "But when I do give the children some freedom and tell them to choose an activity, they don't know what to do. They always end up asking me." It is quite true that children who are accustomed to having decisions made for them may become frustrated and may not know what to do if suddenly they are given the responsibility of making an independent choice. Whatever their reaction, it is unlikely that they will use the opportunity constructively. Children must become accustomed to thinking, deciding and choosing independently on a gradual basis. No one can take a child from a point he or she has not yet reached.

Choice with responsibility is a learning process

One major reason for allowing children to make choices and accept responsibility for those choices is to enable them to gain experience in making their own decisions. The following example illustrates some of the values of this decisionmaking process.

At age 6, Karen was given $3.00 each Monday as an allowance. She could buy small toys, play items or use the money for personal entertainment. One Monday afternoon Karen saw a set of doll clothes that cost $2.87. Without deliberation she bought the set. The next afternoon a friend invited her to the Thursday matinee. Karen wanted to go but she did not have any money.

This is an excellent opportunity for Karen to learn about decisionmaking, if she is allowed to accept the responsibility for her predicament. She must first recognize the problem, ask herself how the problem can be solved, and

come up with possible solutions. The amount of adult guidance Karen will need will depend in part upon her prior experience in solving her own problems. As Karen thinks of alternatives, the following possibilities may seem feasible: (1) stay at home, (2) ask for more money, (3) ask for an allowance advance, (4) borrow from a friend, or (5) earn some money.

As children grow toward wise decisionmaking they will learn to think independently, stay with the task long enough to look at all sides of the issue, analyze the possible effects of each alternative, and then accept the consequences of their decisions. If a mistake has been made, the child must be able to admit the error and have self-confidence to start again and proceed logically.

Inauthentic choices

While providing children with opportunities for making choices with responsibility, it is important to avoid offering inauthentic choices, as in the following situations.

Choice without responsibility. This was discussed in the example of Jamie and the wishing well. If he never has to accept the responsibility for his behavior he will have no need to stop and think about consequences before he acts. Choice without responsibility leads to irresponsibility.

Unreal choice. If adults have already decided the issue before asking, even young children soon come to recognize that the choice is really not theirs. This type of choice can lead to distrustfulness and feelings of unimportance and apathy on the part of the child.

Unlimited choice. When children are allowed to make decisions in areas they are not equipped to handle, they are almost sure to experience disappointment and defeat. Children can learn a great deal if they have to accept the responsibility for throwing their daily or even weekly allowance into the wishing well. But the disadvantages can far outweigh the advantages if, at the age of 5, they have to accept the responsibility of throwing a whole month's allowance away. Young children can be given only small amounts of their allowances at one time. This way their disappointments will not be so long lasting that the whole teaching-learning process is defeated. Unlimited choice or freedom without limits is almost certain to result in frustration and confusion for the child.

Adults have responsibilities, too

Providing children with opportunities to make choices and accept responsibility is not an easy task. The following characteristics seem to be necessary on the part of adults in order for a child to become a responsible self-directing individual.

The adult must be flexible. Adults must realize their own biases and not let these interfere with the children's decisions. (If there are reasons children should not have a choice, do not give them a choice. If there are limits to their choices, state these clearly.)

The adult must be creative. Children often need adult guidance in realizing the many possibilities of choice.

The adult must be responsible. When children are given a choice they need an adult who will support their decision and assist in implementation if necessary. It is also essential that adults make logical decisions and accept responsibility themselves.

If children are allowed to make choices and accept responsibilities that are right for their developmental levels, the values inherent in wise choices and responsible behavior can be vividly manifested in their daily activities and reactions to others. Allowing children to make choices and accept the responsibility for those choices is one of the most important things adults can do in fostering children's growth and development.

Circle Time

Getting Past "Two Little Pumpkins"

Oralie D. McAfee

Nearly every early childhood program includes circle time or group time on the daily schedule. What happens during this time together? Ideas can be introduced, shared, or consolidated. Good literature, music, or dance are enjoyed. Intellectual, social, emotional, or physical concepts and skills may be taught. A cohesive group feeling can be fostered. Games, songs, fingerplays, discussion . . . all are a part of the traditional circle time.

Why, then, if circle times are so popular and seem to have so much learning potential, do children often tune out the group's activities . . . visit with their neighbors . . . lie on the floor . . . play with the nearest toy . . . or even get up and leave?

Children learn about their roles and relationships during group time just as they do in any other event in their lives. In circle time, are they learning to pay attention, to participate, and to function as a group? Do they know when to listen and when to talk? Do they know how to respect the rights of others or to ignore distraction?

Despite the popularity of group time, very little information is available in how teachers think about, plan, and conduct these activities, and what teachers and children actually do at

circle time (Berkeley & Entwhistle, 1979). The teacher's role is often seen as manager of the classroom setting and action (Morrison & Oxford, 1978; Ross, 1983). Some studies suggest that teachers must maintain the group's momentum (Kounin, 1970), while others focus on the variables that influence young children's ability to pay attention (Roedell, Slaby, & Robinson, 1977), or the complexity of classroom interactions (Flanders, 1970; Gump, 1969; Stallings & Kaskowitz, 1974).

Only recently have curriculum resources become available that contain suggestions for groups of young children (Bartlett, 1981; Copple, Sigel, & Saunders, 1979; Hohman, Banet & Weikart, 1979). An exploratory study on the reality and possibilities for group time seemed long overdue.

What happens in group time?

In order to learn more about what takes place in circle time, we interviewed 35 teachers of children ages $2\frac{1}{2}$ through kindergarten (McAfee, 1985). The programs were representative of the diversity in the field in terms of length of day, sponsorship, and population served. From this group, we selected 5 classrooms to observe in-

tensely both teachers' and children's behavior. The most pertinent results of this exploratory study are presented here.

Program quality factors

Our observations confirmed the teachers' reports that their programs were of good quality. For example, almost half of the teachers had a degree in early childhood education, child development, or a related area (Table 1). Teachers' educational levels did not vary by program setting.

Both adult:child ratios and class size were well within state guidelines. More than two-thirds of the classrooms had 1 adult for 10 or fewer children. Class size ranged from 10 (a group of 3-year-olds in a cooperative nursery) to one group of 60 (a team-taught public kindergarten with 2 certified teachers and 2 assistants). Sixty percent of the groups had fewer than 18 children.

Plans for circle

Teachers told us that what they did in group time was most often influenced by two factors—the theme or concepts

---

Oralie D. McAfee, *Ed.D., is Professor of Early Childhood Education, Metropolitan State College, Denver, Colorado.*

Table 1. **Highest level of education completed by teachers**

Education completed	Frequency	Percent
High school	1	3
Associate Degree, ECE	2	6
Some college in another area	3	9
Some college in ECE	4	11
Master's Degree in ECE or related area	4	11
Bachelor's or Master's Degree in another area	9	26
Bachelor's Degree in Early Childhood Education or related area (Elementary Ed.; Child Development)	12	34
	35	100%

Table 2. **Group time activities: Reported and observed**

Activity	Reported as used in group time (35 teachers)[a]		Reported as "going well" (35 teachers)[a]		Observed (5 teachers; 48 observation checks)	
	Number	Percent	Number	Percent[b]	Number	Percent[b]
Books/stories	39	15	22	18	16	33
Music, songs, music-related activities	38	15	22	18	5	10
Exercise, movement, dance	27	10	12	10	0	0
Fingerplays	26	10	19	16	0	0
Discussion	23	9	7	6	4	8
Sharing/show & tell	21	8	5	4	11	23
Lessons and demonstrations	19	7	9	7	0	0
Traditional opening activities (calendar, roll, weather)	18	7	4	3	6	13
Planning & review	16	6	1	1	0	0
Dramatization	13	5	5	4	0	0
Games	7	3	5	4	0	0
Films, filmstrips, slides	4	1	2	2	0	0
Poetry, nursery rhymes	3	1	3	2	0	0
Other (relaxation; person-of-the-week; newstime; transition, etc.)	7	3	5	4	6	12
	261	100%	121	99%	48	99%

[a] Teachers could give more than one response within and across categories. [b] Percent does not total 100 because of rounding.

being emphasized, and children's needs and preferences. Few teachers wrote detailed plans—12 of the 35 said they picked up on what the children were interested in, planned in their heads, or never needed plans. Others reported a combination of approaches ranging from detailed weekly or monthly overviews to sketchy ideas. The most typical written plan listed days of the week in one column and activities in the other. Group time was listed occasionally.

Circle activities

The teachers reported 14 types of activities common in group time. Books/stories and music-related events were the 2 most frequently used categories (Table 2). The type of activity varied little regardless of the children's age, background, or program. While kindergarten teachers mentioned traditional opening activities such as calendar and sharing more frequently, teachers of all ages reported similar events.

We also asked teachers to identify the activities that children actively participated in and enjoyed. Books/stories and music were identified as the most successful. Ironically, sharing/show and tell, mentioned 21 times as a possible activity, was identified only 5 times as one that children participated in and enjoyed. Traditional opening activities and planning and review followed the same pattern.

Classroom observation and examination of teaching plans revealed that only a few of the 14 potential types of activities were implemented. Reading a book and sharing/show and tell were evident in more than half of our observations (Table 2).

Our observations in each classroom included 48 1-min checks of
- teacher methods of monitoring children or the activity, and
- adult and child behavior.

In almost half of these checks, teachers focused on the material they were presenting, one child, or a small group of children within the larger group. More effective methods to monitor and maintain children's attention (such as scanning the group, making eye contact, changing pace and presentation) were used infrequently.

Consequently, the percentage of children appropriately attending in group time ranged from 50% to 88%. When computed according to activity, attention ranged from 65% for sharing/show and tell to 78% for discussion of a Halloween parade with pictures of the children (a high interest activity with a visual focal point).

Teachers dealt with inattention and misbehavior by ignoring it (38%), preventing it, such as by maintaining a brisk pace for the discussion or story (26%), or reminding children of appropriate behavior (11%). Other techniques, such as reinforcement of desired behavior, were observed far less frequently.

Teaching assistants often distracted children by talking to them, engaging in physical contact that pulled children's attention away from the group activity, or talking to another adult—all of which failed to help children focus their attention on the activity.

We saw no out-of-control or disturbed children. However, in four of the classrooms, transitions before and after group time were managed poorly and thus were not conducive to appropriate child behavior.

Problems

The teachers in our survey identified two primary difficulties at group time:

- children's behaviors that disrupt the group, and
- balancing individual needs with those of the group.

They listed an assortment of children's distracting behaviors, including one recent diversion—children who repeatedly open and close the Velcro closures on their shoes!

Active children were seen as more difficult than those who are inattentive, although both behaviors indicate lack of involvement. One teacher commented, "I can't get past two little pumpkins!"

What do teachers see as the cause of these problems during circle time? Teachers cited conditions they believed to be beyond their control in 75% of their responses: children's developmental levels, emotional or behavioral problems, home background, and classroom conditions (group too large, wide age span).

Only 25% of the problems were seen as related to conditions within teachers' control: activities that were inappropriate or insufficient, assistants who need to be trained, or children who still needed help to learn appropriate group behavior.

These responses indicate that this group of teachers seems to be largely unaware that they can plan and implement activities that are more appro-

Circle activities should be appropriate to the age, developmental level, and social functioning of the group.

Constantly monitor how the children respond. Shorten, lengthen, or vary your plans accordingly.

In advance

- Schedule to eliminate distractions.

- Use smooth, orderly transitions.

- Select high interest, appropriate activities.

- Sequence activities to vary the pace.

- Anticipate problems.

During group time

- Monitor the group and alter plans accordingly.

- Identify expected behaviors.

- Give clear, simple directions.

- Maintain the momentum.

- Acknowledge appropriate behavior.

After group time

- Evaluate and make needed changes.

priate to the age, developmental level, or social functioning of the group.

Conclusions

Although our study was exploratory because of sample limitations, we can draw some tentative conclusions from our data.

- These teachers are missing out on the wide variety of activities that are appropriate for groups. They also could benefit by expanding their monitoring and guidance techniques.

- Teachers were concerned about the moment and children's interest or the chosen theme. Long-range goals, or thoughtful choices of activities to achieve identified goals, and flexible plans were not typical of the teachers in this sample.

- It is questionable whether calendar, weather, and show and tell, even with some variations, can be equally ap-

propriate for children ages 3, 4, 5, and 6. The age and development span is wide. Also, we cannot expect children to maintain interest in doing the same things in group time year after year.

- These teachers did not see themselves as active and powerful leaders in group time. When problems arose, they blamed the children, the children's backgrounds, or other conditions beyond their control. On the other hand, when an activity was successful, they credited the activities or "a good group." Their tendency to ignore inattention and inappropriate behavior by children and adult assistants affirms this conclusion.

How to improve group time

What can teachers do to make group time a more positive learning experience for children? The results of our study, other research, and accepted

Paul M. Schrock

best practices in working with young children lead to several recommendations.

Before group time

● Schedule group activities at a time and place free from distractions. Group time usually is more appealing to children if it is scheduled between more invigorating, individual activities, rather than just before or after another group activity. For example, if you plan free play before and small teams after circle time, the pace will be varied enough to help children maintain interest. Also, set up the area so that children face away from an open door or preparations for the next activity.

● Ease children in and out of circle time with smooth, orderly transitions. Alger (1984) offers a wealth of ideas about how to help children move from one activity into another throughout the day. This sense of structure and continuity is important for both children and staff.

● Select and be prepared with high interest activities appropriate to your group's age, experience, and development. Choose from the wealth of available resources to assure variety: poetry, relaxation, fingerplays, films, and movement, for example. If the more traditional activities appeal to the children, find creative ways to present the calendar, weather, or sharing times to keep interest high. Check the weather outdoors, use a large weekly or daily calendar in which children can record their significant events, or include these events on a regular basis but not daily.

● Organize activities in a sequence

To hold attention: whisper, create a sense of excitement, add some mystery, use humor, try suspense, use props. If children's attention cannot quickly be recaptured, it is time to move on.

that helps children learn and do what is expected. Use open-ended songs, chants, fingerplays, or action games as the group assembles to give children time to enter the group gradually as they finish their previous work.

• After the group has gathered, increase children's alertness with an energizing activity: movement or action songs. Follow with a calming activity that helps focus children's attention—a story, demonstration, or discussion. Signal that group time is over by gradually dispersing the group using names, songs, next activities, or other transitional devices.

• Work with assistant teachers and volunteers to help them participate in group time, too. Talk together about how they can help children become part of the group without themselves becoming a distraction. Identify children who might be able to become more involved if an adult sits near them. Anticipate problems before they erupt, and take steps to avoid them.

During group time

• Respond to the group and individuals sensitively. Constantly monitor how the children respond to the activity. Shorten, lengthen, or vary your plans accordingly to keep everyone together. If an activity seems especially important but the group attention has wandered, use it later in the day or week. Make sure you can see and be seen by all the children. Scan the entire group regularly. Stand or move around if it is appropriate. Maintain physical and emotional closeness.

• Coach children on expected group behavior. Demonstrate what they are to do, tell them in a matter-of-fact way, and even practice if it seems appropriate.

• Give clear, simple directions in the sequence in which they are to be done. For example, tell the children the procedure for going to the next activity. "Nikki, Todd, and Chris please get your smocks on because you asked to paint at the easel," rather than announcing, "It's time to go now."

• Maintain the momentum of involvement in the group. Avoid interruptions or delays. Use attention-holding techniques: whisper, create a sense of excitement, add some mystery, use humor, try some suspense, focus children's attention with pictures or props. If children's attention cannot quickly be recaptured, it is time to move on to something else.

• Acknowledge and reinforce appropriate behavior. Ignore minor distractions while you use the attention-holding techniques. If a child becomes disruptive, deal with the problem quickly and quietly. Better yet, if you sense a child may have difficulty in the group that day, talk with the assistant teacher about the need for prevention, or find something else for the child to do.

After group time

• Evaluate what happened, and use what you learn to improve group time in the future. How could transitions be smoother? Would another pace be more suitable? What seems to be an appropriate length of time? How can activities be varied? How can teachers work together to maintain interest? Would smaller groups be more effective?

Circle time is a complex, dynamic interaction among the adults, children, and resources used. You can make group time more effective and enjoyable for children and the staff!

References

Alger, H. A. (1984). Transitions: Alternatives to manipulative management techniques. *Young Children, 39* (6), 16–25.

Bartlett, E. J. (1981). Selecting an early childhood language curriculum. In C. B. Cazden (Ed.), *Language in early childhood education* (pp. 33–75). Washington, DC: National Association for the Education of Young Children.

Berkeley, M. V., & Entwhistle, D. R. (1979). *Kindergarten social climate.* Baltimore, MD: Johns Hopkins University, Center for Social Organization of Schools. (ERIC Document Reproduction Service No. ED 183 287)

Copple, C., Sigel, I. E., & Saunders, R. (1979). *Educating the young thinker: Strategies for classroom growth.* New York: Van Nostrand.

Flanders, N. A. (1970). *Analyzing teacher behavior.* Reading, MA: Addison-Wesley.

Gump, P. V. (1969). Intra-setting analysis: The third grade classroom as a special but instructive case. In E. P. Willems & H. L. Rausch (Eds.), *Naturalistic viewpoints in psychological research.* New York: Holt, Rinehart, & Winston.

Hohman, M., Banet, B., & Weikart, D. P. (1979). *Young children in action.* Ypsilanti, MI: High/Scope.

Kounin, J. S. (1970). *Discipline and group management in the classroom.* New York: Holt, Rinehart, & Winston.

McAfee, O. (1985). *Group time in early childhood centers: An exploratory study.* (ERIC Document Reproduction Service No. ED 251 243). Urbana, IL: ERIC/EECE.

Morrison, S. B., & Oxford, R. I. (1978). Classroom ecology and kindergarten students' task related behaviors: An exploratory study. (ERIC Document Reproduction Service No. ED 153 744)

Roedell, W. C., Slaby, R. G., & Robinson, H. B. (1977). *Social development in young children.* Monterey, CA: Brooks/Cole.

Ross, R. P. (1983). What's happening in elementary school classrooms? *Research on time use, classroom operations, and activity management.* (Catalog No. 197). Urbana, IL: ERIC/EECE.

Stallings, J. A., & Kaskowitz, D. H. (1974). *Follow-through classroom observation evaluation: 1972–1973.* Menlo Park, CA: Stanford Research Institute.

"But what about sharing?"
Children's Literature and Moral Development

Suzanne Lowell Krogh and Linda Leonard Lamme

"Well, if the Little Red Hen did all the work, she oughta get all the cake," Heather declared, looking and sounding very sure of herself.

"But what about sharing?" Mark asked. "We just said that it's good to share." He sounded less sure of himself than Heather did.

Gregg spoke up. "Yeah, it's good to share, but only if you do something for it. Like you have to earn stuff."

"Right!" Heather vehemently agreed. "The animals didn't work so they didn't earn any of the hen's cake."

Then the teacher stepped in with a question designed to increase the complexity of the discussion. "Suppose the dog and the cat helped a lot, but the turkey and the pig helped just a little. How will the hen split up the cake?"

Ricky had an answer immediately. "Everybody gets the same if everybody helped. It doesn't matter how much they did. Otherwise everybody will be yelling and fighting."

"I don't think so," responded Heather in self-confidence. "If the dog and cat work more they should get more. That's fairest."

The discussion continued for a few minutes with about half of these second graders arguing Heather's side while the other half took Ricky's position. Through it all Mark seemed unsure, listening quietly to both sides. Finally, a smile came to his face. "I've got an idea! Everybody should get cake depending on how hard they worked, but one thing's different. The pig and the turkey are bigger so they're gonna need more food to stay alive. It wouldn't be fair for them to starve to death! That means they should get a little more than the dog and cat even if they didn't work quite as hard."

Realizing that no consensus would be reached, the teacher soon drew the discussion to a close, allowing each child to reach an independent and personal decision concerning the various sharing issues suggested by the story.

Parallels in cognitive and moral development

This experience was one in a series in which two classes, a first grade and a second grade, used literature to explore the issue of distributive justice—fairness in sharing situations. The study of this topic has its roots in the work of Piaget (1932), who recognized that children's cognitive development is accompanied by similar stages in moral judgment. Kohlberg (1975) expanded the research on moral development, especially after the age of ten, while Selman (1980) and Damon (1977) related this theory and research to younger children.

Damon's research shows that children progress according to developmental levels in their understanding of the fair distribution of resources. Subsequent studies based on Damon's work indicate that adults can stimulate children's growth in reasoning (Krogh, in press; Enright 1982) as they progress through several stages.

Damon describes these stages as "a sequence of unfolding

Suzanne L. Krogh, *Ph.D., is Associate Professor, Early Childhood Education, University of Florida, Gainesville, Florida.*

Linda L. Lamme, *Ph.D., is Professor, Early Childhood Education, University of Florida, Gainesville, Florida.*

Table 1. Stages of children's moral development (Damon 1977)

Level 0-A: Choices are based on self-interest (ages 3–4).

Level 0-B: Choices are made based on external realities such as size, sex, or perceived attractiveness (ages 4–5).

Level 1-A: Choices are based on strict equality—everyone gets the same (ages 5–6).

Level 1-B: Compromises are made between competing claims (e.g., hardest workers vs. most effective) and special needs (e.g., poverty) are taken into consideration (ages 7–8).

Level 2-A: Equality, reciprocity, and competing claims are all taken into account so that each person is given what is due (ages 8–10).

confusions in the mind of the child" (p. 74). These stages are briefly reviewed in Table 1.

In the discussion of the Little Red Hen, the children reasoned at several of these levels, all of them representative of what might be expected for second graders. Rick's argument that everybody gets the same no matter what the effort places him at level 1-A. Heather's contention that distribution should be based on the work contributed indicates level 1-B reasoning. Although Mark was uncertain during much of the discussion, he finally felt comfortable with a level 2-A argument in which the competing claims of the various animals were considered.

Leading group discussions

This discussion is an example of the ways in which children's literature dealing with social issues can help children reason about topics such as distributive justice. Although on this day Heather and Ricky remained firmly convinced at their levels of understanding, Mark was ready to move on and it was the discussion that helped promote his growth.

While unstructured discussion may also lead to growth in moral development, the sessions in our series were intentionally designed to further children's reasoning abilities. Note that the teacher in the Little Red Hen discussion purposely increased the complexity of the discussion by asking a well-timed question. Based on the research on children's cognitive and moral development, we identified several guidelines that assisted us in conducting our series of discussions, and that we recommend to other teachers.

Limit group size

Interaction among peers or between children and the adult is facilitated when the number of participants is limited. We found that in a group of eight children, everyone could participate actively. In larger groups, not everyone can be in-

volved. Interaction among peers or between children and the adult needs to be firsthand and concrete in order for young children to grow in their ability to understand how others feel (Castle and Richards 1979). This role-taking skill is essential if children are to come to understand the decision-making process of a story's protagonist.

Choose appropriate stories

Literary merit and appropriateness to the developmental levels of the children are equal considerations. If the Little Red Hen's reasoning had been based on self-interest or unrelated factors, these second graders would have had no model for advancing in their moral development. If the reasoning had been too advanced, or the topic more removed from children's experience, they would not have been able to relate to it (Kohlberg 1975). *The Little Red Hen*'s enduring popularity may in part be because her reasoning about distributive justice is a good match for young children.

Keep the discussion concrete

Young children are capable of in-depth discussions, but they need accompanying concrete experiences as well (Schuncke and Krogh 1983). Therefore, while the children were discussing *The Little Red Hen* they were also drawing pictures of the story! Although children's pictures might have been unrelated to the issues, children seemed more comfortable and natural in this setting than they would sitting in a circle, for example. When the same discussion was tried in other groups without the opportunity to draw, children were bored and fidgety.

Build on diversity

Children's moral, social, and cognitive reasoning is expanded through giving and hearing a variety of viewpoints at different levels of development (Kohlberg 1975). If possible, select discussion groups that include a mixture of cognitive abilities, experiences, and other pertinent qualities.

Take unscheduled detours

Because the intent of reading and discussing stories is to help children deal with real life, reality occasionally intrudes into children's discussions. These unscheduled detours may offer even better opportunities to help children apply their newly acquired reasoning and thinking skills.

The teacher of this same second grade class had just read aloud *One Fine Day*, a cumulative tale in which a fox must ask a succession of characters for various items which will lead to getting an elderly woman to sew his tail back on. After some discussion about the sharing aspects of the story, Mark looked up from the picture he was drawing and announced, "I just put the moral of the story on here."

Everyone was interested to know what the moral was, even those who had never heard of one before, so he read aloud, "Say please." Mark's reason for assigning this moral to the story was that if the fox had said "please" to the woman in the first place, he wouldn't have had to go through a whole story full of frustrations!

Gregg looked over Mark's shoulder at the inscribed moral and suggested that he would put the same moral on his own paper. As he carefully studied the words in order to copy the spelling, Mark pulled his paper away, looking quite annoyed. "But that's *my* idea," he said.

Recognizing an opportunity for firsthand experience, but not wanting to pass judgment either, the teacher asked non-commitally, "And you don't want to share your ideas?"

Two other children heard the frequently discussed word *share* and seized the chance. They chanted in unison, "It's good to share, Mark."

"Well," he agreed reluctantly, "I guess so," and returned the paper to the table. Obviously, Mark had shared only because of peer pressure rather than because of growth in his reasoning. You will recall that his earlier discussion of the Little Red Hen showed his thought processes to be more advanced than those of the other children. Now he was faced with the need to put his ideas into practice—difficult for all of us at times!

The following day, the teacher watched Mark with some concern as he again wrote a moral and others asked to copy it. Sighing almost inaudibly, he held the paper up for all to see. "Thanks, Mark!" one or two children said, and he suddenly smiled. Obviously, there was a reward for his sharing, and each day from then on he agreed to show his story morals without hesitation, occasionally reminding the children to thank him.

In a second experience, both ideas of sharing and saying "please" were made concrete when Charles brought a large box of expensive marking pens from home to use during the discussion time. Magnanimously he spread them on the table before the group. "I'm bringing them because it's good to share," he said, "but it's good for you to say 'please,' too. Then I'll want to share them with you."

That day Heather wrote on her picture, "If you share with others they will share with you." This is another example of her 1-B reasoning. From then on, the group challenged itself to find a moral in every story discussed.

Selecting good stories

Before choosing books to discuss, you will want to review the variation of reasoning abilities in your class. We asked volunteers and the school librarian to conduct discussion groups so that we could limit the group size, but chose the books for them to read to ensure that children's development and needs were matched with the stories.

Flexibility in selections is desirable. A useful description of books on the topic of sharing, categorized by reasoning levels, is found in an earlier article (Krogh and Lamme 1983). The books and questions relating to them which we used over the course of four weeks are listed in Table 2.

These questions made it possible for the group to discuss a book in about 15 minutes. Although at times the children reached agreement, more often they retained their disparity of ideas. The discussion leaders made no judgments and did not try to force consensus. In fact, the children showed a nearly unanimous lack of interest in what any adult thought about the issues.

Rewards

Our story discussions took place twice a week for a month. The focus each time was on sharing, with the intent that other social and moral issues would be explored at other times. By focusing on one issue, children are encouraged to think more broadly about the topic than they might otherwise.

An example of how deeply involved the children were in the topic of sharing occurred one day when several children had created their own cumulative tale using *One Fine Day* as a model. After Daniel made the last character in their tale find his pot of gold, he turned to the rest of the group and declared, "I found it, but I'm going to share it with all of you because you helped me!"

It is especially rewarding when the evidence of growth through classroom experience is apparent in children's behavior. Using books gives children an opportunity to analyze

Table 2. Books and questions used to stimulate discussion of sharing.

Angus and the Cat (Flack 1931)

A Scotty dog learns to share in order to keep his friend, a cat.

Why was Angus annoyed with the new cat?

Have you ever been jealous and not wanted to share?

Who should have most of the sunlight (or milk)? Why?

The Little Red Hen (Galdone 1973)

A hen chooses not to share any cake with the other animals because they refused to help her bake it.

Should the Little Red Hen have shared? Why?

Should anyone get more than anyone else?

John Brown, Rose and the Midnight Cat (Wagner 1977)

A dog refuses to share his owner with an intruding cat, but must change his mind.

Why did John Brown pretend the cat wasn't there?

Why did John Brown change his mind and let the cat in?

How did he feel about sharing Rose? Why?

The Mannerly Adventures of Little Mouse (Keenan 1977)

A young mouse learns that the essence of manners may be willingness to share.

How did Little Mouse feel after he had shared treats with everyone in the family?

Which family members deserved the most? Why?

Morris's Disappearing Bag (Wells 1975)

Older siblings refuse to share with Morris until it is learned that he has something to share back.

Do you have a toy that you don't like to share? Why is this toy so special?

What toys do you like to share with others?

Why didn't the brothers and sisters want to share with Morris?

One Fine Day (Hogrogrian 1971)

A fox needs to have his tail stitched back on and must find characters willing to share materials and skills.

Why wouldn't each character give the fox what he needed without getting something in return?

Which character wanted to share and why was he the only one?

Pet Show (Keats 1972)

A young boy shares his first-prize ribbon with an elderly lady even though she didn't earn it.

Why did Peter decide to share the prize?

How did Peter feel after he had let the lady keep the ribbon?

Peter's Chair (Keats 1967)

A boy resists sharing his old possessions with a new baby sister.

How did Peter feel when all of his belongings were painted pink for his sister?

Why did Peter decide to share his chair with her after all?

---

the role models which literature provides. Not only do children advance in their reasoning, then, but they also grow to appreciate literature and comprehend stories more fully.

"... Values do not come from injections by persons in authority or by superficially copying society's patterns. They must be searched for, tried out, discussed and analyzed. Alternatives must be scrutinized and weighed" (Riley 1984, p. 17).

How important it is to include moral issues such as sharing in the early primary curriculum! As Riley continues, "If we expect to survive as a people capable of establishing and holding values consistent with a humanitarian philosophy, we must re-examine the ways in which we are educating our children. It is essential that children grow into adults who not only can read and write but who are curious and imaginative and capable of making choices based on ethical values" (p. 39).

References

Castle, K. and Richards, H. "Adult/Peer Interactions and Role-Taking Ability Among Preschool Children."*Journal of Genetic Psychology* 135 (September 1979): 71–79.

Damon, W. *The Social World of the Child*. San Francisco: Jossey-Bass, 1977.

Enright, R. "A Classroom Discipline Model for Promoting Social Cognitive Development in Early Childhood." *Journal of Moral Education* 11 (October 1981): 47–60.

Flack, M. *Angus and the Cat*. New York: Doubleday, 1931.

Galdone, P. *The Little Red Hen*. New York: Seabury, 1973.

Hogrogrian, N. *One Fine Day*. New York: Collier, 1971.

Keats, E. J. *Peter's Chair*. New York: Harper & Row, 1967.

Keats, E. J. *Pet Show*. New York: Collier, 1972.

Keenan, M. *The Mannerly Adventures of Little Mouse*. New York: Crown, 1977.

Kohlberg, L. "The Cognitive-Developmental Approach to Moral Education." *Phi Delta Kappan* 56, no. 10 (June 1975): 670–678.

Krogh, S. "Encouraging Positive Justice Reasoning and Perspective Taking Skills: Two Educational Interventions." *Journal of Moral Education,* in press.

Krogh, S. and Lamme, L. "Learning to Share: How Literature Can Help." *Childhood Education* 59, no. 3 (January–February 1983): 188–192.

Piaget, J. *The Moral Judgment of the Child*. New York: Free Press, 1965 (first published in 1932).

Riley, S. *How to Generate Values in Young Children*. Washington, D.C.: National Association for the Education of Young Children, 1984.

Schuncke, G. and Krogh, S. *Helping Children Choose*. Glenview, Ill.: Scott, Foresman, 1983.

Selman, R. *The Growth of Interpersonal Understanding*. New York: Academic Press, 1980.

Wagner, J. *John Brown, Rose and the Midnight Cat*. New York: Bradbury, 1977.

Wells, R. *Morris's Disappearing Bag*. New York: Dial, 1975.

Why Not Holiday Performances?

Q. Each year most of our preschool parents and some of our teachers want the children to perform—Thanksgiving, Hanukkah, and Christmas programs; preschool graduation; or a visit to the Mayor's office during the Week of the Young Child! We all want the children to be involved and to learn from these events, but performances always end up with squirming children, at least one child in tears, and demanding parents. What do you suggest?

A. We all have heard the persistent "shhhhhs", seen the class ham steal the show from the appointed star, and observed a parent urgently prod an unwilling performer. Despite these trying experiences, it is still difficult to help adults see why rehearsed performances exploit children and have little positive value for them.

Young children are natural performers—when they can be enthusiastic and spontaneous. You can build on these qualities by developing any holiday event with these guidelines in mind.

- Help children plan the festivities and carry out their plans.
- Keep the occasion simple and short.
- Involve the parents in the activities.
- Let children choose whether to participate.

Have you asked the children what they feel would be an appropriate way to celebrate? Their creative suggestions might lead to an art fair, a parent breakfast, a puppet show, or a chance to teach parents words to their favorite songs! You will most likely find that the content will be drawn from their typical activities and interests.

Once children decide *what* to do, they can plan *how* to make the event a success. In preparation, children might select, purchase, and prepare food; build a puppet stage and construct puppets and props; or collect and paste photographs taken throughout the year in a book for each family.

Teachers, parents, or older siblings might be asked to narrate a story, take photos, type words for favorite songs, or provide transportation for shopping.

If more than one classroom is involved, small committees could be established to coordinate plans. Teachers can work closely with children to keep plans realistic—a pumpkin-carving party may be affordable, but swimming at the beach (which is three hours away) might not be quite as feasible!

If the children choose some type of presentation, keep in mind that the actual performance will probably lose interest for the children after about 15 minutes. Children are not good audiences, nor do they benefit from rehearsals, except to see the area in which the event will be held. Plan accordingly if several groups are involved.

Give children the choice of whether to participate, both in advance, and again just before the activity. Be sure to talk with any children who seem reluctant.

Refreshments are an excellent way to expand the event so that everyone feels it was worth their efforts. Parents and teachers will welcome this informal opportunity to get to know each other better, too.

Most of us have become accustomed to children's performances, so this short list of what *not* to do might help us plan activities that are more appropriate for young children.

DO NOT ... plan the event yourself ... assign parts for each child to memorize ... single out one or two children as stars ... rehearse children until they become robots ... demand intricate or delicate costumes ... serve unhealthy food ... make all the children prepare identical gifts for the honored person ... make all the decorations yourself so they look perfect ... display only the neatest and most advanced art or writing samples ... plan the event at an inconvenient time ... keep children sitting quietly until it is their turn to perform.

We gratefully acknowledge Sue Bredekamp's contributions in the preparation of this column.

The Unpopular Child

Jaipaul L. Roopnarine and Alice S. Honig

"Nya, nye, nye. You can't come to my birthday party," chanted Chantal as Louise walked over to watch Chantal and Tonya cook popcorn with their wooden beads in a pot.

"I'll help you build your garage, Deanna. Here's some big, big blocks, O.K.?" offered Elena eagerly. Deanna, a preferred playmate among the 5-year-olds, smiled and chatted happily.

The children lined up at the water fountain in the park near their child care center. Mr. Lem lifted each thirsty child up for a drink. He did not notice as Sacha pushed Denny away from the end of the line and announced "You can't get on our line." Denny, shy and discouraged, moved back uncertainly.

"Larry, you be the daddy and I'll be the mommy and Joey will be the baby," announced Mona with vigorous authority. Joey protested weakly that he would like to be the daddy this time. Larry and Mona shook their heads and chorused "Nope, you got to be the baby." Joey wanted badly to be part of this family game, so once again he accepted the role of baby in deference to his playmates.

Why are some children popular and well-liked, while others are infrequently chosen as preferred playmates? How can teachers help children learn social skills so they too can be chosen as accepted playmates?

Social competence with peers is critical for social and personality development (Hartup, 1983). Deprivation studies with young primates suggest that if they lack contact with playmates during the first few months of life, the formation of subsequent peer and sexual relationships with other animals can be seriously impaired as they mature (Harlow, 1969; Suomi & Harlow, 1975).

In humans, lack of social competence with peers during early childhood is related later on to mental health problems (Cowen, Pederson, Babigian, Izzo, & Trost, 1973), suicide (Stengel, 1971), dropping out of school (Ullman, 1957), and delinquency (Roff, Sells, & Golden, 1972).

Given the importance attributed to social competence with peers for social development and the implications of social competence for later mental health, researchers have begun to examine 1) why some children are perceived as popular or unpopular by peers, and 2) the behavioral problems unpopular children might encounter during group interactions.

This review of research will address some very basic questions regarding unpopular children.

● What constitutes unpopularity in the peer group?

● What types of interaction patterns do unpopular children engage in with peers compared to their more popular counterparts?

● What types of parent-child interaction patterns tend to result in popular or unpopular children?

● What can researchers, parents, and teachers do to help the unpopular child?

---

*This is one of a regular series of Research in Review columns. The column in this issue was written and edited by **Jaipaul L. Roopnarine**, Ph.D., Assistant Professor, and **Alice S. Honig**, Ph.D., Professor, Department of Child and Family Studies, Syracuse University, Syracuse, New York.*

Lack of social competence with peers during early childhood is related later on to mental health problems, suicide, dropping out of school, and delinquency.

What is unpopularity?

Unpopularity refers to the social condition of children who are seen by most classroom peers as people they would least prefer to play with. Sociometric techniques (Asher, Singleton, Tinsley, & Hymel, 1978; Peery, 1979) are commonly used to assess popularity in the peer group. Each child is shown a board with photographs of classmates. Typically, a child is asked to name the child in each picture correctly and then a) to choose from the pictures children they would most or least prefer to play with, or b) to answer a series of positive and negative questions regarding the children, such as

Find someone you like very much at school.

Whom don't you like to play with outside?

When you can do what you want to do, whom do you like to do it with?

Whom don't you like to sit next to for stories on the rug?

Each child in the classroom is rated or ranked based on how frequently she or he is chosen in the responses. Another way to measure popularity has been to examine general rates of interactions with peers over extended periods of time. Those children who interact with peers less than one-third of the observed time are considered unpopular or socially isolated (Furman, Rahe, & Hartup, 1979; Roopnarine & Field, 1984).

Researchers sometimes subdivide the unpopular group into children who are rejected or neglected. Rejected children are those whom most classmates dislike to play with and whose bids for social interactions are often rebuffed. Peers and teachers describe them as disruptive and aggressive. On the other hand, neglected children are those who are isolated and frequently shy or withdrawn and ignored by classmates in play.

Peer interactions and unpopularity

Social networks

Not surprisingly, when the social networks of popular and unpopular children are examined in classroom settings, popular children are found to initiate and receive positive interactions primarily with other children who are popular. Similarly, unpopular children initiate behaviors mostly with unpopular peers (Benson & Gottman, 1975). Rejected children, compared to popular or moderately popular children, play in smaller groups than do popular children. Also, they play with children who are younger and/or unpopular (Ladd, 1983).

Thus there seems to be a strong within-group reciprocity in play, based on popularity. If this is truly the case, then unpopular children's attempts to interact with more competent peers may well be frustrated unless perceptive adults notice such problems and try to help children overcome them.

For example, Joan Sprigle, in the Learning to Learn early intervention program in Florida, taught specific concepts, such as color or sound discrimination, to small groups of three children in a setting separate from the classroom. The children were carefully chosen so that two of the three would be good social role models for the third. The goal of these small tutorial groups was to enhance positive social interactions among preschool peers as much as it was to increase cognitive competence (Van de Riet & Resnick, 1973).

Sex of child

Research conducted in homes and early childhood programs reveals marked differences in the way young children are responded to as a function of the sex of the child (Honig, 1983). Does popularity vary with sex of the child? McCandless and Marshall (1957) studied sex differences in social participation and acceptance among preschoolers. Popular girls were more likely than popular boys to interact with peers. By contrast, gender had no effect on the popularity of preschool children when they were perceived as physically attractive by adult raters in a study by Chung (1978).

Same sex playmate preference has been reported as early as 20 months of age (Rubenstein, 1984). In general, during the preschool years, perceived similarity—of sex of children, interests, and linguistic background—seems to become a major determinant of peer interactions and popularity preference. Rubenstein cautions that

> It may require different strategies and different skills to initiate a relationship with a peer who is predisposed to respond positively because of similarities . . . than with a peer who is disposed to react less favorably because of differences (p. 134).

Thus, teachers have to become sensitive observers of different characteristics that may interfere with full peer group acceptance. In classrooms with mixed ages, ethnicity, or language skills, and in classrooms with mainstreamed children, teachers will need to be alert to children's perceptions and expectations of differences that may lead to certain children being preferred and unpreferred playmates. Teachers can assume central roles in helping children see the potential each child has to be a positive play partner.

Ways to improve children's social skills

- Help families focus on positive discipline techniques.
- Encourage children to participate in small groups at first.
- Use puppets, reverse role playing, or books to show children other interaction styles.
- Ensure peer interactions for very young children.
- Enhance children's self-esteem, provide clear rules with reasons, and model warm, nurturant attentiveness.
- Make prosocial development an integral part of the curriculum.

Popular children interact primarily with other popular children.

Behavioral differences

How do popular children differ from rejected and neglected children in behavioral interactions with peers? Rejected children engage in more verbal and physical aggression. Their attempts to engage in social interaction are rebuffed more often than those of popular children (Dodge, Coie, & Brakke, 1982; Moore, 1967). Rejected children often wander; they engage in unoccupied and hovering behaviors. Moreover, unpopular children disagree more with peers and are less likely to provide a good reason for their disagreement. They are more likely to be ignored by groups they enter and more likely to call attention to themselves than popular children (Putallaz & Gottman, 1981).

Lastly, popular children seem to give and receive more positive reinforcements than unpopular children. Hartup, Glazer, and Charlesworth (1967) observed 32 children in two nursery classes, initially over a 5-week period and then a second time 20 weeks later. A picture sociometric interview was conducted with each child following the second observations. Children received more positive reinforcements from liked than from disliked peers. Giving positive reinforcement to a peer was correlated with social acceptance, .70 and .67 respectively, in the two preschool classrooms observed. Giving negative reinforcement correlated with social rejection .80 in the first classroom.

Thus, if preschoolers are annoying or assaultive, they are far more likely to be unpopular. Hartup, Glazer, and Charlesworth note that "the frequency with which the children dispensed positive reinforcement to peers and the degree of acceptance by the peer group were relatively stable over the period of five months" (p. 102).

Children's giving negative reinforcement and rejection scores were not stable over time. This is encouraging news. Perhaps teachers actively try to change poor peer relationships, and this may account for the lack of stability. Happily, positive peer reinforcement was far more frequent than negative peer reinforcement in the classrooms.

A French ethologist, Montagner, has observed peer social behaviors of children aged 6 months to 6 years for about 15 years. He notes that as early as the second year of life, some children regularly use more aggressive gestures than gestures that could be classified as pacifying or attaching. These tiny gestures seem to spell the difference between success and failure in the peer group or between unpopularity and friendship formation.

The secret of success with peers, according to Montagner (Pines, 1983) is to use many gestures from the pacifying or attaching category. Examples are: clapping one's hands, offering a toy, a tilt of the head combined with a smile, and a

Janet Worne

Children who have friends are more verbal and more likely to take turns submitting and directing during interactions. They are more likely to engage in fantasy play.

problems forming and maintaining interpersonal relationships. The interactions of children who do and do not have friends are quite different.

Children who have friends are more verbal and more likely to take turns submitting and directing during interactions. They are more likely to engage in fantasy play. Children who do not have friends tend to watch the activities of children with friends, and fight with children who do not have friends (Roopnarine & Field, 1984). It seems that findings for unpopular children and for children without friends are quite similar. But it is uncertain whether friendship formation and popularity in the peer group can be considered equivalent.

Parenting practices and popularity

Parental childrearing practices have been related to young children's popularity within peer groups. Fathers of popular boys evaluate their sons' behaviors more positively. These fathers provide more positive reinforcement for their sons, discourage aggressive behaviors, and use very little punishment or deprivation of privileges (Winder & Rau, 1962).

Likewise, warm and positive relationships have been found between popular children and their parents (Elkins, 1958), and affection and the use of induction (reasoning) as a discipline technique may also contribute to positive perceptions of the child by peers (Hoffman, 1973, 1975).

Using a picture sociometric choice technique, Peery, Jensen, and Adams (1984) contacted the parents of 43 middle class preschool children identified as either 1) popular—with high social impact and positive social preference, 2) amiable—low social impact and positive social preference, 3) isolated—low social impact and negative social preference, and 4) rejected—high social impact and negative social preference for the child by peers.

The PARI (Parent Attitude Research Instrument, Schaefer & Bell, 1958) was sent home to the parents of each child. PARI questionnaires were obtained from 39 parents. Fathers of 6 of the 14 rejected preschoolers did not return the questionnaires despite repeated follow-up request.

Analyses of the PARI responses received revealed that rejected and isolate preschool children were more likely than popular or amiable children to have mothers who had poor self-concepts about their mothering role and used praise infrequently when their children were behaving nicely. They also failed to promote their children's independence. The fathers of isolated and rejected preschool children, in contrast to fathers of popular and amiable children, reported very definite behavioral expectations for their children, yet had weak interactions with the children, disliked the intrusiveness of young children, and viewed childrearing as a mother's duty and responsibility.

Subsequently, Roopnarine and Adams (1985) have shown that unpopular children were more compliant to authoritarian, imperative teaching strategies of their parents, but more likely to ignore the suggestions of their parents compared to popular children.

friendly extended hand. Those children who become leaders of peers engage in these attractive gestures more often. The most popular children, however, also participate in many competitions for attractive toys or for play spaces. On the other hand, children who mix signals, such as combining a threatening or aggressive gesture with a friendly one, are treated as aggressive; they are highly unpopular with peers. Furthermore, children who engage in a lot of self-stimulation tend to be isolates in the classroom.

In sum, then, unpopular children seem to engage in behaviors that appear less conducive to meaningful social interaction. Instead, they behave in ways that repel other children. Their aggressive displays increase the likelihood that children who are more socially competent will exclude them in play. Children who are unpopular may be in that position both because of their own behaviors and additionally because of rejection or exclusion by peers.

Individual friendship formation

Because popularity and friendship formation share common attributes, unpopular children sometimes have more

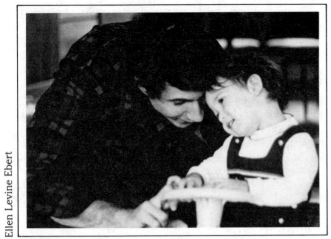

Children who are more apt to be popular among peers have parents who are warm and supportive. Parents who use authoritarian parenting styles often have children who are relatively distrustful, withdrawn, discontent, and less popular with peers.

Patterns of attachment relationships during infancy have also been shown to be related to peer relationships in preschool. Sroufe (1983) observed the peer interactions of 47- to 57-month-old preschoolers in two classrooms. As infants, the children had been classified, according to the Ainsworth Strange Situation method, as either securely, avoidantly, or ambivalently attached to their mothers. The two latter groups were insecurely attached as babies.

In the preschool, teachers were blind to the initial attachment classifications of the children. Yet, teacher rankings of social competence favored the secure children. The teachers ranked the secure children significantly higher in number of friends. Sociometric assessments of the preschoolers correlated highly (.56 and .85 for the two classrooms) with teacher rankings. The preschoolers who had been securely attached to their mothers in infancy held the majority of the high rank peer-nominated positions of popularity in both classes. Both insecurely attached groups of children showed a lack of empathic response to peer distress. Empathy was, however, characteristic of the peer responses of the secure children. Thus, peer popularity, capacity for positive empathic response to peers in distress, and early parental attachment with infants were all found to be interrelated.

Finally, Chung (1978) asked parents to describe their child-rearing practices and had peers rate their preschool classmates' popularity through a picture sociometric choice procedure. The parents of preschoolers who were chosen as popular showed more agreement in childrearing practices, more positive affection for their children, and more encouragement of child autonomy than did the parents of unpopular preschoolers.

These researches suggest that children who are more apt to be popular among peers have parents who are warm and supportive. Those who are unpopular have parents who have more negative childrearing attitudes and behaviors.

Baumrind (1977) has shown through home observation, interview, and teacher ratings, that children whose parents use authoritarian parenting styles have children who are relatively distrustful, withdrawn, discontent, and less popular with peers. Social orientation learned within the family seems to affect how children are viewed by peers in classroom settings. Children who have learned a judicious balance between rights and responsibilities are preferred by playmates. Children who have learned to balance assertiveness with cooperation are more popular.

Helping children develop social skills

Attempts to improve the social skills of unpopular children have been narrow in focus. Researchers have usually chosen peers as behavior change agents. For example, Koch (1935) chose seven very unsocial children and paired each unpopular child with a sociable nursery school peer for a special 30-minute session with toys daily for 20 days. Increased sociability of the isolate child was reported.

In similar work, Furman, Rahe, and Hartup (1979) chose 24 isolate preschoolers (48 to 68 months of age) from seven child care centers. Then they provided one of three conditions to the isolate children: 1) time together with two peers of the same chronological age, 2) time together with two much younger (12 to 20 months younger) sociable children, or 3) no treatment. The classroom teachers were neither informed of the labeling of the isolate children nor did they know the purpose of the special sessions, since children were often taken out of the room for special experiences.

Isolates who were paired with younger playmates gained more than those assigned to same-age children (much as Suomi and Harlow found in their work with socially isolate young monkeys!). Of the 8 children in group two, 7 improved their peer interaction rate by 50% or more. Those exposed to same-age peer interaction did not differ from the control children in social interaction scores. The play sessions with younger preschoolers evidently provided the isolates with positive social experiences and opportunities for assertive interactions—a rarity for them.

Parents, teachers, and peers can all assist children to develop social skills in the peer group. Adults can make a special effort to notice when children are being rejected by peers, scapegoated, assaultive and then disliked and rejected by peers, or isolated and uninvolved in play groups. Based on observations of children's social skills, parents and teachers can then take several steps to help children develop more appropriate behaviors.

● Include parents in program efforts to help improve unpopular children's social skills. Work with families can focus on positive discipline techniques and nonpunitive ways to encourage cooperation (Honig, 1985a; 1985b; 1985c).

● When teachers identify young children who are socially withdrawn, encourage them at first to participate more comfortably in small groups of two or three children rather than trying to force participation in larger groups.

● Puppetry, reverse role playing, and books about lonely or shy animals and children who learn to make friends can be used to enhance the social repertoire of unpopular children.

- Encourage parents of young children who are not exposed to peer groups to make special efforts to find a play group. Judicious doses of peer interactions can assure that toddlers have opportunities to engage in positive social experiences with peers and toys and to form early friendships.

- Parents, center staff, and family day care providers can sharpen their interaction skills and modes of functioning with children. Adults should strive to enhance young children's self-esteem, provide clear rules with reasons, and model warm, nurturant attentiveness.

- Emphasize prosocial development as an integral part of the curriculum, beginning in infancy. In addition to demonstrating positive behaviors, encourage and appreciate budding signs of interpersonal understanding, empathic responsiveness, and other indicators of social competence in young children (Honig, 1982).

References

Asher, S., Singleton, L., Tinsley, B., & Hymel, S. (1978). A reliable sociometric measure of preschool children. *Developmental Psychology, 15,* 443–444.

Baumrind, S. (1977). Some thoughts about childrearing. In S. Cohen & T. Comiskey (Eds.), *Child Development: Contemporary Perspectives.* Itasca, IL: F. E. Peacock.

Benson, G., & Gottman, J. (1975). *Children's popularity and peer social interaction.* Unpublished manuscript, Indiana University.

Chung, M. J. (1978). *A study of popularity, physical attractiveness, social behavior and child rearing practices in preschool children.* Dissertation, Syracuse University.

Coie, J. D., Dodge, K. A., & Coppotelli, H. (1982). Dimensions and the types of social status: A cross-age perspective. *Developmental Psychology, 18,* 557–570.

Cowen, E. L., Pederson, A., Babigian, H., Izzo, L. D., & Trost, M. A. (1973). Long-term follow-up of early detected vulnerable children. *Journal of Consulting and Clinical Psychology, 41,* 438–446.

Dodge, K. A., Coie, J. D., & Brakke, N. P. (1982). Behavior patterns of socially rejected and neglected preadolescents: The role of social approach and aggression. *Journal of Abnormal Child Psychology, 10,* 389–410.

Elkins, D. (1958). Some factors related to the choice status of ninety eighth-grade children in a school society. [Monograph]. *Genetic Psychology, 58,* 207–272.

Furman, W., Rahe, D., & Hartup, W. (1979). Rehabilitation of socially withdrawn preschool children through mixed-age and same-age socialization. *Child Development, 50,* 915–922.

Harlow, H. F. (1969). Age-mate or peer affectional system. In D. S. Lehrman, R. A. Hinde, & E. Shaw (Eds.), *Advances in the Study of Behavior* (Vol. 2). New York: Wiley.

Hartup, W. W. (1983). Peer relationships. In E. M. Hetherington (Ed.), *Carmichael's Manual of Child Psychology.* New York: Wiley.

Hartup, W. W., Glazer, J. A., & Charlesworth, R. (1967). Peer reinforcement and sociometric status. *Child Development, 38,* 1017–1024.

Hoffman, M. L. (1973). Altruistic behavior and the parent-child relationship. *Journal of Personality & Social Psychology, 31,* 937–943.

Hoffman, M. L. (1975). Developmental synthesis of affect and cognition and its implications for altruistic motivation. *Developmental Psychology, 11,* 607–622.

Honig, A. S. (1982, July). Research in review: Prosocial development in children. *Young Children, 37* (5), 51–62.

Honig, A. S. (1983, September). Research in review: Sex role socialization in early childhood. *Young Children, 38* (6), 57–70.

Honig, A. S. (1985a, January). Research in review: Compliance, control, and discipline (Part I). *Young Children, 40* (2), 50–58.

Honig, A. S. (1985b, March). Research in review: Compliance, control, and discipline (Part II). *Young Children, 40* (3), 47–52.

Honig, A. S. (1985c). *Love and Learn: Discipline for Young Children.* Washington, DC: National Association for the Education of Young Children.

Koch, H. (1935). The modification of unsocialness in preschool children. *Psychological Bulletin, 32,* 700–701.

Ladd, G. (1983). Social networks of popular, average, and rejected children in school settings. *Merrill-Palmer Quarterly, 29,* 283–307.

McCandless, B. R., & Marshall, R. (1957). A picture sociometric technique for preschool children and its relation to teacher judgment of friendship. *Child Development, 28* (2), 139–147.

Moore, S. G. (1967). Correlates of peer acceptance in nursery school children. In W. W. Hartup & N. L. Smothergill (Eds.), *The Young Child.* Washington, DC: National Association for the Education of Young Children.

Peery, J. C. (1979). Popular, amiable, isolated, rejected: A reconceptualization of sociometric status in preschool children. *Child Development, 50,* 1231–1234.

Peery, D., Jensen, L., Adams, G. (1984). *Relationships between parent's attitudes regarding child rearing and the sociometric status of their preschool children.* Unpublished manuscript, Brigham Young University, Salt Lake City.

Pines, M. (1984). Children's winning ways. *Psychology Today, 18,* 58–65.

Putallaz, M., & Gottman, J. (1981). An interactional model for children's entry into peer groups. *Child Development, 52,* 986–994.

Roff, M., Sell, S. B., & Golden, M. (1972). *Social adjustment and personality development in children.* Minneapolis: University of Minnesota Press.

Roopnarine, J., & Field, T. (1984). Play interactions of friends and acquaintances in nursery school. In T. Field, J. Roopnarine, and M. Segal (Eds.), *Friendships in normal and handicapped children.* Norwood, NJ: Ablex.

Roopnarine, J., & Adams, G. (1985). *The interactional teaching patterns between mothers and fathers and their popular, moderately popular, or unpopular preschool children.* Unpublished manuscript, Syracuse University.

Rubenstein, J. (1984). Friendship development in normal children: A commentary. In T. Field, J. Roopnarine, & M. Segal (Eds.), *Friendships in normal and handicapped children.* Norwood, NJ: Ablex.

Schaefer, E., & Bell, R. Q. (1958). Development of a parental attitude research instrument. *Child Development, 29,* 339–361.

Sroufe, L. A. (1983). Individual patterns of adaptation from infancy to preschool. In M. Perlmutter (Ed.), *Proceedings of Minnesota Symposium on child psychology.* Hillsdale, NJ: Erlbaum.

Stengel, E. (1971). *Suicide and attempted suicide.* Middlesex: Penguin.

Suomi, S. J., & Harlow, H. F. (1975). The role and reason of peer relationships in rhesus monkeys. In M. Lewis & L. Rosenblum (Eds.), *Friendship and peer relations.* New York: Wiley.

Ullman, C. (1957). Teachers, peers and tests as predictors of adjustment. *Journal of Educational Psychology, 48,* 257–267.

Van de Riet, V., & Resnick, M. B. (1973). *Learning to learn: An effective model for early childhood education.* Gainesville, FL: University of Florida Press.

Winder, C. L., & Rau, L. (1962). Parental attitudes associated with social deviance in preadolescent boys. *Journal of Abnormal & Social Psychology, 64,* 418–424.

Dealing with Difficult Young Children

Strategies for Teachers and Parents

Anne K. Soderman

Young children's personality development remains one of the most intriguing and widely debated issues for both parents and teachers. This article will review what we know about individual temperament and recommend ways to understand and build upon children's strengths.

Individual temperament

Generations of parents and child development professionals have recognized that children exhibit individual personality traits. As early as 1924, Gesell wrote that

> The personality of the child grows like an organic structure.... Original nature ... provides certain tendencies or materials, but the final patterns of personality are the result of education and experience. (p. 3)

Much of the research on temperament has been conducted only in the past two decades. Thomas, Chess, and Birch (1968) collected parent interviews and observed 136 children in natural settings from infancy to preadoles-cence. They identified nine characteristics of temperament that they clustered into three basic types.

- *Easy* children were moderately low in intensity, adaptable, approachable, predictable with body functions, and positive in mood (40 percent of the sample).
- *Difficult* children were often negative in mood, adapted slowly to change, had unpredictable biological functions, and frequently exhibited intense reactions (10 percent of the sample).
- *Slow-to-warm-up* children took longer to adapt than the easy children and demonstrated low activity and intensity levels (15 percent of the sample).

Children who did not appear to fit in any of these categories comprised the remaining 35 percent of the group.

A flurry of responses followed, many of which either challenged or extended this pioneering work. For example, Bates (1980) criticized the research methodology of asking parents to assess their own children. He held that difficult temperament in children is an adult social perception with only a "modest empirical foundation."

Early infant behaviors (such as susceptibility to emotional stimulation; strength and speed of response; and quality, fluctuation, and intensity of mood) were examined closely for indications that they might predict later personality traits (Goldsmith and Gottesman 1981; Als 1981; Dunn and Kendrick 1980). Plomin (1982) praised the Thomas, Chess, and Birch study because it balanced the tendency throughout the 1950s and 1960s to blame children's behavioral problems on their mothers.

In a rebuttal supporting the validity of their earlier findings, Thomas, Chess, and Korn (1982) argued that their within-the-child definition of difficult temperament was not only valid but also practical in looking at later behav-

***Anne K. Soderman**, Ph.D., is Assistant Professor in the Department of Family and Child Ecology, Michigan State University, East Lansing, Michigan.*

Peter Waugh

Young children's behaviors are continually being modified or intensified depending on adults' responses.

ioral difficulty in children. They noted that

the concept of difficult temperament as a within-the-infant characteristic in no way implies a fixed immutable trait ... but can be modified or altered by post-natal genetic or maturational influences, situational context, or the effect of the child-environmental interactional process. (p. 15)

Meanwhile, Brazelton (1978) observed that an infant's personality may be a determining factor in whether adults react to the child positively or negatively. In an effort to identify infants likely to encounter difficulties in relationships because of their temperament, Brazelton and his colleagues created the Neonatal Behavioral Assessment Scale (NBAS) (1973). This scale elicits and measures whether infants can calm themselves, whether they can shut out disturbing stimuli, their need for stimulation, their level of sociability, and the organization and predictability of their behavior. Although the instrument does not necessarily predict later development, it does offer reliable information about new-

born behavior that may cause potential bonding problems (Gander and Gardiner 1981).

Children's temperament affects how others react to them and influences their personality development.

Another tool for assessing temperaments in infants and preschool children is a questionnaire designed by Carey and McDevitt (1978). It is based on the nine characteristics identified by Thomas and Chess (1977). According to Powell (1981), principal uses of the questionnaire are to serve as a basis for a general discussion of a child's temperament so that the child's needs can be met better, and to help with clinical

problems "of which infant temperament can be a part" (p. 111).

In summary, we know that

• very early in life infants have identifiable personalities

• some traits of children's personalities produce behaviors that are perceived by others as ranging from easy to difficult

• young children's behaviors are continually being modified or intensified depending upon adults' responses

Influences on behavior

The child's own traits and behaviors, environmental influences, and adults' perceptions and reactions all affect long term personality development. Thomas, Chess, and Korn (1982) remind us that

To debate whether a child's characteristics or parental perceptions or other environmental influences are more important is antithetical to the view which sees them *all* as all-important in a constantly evolving sequence of interaction and mutual influence. (p. 15)

When children are difficult, less confident adults will doubt themselves, feel guilty, and be anxious about the child's future and their relationship. Unless the difficult behaviors (or perceptions of difficult behaviors) can be satisfactorily modified, a sense of helplessness often begins to influence all interactions with the child. Dreams of being a competent parent or teacher may yield to the harsh reality that the child is unhappy, out of control, and not developing to full potential. Initial pride over the child's assertiveness may turn to disapproval and even rejection. Burned out adults are often the result. Such adult responses, in turn, have a marked effect on whether additional stress will be put upon the child.

Does labeling children *difficult* have a harmful effect in itself? Such identification may damage children if parents and teachers do not approach the child's behavior in a positive way that will build on the child's strengths (Rothbart 1981).

While this concern about the effect of labeling is a valid issue, there is no question that some children *are* more pleasant and sociable than others. Elkind (1981) has pointed out that chil-

Unless we know what to expect of children, it is easy to label a child difficult when in reality the child is exhibiting normal behaviors.

dren are members of a hurried society. Children who cannot adapt to tight schedules, rigorous learning programs, and a fast pace, or who become easily frustrated when stressed, will most likely have difficulty functioning well.

Knowing what to look for in children's behavior, and how to interpret it, can help us find ways to help children cope.

Temperamental characteristics

Regardless of the cause of the behavioral difficulty, the practical implications for difficult children appear very early. Children are active agents in their own socialization, and their temperament affects how others react to them and influences their further personality development. Several temperamental characteristics, and adult perceptions or misperceptions of them, all influence children's personality. Important questions to keep in mind when considering each of these traits are:

• Is the behavior developmentally appropriate for the child's age? Does the behavior exceed what might reasonably be expected when the child's experiences are taken into account?

• Does the child consistently exhibit one or more of these difficult behaviors?

• How much does the adult's behavior style contrast with that of the child?

Unless we know what to expect of children at each age, it is easy to label a child difficult when in reality the child is exhibiting normal behaviors which may vary from day to day and are related to the child's experiences. Likewise, if the adult's personality or energy level is very different from the child's, it is easy to misperceive the meaning of the child's behaviors. The behaviors described here represent extremes along a continuum. Readers are cautioned to carefully consider each of the questions above when reviewing these possible indicators of behavioral difficulty.

Activity level

This trait refers to the proportion of a child's motor activity and inactivity. Are quiet and active behaviors balanced? A difficult child may be viewed as excessively active, always on the go, unable to sit still, or always touching something. At the other extreme, a child may be seen as too passive, with no spirit or motivation, who just sits. Young children are generally full of healthy energy!

Rhythmicity

The child's internal biological time-clock is the key to rhythmicity. Are sleep, hunger, eating, and elimination patterns predictable or unpredictable? Does a toddler or preschool child have difficulty settling down easily for scheduled rest or sleep, only to fall asleep at other times? Children who have a healthy sense of independence can often frustrate adults who are eager to maintain a tight schedule!

Approach/withdrawal

A child's *initial* responses to new objects, people, or foods may indicate that the child is approachable or withdrawn. Children who are too approachable may seem to have no fear or may be willing to accept any suggestion regardless of its appropriateness. Repeated crying, clinging, or avoiding almost all new experiences may indicate that the child is too withdrawn.

This trait affects children's decision making patterns; their ability to prevent overstimulation; and their need to escape uncomfortable, difficult, or unpleasant situations. It can be particularly problematic for adults and children who function differently from each other, or who have a contrasting base of experiences.

Adults should give children every reasonable chance to assess the situation, figure out what should be done, and then experience the consequences of their decisions.

Adaptability

Adaptability is an indication that the child responds positively to change. Some children will find it difficult to accept a change in routine, a new sibling, or other important events, even when given time to adjust. Others may hold grudges, or be considered stubborn or resistant. Refusal to care for themselves, or to advance in skill level of an activity, may indicate that the child has a great deal of difficulty adapting. Early school adjustment may be particularly problematic.

Intensity of reaction

Energy level and response to stimuli are related to impulse control. Situations which call for an emotional response are especially indicative of the child's ability to cope. Some children may act without thinking, react quickly with anger, grieve too long after a loss, or become too excited when happy. These children are most often described as aggressive. At the other extreme are children who have a bland exterior—they hide their emotions or exhibit little intensity in emotional situations.

Responsiveness threshold

The level of stimulation necessary to evoke a response may also indicate difficult behaviors. Some children are extremely sensitive to or overstimulated by noise, touch, smell, temperature, light, color, or similar factors, while others will respond slowly or not at all to the same stimuli. Experience can play a large part in a child's responsiveness threshold. A child living on a busy city street may not hear a blaring siren, while such a sound in more isolated areas may rightly cause a frightened reaction.

Mood

This trait deals with a balance between behaviors that are joyful, friendly, and satisfied with those that are not positive. Some children will express a range of moods, while others will react similarly to nearly every situation. They may complain, whine, cry frequently, or fuss. Bad days are frequent, and adults may go out of their way to avoid conflict. Parents and teachers may feel guilty because the child rarely looks happy or joyful.

Attention span and resistance

How much time does the child spend pursuing an activity, especially one with obstacles? Can the child return to the activity if interrupted? Some children seem scattered, cannot attend to any task, and move rapidly without any true involvement. Others may be obsessed with one specific activity, such as completing puzzles or playing with a single toy. Age of the child and appropriateness of the activities are important factors here.

Distractibility

Closely related to attention span and resistance is the child's vulnerability to interference when pursuing any activity. Some children may become so completely absorbed that they forget to use the bathroom, or may resist distraction even from a prohibited activity. Others will be unable to shut out typical distractions such as noise. In infancy and toddlerhood distractibility may be an asset when children need to be distracted! In older children, however, distractibility may interfere with the child's ability to attend to responsibilities.

Strategies for parents and teachers

You probably recognize some of these difficult behaviors in nearly every child you know! Many of these behaviors can be difficult for an adult to deal with at the moment, but may not indicate that the child has any long term personality problem. A pattern of these behaviors may indicate more serious difficulties, however, and consultation with a specialist is recommended for those children. The recommendations here will focus on ways adults can help children cope with occasional difficulties.

The way in which parents and teachers deal with young children's difficult behavior can have a lasting effect on the children's emerging personality. May (1981) discusses the fragile balance between power and powerlessness in altering interpersonal relationships. Adults can intensify children's difficulties and increase stress if they respond inappropriately. Examples of inappropriate responses would be for the adult to

- ignore difficult behaviors
- coerce children to comply with adult expectations
- shame or compare children to others
- label children with derogatory words
- inflict verbal or physical punishment

Positive change requires that the adult keep children's self-esteem intact while helping them become knowledgeably involved in the process of modifying their own behavior. Adults can help children cope with their own behaviors by using a variety of strategies.

Respect the child

Individual differences exist as a result of both heredity and the environment. Children's difficult behaviors do not necessarily indicate that the child is intentionally being difficult, is stubborn, or that the adult is inadequate. Instead, the adult can respect the child by closely assessing the situation and working out a plan to help the child cope.

Evaluate behavior objectively

Our own temperamental style and personality play a critical role when we evaluate any child's positive or negative qualities. How do our behavior and expectations affect the child? As adults, we may need to change our behaviors before we can effectively work with a difficult child.

Structure the environment

A close look at the environment may reveal the causes of some difficult behaviors. Are children asked to sit quietly for longer periods than they can legitimately manage? Are noise levels too high or is lighting too harsh? Changing the pace of the day to balance vigorous and calm times, providing a place for quiet activities, or rearranging traffic patterns, for example, may establish a climate for more appropriate behaviors.

Set effective limits

Unless children know the limits, and those limits are reasonable, difficult behaviors are likely to follow. Review the rules you have set to make sure they are appropriate, and then discuss them with the children. Natural and logical consequences should result when children do not observe the limits, such as loss of the privilege to use an item.

© 1986 Michael Siluk

Our reactions to difficult behavior can sow feelings of inferiority and insecurity, or competence and strong self-esteem.

Often a subtle cue from the adult is all that is needed to remind children before their behavior becomes unacceptable.

Use positive interactions

Once we understand how the child interacts with others, we can help children modify their behaviors. With very young children who may be egocentric, for example, adults can state how the child's behavior affects the feelings of others. Rather than expecting an immediate change, you may want to identify steps for making progress.

Be patient

Helping children to modify their behavior, or modifying your own, is a long range goal. During the process, there must be opportunity to correct behaviors in a nonthreatening atmosphere. Instead of redirecting children too quickly or making decisions for them, adults should give children every reasonable chance to assess the situation, figure out what should be done, and then experience the consequences of their decisions.

Work with colleagues and parents

Most teachers and parents are doing the best job they know how to do. If, however, we see negative interaction styles between other adults and a difficult child, we need to approach those adults as partners in trying to help the child cope more effectively. We can note areas of interaction that are difficult for us and stress the normal variations that may be found in young children. It is important for us to understand that a child's behavior, while it may be irritating, can be quite innocent. Our reactions to that behavior, therefore, can sow feelings of inferiority and insecurity or, on the other hand,

competence and strong self-esteem.

Once we go beyond feeling guilty or trying to blame someone about a child's behavior, we can work more cooperatively with others.

Conclusions

Many of the recommendations here are common sense techniques that apply to all human relationships—it is the consistent and intentional use of these strategies that make a difference in children's personality development. Our attitudes toward children, adults, and ourselves play a key role in ensuring successful collaborative efforts to help children become more effective in their relationships.

Bibliography

Als, H. "Assessing Infant Individuality." In *Infants at Risk: Assessment and Intervention,* eds. C. C. Brown and T. B. Brazelton. Boston: Johnson & Johnson, 1981.

Bates, J. E. "The Concept of Difficult Temperament." *Merrill-Palmer Quarterly* 26, no. 4 (October 1980): 299–319.

Brazelton, T. B. "Introduction," In *Organization and Stability of Newborn Behavior: A Commentary on the Brazelton Neonatal Behavior Assessment Scale,* ed. A. Sameroff. *Monographs of the Society for Research in Child Development* 43, no. 5–6 (1978): 1–13.

Buss, A. H. and Plomin, R. A. *A Temperamental Theory of Personality.* New York: Wiley, 1975.

Carey, W. B. and McDevitt, S. C. "Revision of the Infants' Temperament Questionnaire," *Pediatrics* 61, no. 5 (May 1978): 735–739.

Dunn, J. and Kendrick, C. "Studying Temperament and Parent-Child Interaction: Comparison of Interview and Direct Observation." *Developmental Medicine and Child Neurology* 22, no. 4 (August 1980): 484–496.

Escalona, S. K. *The Roots of Individuality: Normal Patterns of Development in Infancy.* Chicago: Aldine, 1958.

Elkind, D. *The Hurried Child.* Reading, Mass.: Addison-Wesley, 1981.

Freedman, D. G. "Infancy, Biology, and Culture," In *Developmental Psychobiology: The Significance of Infancy,* ed. L. P. Lipsitt. Hillsdale, N. J.: Erlbaum, 1976.

Gander, M. J. and Gardiner, H. W. *Child and Adolescent Development.* Boston: Little, Brown, 1981.

Gardner, H. G. *Developmental Psychology.* Boston: Little, Brown, 1981.

Gesell, A. "The Development of Personality: Molding Your Child's Character." *The Delineator* (April 1924).

Goldsmith, H. H. and Gottesman, I. I. "Origins of Variation in Behavioral Style: A Longitudinal Study of Temperament in Twins." *Child Development* 52, no. 1 (March 1981): 91–103.

May, R. *Power and Innocence: A Search for the Sources of Violence.* New York: Dell, 1981.

McDevitt, S. C. and Carey, W. B. "The Measurements of Temperaments in 3–7 Year-Old Children." *Journal of Child Psychology and Psychiatry* 19, no. 3 (July 1978): 245–253.

Plomin, R. "The Difficult Concept of Temperament: A Response to Thomas, Chess, and Korn." *Merrill-Palmer Quarterly* 28, no. 1 (January 1982): 25–33.

Powell, M. *Assessment and Management of Developmental Changes and Problems in Children.* St. Louis: Mosby, 1981.

Rothbart, M. K. "Measurement of Temperament in Infancy." *Child Development* 52, no. 2 (June 1981): 569–678.

Sheldon, W. H. *The Varieties of Human Physique.* New York: Harper & Row, 1940.

Sugarman, G. I. and Stone, M. N. *Your Hyperactive Child.* Chicago: Henry Regnery Co., 1974.

Thomas, A. and Chess, S. *Temperament and Development.* New York: New York University Press, 1968.

Thomas, A.; Chess, S.; and Birch, H. G. *Temperament and Behavior Disorders in Children.* New York: New York University Press, 1968.

Thomas, A.; Chess, S.; and Korn, S. J. "The Reality of Difficult Temperament." *Merrill-Palmer Quarterly* 28, no. 1 (January 1982): 1–20.

Torgersen, A. M. and Kringlen, E. "Genetic Aspects of Temperamental Differences in Infants." *Journal of American Academy of Child Psychiatry* 17, no. 3 (Summer 1978): 433–444.

Black Children: Their Roots, Culture, and Learning Styles

Research in Review

Janice Hale-Benson

The research we conduct and our resultant knowledge depends on the questions we ask, the methods we deem appropriate and fruitful, and the patterns of relationships and structures we are able to discover among the data. These empirical practices are heavily influenced by the assumptions, values, and the cultural filters of both the community of researchers and its individual members. It is important that we are reminded of these relationships as we seek to use and apply what we have learned. Janice Hale's position paper challenges much of social science research about Black children's development, and calls for research generated from a Black cultural perspective. Her discussion of cultural influences on children's development helps us to view existing research and its educational implications in a more critical manner. Her contribution to this column and to the profession rightly indicates where knowledge is inadequate and suggests feasible remedies.

J.H.S., Jr.

DuBois (1903) described the Black person in America as possessing two "warring souls." Black people are products of their Afro-American heritage and culture. However, they are also shaped by the demands of Anglo-American culture. Those who share the spirituality of the Black experience share it mentally and emotionally. Black people transform every cultural mode they interact with: language, music, religion, art, dance, problem solving, sports, writing, or any other areas of human expression.

The purpose of this article is to describe this spirituality or "soulfulness" and to demonstrate its relationship to the cognitive development of Black children, including the conflict that ensues when Black children are evaluated from an Anglo-centric framework.

Cultural style

Hilliard (1976) set forth some basic assumptions about human behavioral styles, or the framework from which people view the world. He reviewed several styles, and concluded that "every style is necessary, valuable and useful in human experience if society is to function fully" (p. 43). While style is evident in all areas of an individual's behavior, one can learn aspects of other styles. Hilliard also stated that strong relationships exist between style and socioeconomic level and between style and cultural or ethnic group membership. He found no evidence, however, of a relationship between basic intelligence and style.

Elements of Afro-American cultural style were also identified by Hilliard (1976). He stated that Afro-American people

- tend to view things in their entirety and not in isolated parts;
- seem to prefer inferential reasoning rather than deductive or inductive reasoning;
- tend to approximate space, number, and time instead of aiming for complete accuracy;
- appear to focus on people and their activities rather than objects. Many Black students have chosen careers in the helping professions even though these types of jobs are scarce and the curriculum is rigorous.
- have a keen sense of justice and quickly perceive injustice;
- tend to prefer novelty, personal freedom and distinctiveness, such as in music and styles of clothing; and
- in general tend not to be "word" dependent, but are proficient in nonverbal as well as verbal communication.

Akbar (1975) described the Afro-American child (see Figure 1).

Janice Hale-Benson, Ph.D., is Coordinator of Early Childhood Education Programs at Cleveland State University, Cleveland, Ohio.

This is one of a regular series of columns edited by Joseph H. Stevens, Ph.D., Professor, Department of Early Childhood Education, Georgia State University, Atlanta, Georgia.

Cohen (1971) delineated two styles of learning and of schools in terms of differences in methods for selecting and classifying information. Hilliard (1976) summarized the characteristics of the analytical and relational styles (see Figure 2).

Most schools require an analytical approach to learning (Cohen 1971). Children who function with a different cognitive style or who have not developed analytical skills will be poor achievers early in school and will do worse as they move to higher grade levels.

Not only does the school reward development of the analytic style of processing information, but the overall ideology and environment of the school reinforces behaviors associated with that style.

Aspects of analytic style can be found in the requirements that the pupil learn to sit increasingly long periods of time, to concentrate alone on impersonal learning stimuli, and to observe and value organized time-allotment schedules. (Cohen 1971, p. 829)

The differences between children who function with relational and analytic styles is so great that children whose cognitive organization is relational are unlikely to be rewarded with grades regardless of their native ability, the extent of their learning, or their experiences. In fact, they will probably be considered deviant and disruptive in the analytically oriented learning environment of the school (Cohen 1971).

Hilliard (1976) agreed that most schools support the analytic cognitive style, and contrasted these schools with those based on the relational cognitive style (Figure 3).

Origins of cognitive style

Cohen (1971) suggested that children develop cognitive styles based upon the socialization they receive in their families and friendships. Children who live in structured families with "formal" styles of group organization have been observed to function with the analytical cognitive style. Those children who live in more fluid or "shared-function" primary groups are more likely to exhibit the relational cognitive style.

Although that explanation has some merit, more work is needed to describe the socialization of Black children that leads to their distinctive cognitive styles.

Figure 1. The Afro-American Child

Is highly affective

Uses language requiring a wide use of many coined interjections (sometimes profanity)

Expresses herself or himself through considerable body language

Relies on words that depend upon context for meaning and that have little meaning in themselves

Prefers using expressions that have several connotations

Adopts a systematic use of nuances of intonation and body language such as eye movement and positioning

Prefers oral-aural modalities for learning communication

Is highly sensitive to others' nonverbal cues

Seeks to be people oriented

Is sociocentric

Uses internal cues for problem solving

Feels highly empathetic

Likes spontaneity

Adapts rapidly to novel stimuli

Carvis Bullock

Schools should support the natural energy level of Black children who need an active environment for successful learning.

Affective orientation

The cognitive styles of Black people seem to place a greater degree of emphasis upon affect than Anglo-Americans. Some scholars have suggested that the emotion-charged, people-oriented quality of Black expression is a part of the African heritage.

Knowledge in Western societies is largely derived from such propositions as "I think, therefore, I am." The non-Western heritage of Afro-Americans suggests that knowledge stems from the proposition that, "I feel, therefore I think, therefore, I am." (Dixon and Foster 1971, p. 18)

The uniqueness of Black culture can be explained in that it is a culture whose emphasis is on the nonverbal ... in Black culture, it is the experience that counts, not what is said. (Lester 1969, p. 87)

This does not mean that Black people do not think or conceptualize their experience symbolically. Intellectual analysis disconnected from feelings leads to incomplete knowledge of the world (Haskins and Butts 1973).

There are research studies (Gitter, Black, and Mostofsky 1972; Young 1970) that have found Black children to be more feeling oriented, people oriented, and more proficient at nonverbal communication than White children. It is important to determine the implications of these attributes for their cognitive development (Gitter, Black, and Mostofsky 1972).

Young (1970) suggested that White

Figure 2.   Analytical and Relational Cognitive Styles (compiled from Rosalee Cohen)

Analytical Style

Stimulus centered
Parts-specific
Finds non-obvious attributes
Abstracts common or generalizable principle of a stimulus
Notices formal properties of a stimulus that have relatively stable and long lasting meanings
Ignores the idiosyncratic
Extracts from embedded context
Names extracted properties and gives them meaning in themselves
Relationships tend to be linear
Relationships which are noticed tend to be static and descriptive other than functional or inferential
Relationships seldom involve process or motivation as a basis for relations
Perception of conceptual distance between observers and observed
An objective attitude—a belief that everything takes place "out there" in the stimulus
Stimulus viewed as formal, long lasting and relatively constant, therefore there is opportunity to study it in detail
Long attention span
Long concentration span
Greater perceptual vigilance
A reflective attitude and relatively sedentary nature
Language style is standard English of controlled elaboration
Language depends upon relatively long lasting and stable meanings of words
Language depends upon formal and stable rules of organization
Communications are intended to be understood in themselves, i.e., without dependence upon non-verbal cues or idiosyncratic context
"Parts of speech" can readily be seen in nonsense sentences
Analytic speech characterized by "hesitation phenomena," pauses for verbal planning by controlled vocal modulation and revision of sentence organization to convey specific meaning, since words have formal meanings
Sometimes view of self expressed as an aspect of roles such as function to be performed
View of self tends to be in terms of status-roles

Relational Style

Self-centered
Global
Fine descriptive characteristics
Identifies the unique
Ignores commonalities
Embedded for meaning
Relevant concepts must have special or personal relevance to observer
Meanings are unique depending upon immediate context
Generalizations and linear notions are generally unused and devalued
Parts of the stimulus and its non-obvious attributes are not given names and appear to have no meaning in themselves
Relationships tend to be functional and inferential
Since emphasis is placed on the unique and the specific, the global and the discrete, on notions of difference rather than on variation or common things, the search for mechanisms to form abstract generalizations is not stimulated
Responses tend to be affective
Perceived conceptual distance between the observer and the observed is narrow
The field is perceived as responding to the person
The field may have a life of its own
Personification of the inanimate
Distractable
Emotional
Over-involved in all activities
Easily angered by minor frustrations
Immediacy of response
Short attention span
Short concentration span
Gestalt learners
Descriptive abstraction for word selection
Words must be embedded in specific time bound context for meaning
Few synonyms in language
Language dependent upon unique context and upon many interactional characteristics of the communicants on time and place, on inflection, muscular movements and other non-verbal cues
Fluent spoken language
Strong colorful expressions
Wide range of meaningful vocal intonation and inflection
Condensed conditions sensitivity to hardly perceptible variations of mood and tone in other individuals and in their surroundings
Poor response to timed, scheduled, preplanned activities which interfere with immediacy of response
Tends to ignore structure
Self descriptions tend to point to essence
(Hilliard 1976, pp. 36–38)

---

children are object oriented and have numerous opportunities to manipulate objects and discover properties and relationships. Consequently, this society's educational system is very object oriented, and classrooms are filled with educational hardware and technology —books, listening stations, learning centers, televisions, programmed instruction, learning kits, and so forth.

In contrast, research with Black children has found them to be more people oriented. Most Black children grow up in large families where they have a great deal of human interaction. While traveling in Africa, I was interested in the kinds of dolls with which the children of Ghana play. One mother informed me that African children do not play with dolls, they play with their mother's babies!

This high degree of people orientation may account for the indifference with which some Black children regard books and other materials. It may also explain why some teachers complain that Black children will not work independently, but will cling to the teacher. I observed a classroom in which there were children who would work only when older children assisted them individually. This cultural trait should be acknowledged by providing more human interaction in the learning process.

Young (1970) provided evidence about childrearing practices that influence this people orientation.

Even though household composition varies widely in the Black community, each is almost certain to contain many different types of people of all ages to hold and play with the baby. In many cases, the physical closeness between infants and adults is reinforced by the fact that they are often observed to sleep with their parents or either parent alone. There is a kind of rhythm found between eating and napping with short periods of each activity found with frequent repetition. This rhythm is very different from the disciplined long span of attention cultivated in middle-class childrearing and expected in schools. (p. 276)

Because Black babies are held so much of the time, there is an immediate response to urination and bowel movements. Hence, from an early age, there is an association in the infant's mind

between these functions, and action from the mother. Consequently, when the mother seeks to toilet train the child (in the early and stringent manner that has been observed in the Black community), the child is accustomed to her direct involvement in this process. In contrast, the transition is more startling for middle-class American infants whose functions typically occur alone. The mother begins to interfere with bowel and bladder activity after many months of only cursory attention. There is greater continuity, then, in the behavior of Black mothers.

Young contrasted the highly personal interaction with the low object orientation found in Black families. She noticed that the few objects given to the babies were plastic toys that may have been picked up in the supermarket while shopping. Also, when babies reached to grasp an object or feel a surface, they were often redirected to feeling the holder's face or engaged in a game of rubbing faces as a substitute. This inhibition of exploration is possible because:

there are always eyes on the baby and idle hands to take away the forbidden objects and then distract the frustrated baby. The personal is thus often substituted for the impersonal. (p. 279–280)

This affective orientation may be a critical factor that is overlooked in traditional educational settings. Rapport with the teacher in educational settings and rapport with the examiner in testing settings seems to be strongly related to academic performance for Black students and not very critical for Whites. Zigler and his colleagues (Zigler and Butterfield 1968; Zigler, Abelson, and Seitz 1973) found that when a good rapport was established with an examiner during a standardized testing session, the Black children exhibited significantly superior test performance than when it was not. Such a difference was not found in the White middle-class sample.

Piestrup (1973) identified some factors which created good rapport in the teacher-Black student interaction, including warmth, verbal interplay during instruction, rhythmic style of speech and distinctive intonation in

speech patterns. When those factors were present, first-grade Black pupils showed increased reading proficiency.

Contrasts between Nigerian and Western cultures

It may be useful to examine some aspects of African culture to identify antecedents of the affective orientation of Afro-Americans. Esen (1973) analyzed the childrearing practices found in Nigeria and pointed out differences in United States and African cultures. He referred to the clusters of African attitudes and modes of response as the "care syndrome." Most Africans grow up in a small rural community and are imbued from early childhood with an empathetic concern for others. In contrast, children who grow up in Western societies often do not know their neighbors, do not care about the people in their communities, and do not offer help to those who are in even desperate need.

Esen suggested that the African modes of childrearing give rise to the development of humane attitudes and the care syndrome. Unlike Western childrearing, African socialization emphasizes the closeness of people. Physical and psychological closeness is reinforced by encouragement of body contact between people. Most African children are breast fed and are nursed for longer periods of time than in other societies. Before and after children learn to walk, they are held a great deal of the time by an older sibling. In most cases, infants sleep with their mothers until a new baby arrives. African children learn early in childhood to embrace relatives and friends in greeting them or thanking them for a special favor. Thus, the children grow up in a social network characterized by physical closeness, acceptance, and care. African children expect to receive affection and comfort and learn to give it when it is needed by others. By the time African children are 6 years old, they begin to take responsibility for providing care for a younger sibling. They carry the child on their backs, cradle the child on their laps, and learn to respond with body contact and carrying

Black children tend to be more feeling oriented, people oriented and more proficient at nonverbal communication than White children.

African languages seem to express caring and feeling to a greater extent than Western languages, too.

The extended family system also supports the care syndrome. Children see parents, grandparents, uncles, aunts, and cousins as a part of everyday life. The survival of the family depends upon how the members care about and provide for each other.

The nuclear family structure of father-mother-child in Western culture does not encourage this extended caring network. Grandparents usually must fend for themselves during their last years or be sent to retirement homes filled with strangers and impersonal relationships.

Brazelton, Young, and Bullowa (1971) supported Esen's thesis in a study in which they compared infants born to Zambian mothers and infants born to White American mothers. The health of the Zambian mothers was not optimal, so the Zambian infants weighed less, were shorter, and less healthy than the White infants.

The two groups of infants were examined on days 1, 5, and 10 after birth. On the day one examination, the Zambian infants scored significantly lower on following with eyes, motor activity, irritability, rapidity of buildup, and alertness. By day 10, however, the Zambian babies had surpassed the American infants in cuddliness, reactivity to stimulation, alertness, social interest, and consolability. The Zambian mothers' high-contact, loving environment for their babies provided more handling and feeding contact with their infants than the American mothers.

Nonverbal communication

Lower-class families have been reported to have a minimal amount of verbal exchange (Young 1970). She stated that this is because of the abundance of communication in other forms. She observed that people in these families look deeply into each other's eyes, not speaking, but seeming to communicate fully. Parents use this technique to impress a point on a child. Black people often avoid meeting the eyes of Whites, and this has been inter-

behavior to fit the needs of the child.

Esen believed that in Western society, objects come between children and their mothers. Babies are more prone to be bottle fed, pushed around in baby carriages, placed in playpens to play alone, and left in separate rooms in a different bed for sleeping. These gadgets come physically between babies and their mothers' bodies and interfere with the physical and psychological body warmth that is provided in Africa.

From the African viewpoint, Western children are socialized into a life of detachment and impersonalness. These early attitudes are also expressed later in the detached urban environment. People are seen as things in the distance or numbers in the computer. A basic aloofness toward people begins with the distance from the mother created by the feeding bottle and the baby carriage.

Esen suggested that the care syndrome is reflected in the use of language among African people. One key indicator is the system of elaborate and emotional greetings. Greetings always include inquiries about people who are important to the person, in contrast to Western greetings which discuss the weather and rarely inquire about human life and conditions.

The closest they ever seem to come to some concern for the individual is with "How are you?" And even that in American usage has become impersonalized into a mere "Hi." (p. 208)

Reducing Stress

Betty C. Ford

preted as a gesture of nonequality or nonattention. However, Young suggested that it may instead be a gesture of noncommunicativeness. The gaze of Whites is avoided to cut off that intense level of communication that Black people share with each other. Or, because it is a part of African heritage to respect elders, to look an authority figure directly in the eye is considered defiant and disrespectful.

Other forms of Black nonverbal communication are the mother's caressing of the baby, and children sitting in a circle rubbing bare feet. Young also noted what she called a "mutuality" in family relations exhibited in remarks that pass between mothers and children.

"I'm tired," the 3-year-old girl complains. "I'm tired too," her mother responds. "I want some ice cream," the 8-year-old says wistfully as the ice cream truck passes. "I want some too," is the mother's way of saying no. This echoing of words and tone of voice is a common speech pattern. One does not see mothers and children clash and contend. (p. 296)

Two other studies (Newmeyer 1970; Gitter, Black, and Mostofsky 1972) supported the hypothesis that Black culture develops proficiency in nonverbal communication. Newmeyer had a group of young Black and White males act out a number of emotions nonverbally. The Black children were better at enacting the emotions so that others perceived them correctly. Gitter, Black, and Mostofsky conducted a study with Black and White college students. Each student was shown still photographs of professional actors attempting to portray each of seven emotions. The Black students made significantly more correct judgments of the emotions portrayed.

Physical development

Morgan (1976) suggested that Black infants are superior in all aspects of development when the mothers have adequate prenatal care. He also pointed out that Black children are more active and have more physical energy than White children.

Black lower-income mothers have

Figure 3. The School

As it is in general (Analytical . . .)	As it could be (Relational . . .)
Rules	Freedom
Standardization	Variation
Conformity	Creativity
Memory for specific facts	Memory for essence
Regularity	Novelty
Rigid order	Flexibility
"Normality"	Uniqueness
Differences equal deficits	Sameness equals oppression
Preconceive	Improvise
Precision	Approximate
Logical	Psychological
Atomistic	Global
Egocentric	Sociocentric
Convergent	Divergent
Controlled	Expressive
Meanings are universal	Meanings are contextual
Direct	Indirect
Cognitive	Affective
Linear	Patterned
Mechanical	Humanistic
Unison	Individual in group
Hierarchical	Democratic
Isolation	Integration
Deductive	Inductive
Scheduled	Targets of opportunity
Thing focused	People focused
Constant	Evolving
Sign oriented	Meaning oriented
Duty	Loyalty

(Hilliard 1976, p. 41)

---

been criticized for not providing enough toys for their children (Morgan 1976). Compensatory education programs often purchased toys and playthings to distribute to these families. Morgan indicted such efforts.

Little thought was given to the fact that the tinker toy concept dictates that children are expected to sit in the crib or thereabouts and play quietly with their toys until their favorite TV program comes on. Without these toys, of course, mother and child touch, exchange various forms of communications and learn from one another. (p. 133)

Morgan (1976) maintained that the schools do not support the natural energy level of Black children who need an active environment for successful learning. He stated that this is particularly true of lower-income children whose parents emphasize survival skills rather than conformity, docility, and

quiet manners which are more typical of middle-class childrearing where upward mobility is sought.

Black children enter school for the first time with excitement and enthusiasm. However, the school crushes the freedom and creativity of children who cannot channel their energy until given permission to release it. Consequently Black children elicit more punishment and are labeled hyperactive more frequently because of their high motoric activity (Morgan 1976).

Morgan (1976) believed that Black mothers often ignore their children's motoric precocity and do not seek to extend it because development in that area might interfere with the child's ability to be integrated into the school system of White low motor expectations. This situation, he maintained, is detrimental to the natural learning styles of Black children.

The Black child in school

Morgan (1976) suggested that Black children need schools that are "uncrowded, open and airy with a great deal of natural light, [and] plenty of private space for teachers and learners" (p. 130). He also suggested that model classrooms should be established for research purposes where "special non-punitive environments are created as centers of learning for children who require more free space and movement than what schools normally allow" (p. 130).

Boykin (1978) suggested that the Black home environment provides an abundance of stimulation, intensity, and variation through high noise levels and large numbers of people. This has been analyzed as "overstimulation" and as creating "conceptual deafness" by some social scientists (Marans and Lourie 1967; Goldman and Sanders 1969; Wachs, Uzgiris, and Hunt 1971). However, Boykin hypothesized that this stimulating home environment produces greater psychological and behavioral verve in Black children than children from a White middle-class setting.

Black children may learn faster with techniques that incorporate body movement into the learning process. Guttentag (1972) and Guttentag and Ross (1972) found that Black preschool children possess a greater movement repertoire than both lower- and middle-class White preschoolers. They also showed that Black children learned simple verbal concepts easier when they utilized movement than when they were taught by a more traditional format. Massari and Meyer (1969) also found that the children who could inhibit movement had higher IQ scores.

Boykin (1977) found that varying the format in problem-solving tasks presented to Black and White children did not make a difference in the performance of the White children. However, the Black children performed markedly better with the varied format.

Thus, especially for Black children, schools are rather unstimulating and monotonous places to be (Silberman 1970; Holt 1964). Boykin suggested that the reason White children are more successful at academic tasks than Black children is that they have a greater tolerance for monotony. Perhaps Black children are not as successful in school because they are relatively more intolerant of monotonous, boring tasks, and the sterile unstimulating school environment.

The effectiveness of the use of rhythm in speech and verbal interplay by teachers of Black children may also connect culturally with Black children who interact rhythmically with their mothers at home. Young (1970) observed a "contest" style of speech between Black mothers and children in which they volley rhythmically and the child is encouraged to be assertive and to develop an individual style. Young suggested there is a distinctive manner by which Black mothers give directions for household tasks that approximates the call and response patterns found in Black music. (A mother's communication of directions for household tasks uses few words, and tasks for which she has to give instructions are broken down into small units with brief directions for each short task following completion of the previous one.)

Boykin (1978) concluded that affective stimulation and vivacity are necessary for the Black child to be motivated to achieve in an academic setting. He suggested that this is the reason why Black children become turned off by the sterile, boring school environment and seek other arenas for achievement and expression. He suggested that "perhaps we can facilitate the academic/task performance of the Black child if we increase the 'soulfulness' of the academic task setting."

Looking toward the future

What do we need to know about Black culture in order to design learning environments for Black children? We must conduct a wide-ranging examination of all aspects of at-home interaction that can provide descriptive information about the world view of the Black child. These areas especially deserve attention from Black researchers who wish to lead the work that defines their own culture and learning styles.

Movement. An examination of the amount and utilization of space that is occupied during children's play is needed. It would be interesting to determine the amount of time Black children spend in quiet activities as compared with active movement, because this would have implications for the length of time adults should require children to sit and concentrate on tasks.

Dance. How much reinforcement are Black children given as toddlers to dance in addition to encouragement to walk? Could early expressions of rhythm through dance have any influence upon the physical precocity of Black children? Does early proficiency in dance affect mathematical ability?

Music. What are the stages by which Black children respond to music? How prevalent is music in the Black environment? What is the preferred type of music? How often are songs sung to children and by children? What songs are sung? Why are Black children remarkably able to memorize popular songs? How can that ability be transferred to other types of learnings?

Home environment. Any description of environments in which Black children live, play, and develop should encompass artistic descriptors as well as indicators of affluence and educational enrichment. Note should be taken of color preferences in Black homes as well as any other distinctive features in decor, furniture styles, and arrangement. This information may be useful in designing learning environments for Black children. For example, Black children may learn most effectively or exhibit distinctive moods based upon the colors of the classroom walls.

Fashion. Black people have emphasized personal distinctiveness in their dress, and Black males in particular have influenced the fashion industry by setting trends such as wide-leg pants and bright colors in suits and shirts. A study of the types of clothing worn by Black children for various occasions might reveal the extent to which children are dressed according to the tastes of their parents, and at what age the children begin to express preferences and make choices. Those choices could be analyzed to determine how much influence the Black cultural milieu has on Black children's dress.

Folklore. An ethnographic study of expressive styles should record the folklore of Black children. Most studies of the language of Black children have been from a linguistic perspective, but it may also be useful to study the verbal skills of Black children. There are also stylistic dimensions of the oral tradition in Black culture as described by Silberman (1970): call and response, rhythmic patterns, spontaneity, and concreteness. Games, stories, chants, jump rope rhymes, curse words, and "playin' the dozens" could be analyzed to ascertain the psychological processes they reflect. It is also important to understand the way in which the culture of the Black community affects the fantasy of Black children.

Nutrition. A study of Black children's nutrition may be important in interpreting their behavior. Any study of foods popular with Blacks should encompass food selection and spicing. This information has obvious implications for health services. It would also be helpful in planning menus and nutrition education programs for Black children.

Rookwood (1978) suggested investigating the mealtime patterns of Black families. Teachers are often encouraged to serve meals family style. Rookwood observed a teacher in a Head Start center who had the children eat one by one. When questioned about the practice, the teacher replied that this pattern of eating was more similar to the style of eating of many of the children at home wherein family members "catch a plate" whenever they arrived and were hungry. She found that the children played less at the table, ate more, and seemed to feel better. The teacher stated that children eat better when they can concentrate on eating rather than telling the teacher the color of the peas.

Magical-spiritual beliefs. Rubin (1975) noted a deep concern with the spiritual and the supernatural among Black children. Examining these modes will help to better understand the world view of the Black child and determine the implications for concept development

The story has been told of a child named Akin who was accustomed to hearing bedtime stories each night that told of Tarzan and the Lion. In each episode, Tarzan always defeated the Lion. So, one night, Akin asked his mother when the Lion was going to win. His mother closed the book and sighed, "Honey, I guess the Lion will beat Tarzan when lions begin to write books."

References

Akbar, N. Address before the Black Child Development Institute Annual Meeting, October 1975, San Francisco, California.

Boykin, A. W. "Experimental Psychology from a Black Perspective: Issues and Examples." In *Final Report from the Third Conference on Empirical Research in Black Psychology,* ed. W. Cross. Washington, D.C.: National Institute of Education, 1977.

Boykin, A. W. "Psychological/Behavioral Verve in Academic/Task Performance: Three Theoretical Considerations." *Negro Education* (1978): 343–354.

Brazelton, T. B.; Young, G. G.; and Bullowa, M. "Inception and Resolution of Early Developmental Pathology: A Case History." *Journal of the American Academy of Child Psychiatry* 10, no. 1 (January 1971): 124–135.

Cohen, R. "The Influence of Conceptual Rule-Sets on Measures of Learning Ability." In *Race and Intelligence.* Washington, D.C.: American Anthropological Association, 1971.

Dixon, V. J., and Foster, B. G. *Beyond Black or White.* Boston: Little, Brown, 1971.

DuBois, W. E. B. "Of Our Spiritual Strivings." In *The Souls of Black Folks.* New York: The New American Library Incorporated, 1903.

Esen, A. "The Care Syndrome: A Resource for Counseling in Africa." *Journal of Negro Education* 42, no. 2 (Spring 1973): 205–211.

Gitter, A. G.; Black, H.; and Mostofsky, D. I. "Race and Sex in Perception of Emotion." *Journal of Social Issues* 28 (1972): 63–78.

Goldman, R., and Sanders, J. "Cultural Factors and Hearing." *Exceptional Children* 35 (1969): 489–490.

Guttentag, M. "Negro-White Differences in Children's Movement." *Perceptual and Motor Skills* 35 (1972): 435–436.

Guttentag, M., and Ross, S. "Movement Responses in Simple Concept Learning." *American Journal of Orthopsychiatry* 42 (1972): 657–665.

Haskins, J., and Butts, H. F. *The Psychology of Black Language.* New York: Barnes & Noble, 1973.

Hilliard, A. "Alternatives to IQ Testing: An Approach to the Identification of Gifted Minority Children." Final report to the California State Department of Education, 1976.

Holt, J. *How Children Fail.* New York: Dell, 1964.

Lester, J. *Look Out Whitey! Black Powers Gon' Get Your Mama!* New York: Grove, 1969.

Marans, A., and Lourie, R. "Hypotheses Regarding the Effects of Childrearing Patterns on the Disadvantaged Child." In *Disadvantaged Child,* ed. J. Hellmuth. Seattle: Special Child Publications, 1967.

Massari, H. L., and Meyer, J. "Activity Level and Intellectual Functioning in Deprived Preschool Children." *Developmental Psychology* 1 (1969): 286–290.

Morgan, H. "Neonatal Precocity and the Black Experience." *Negro Educational Review* 27 (April 1976): 129–134.

Newmeyer, J. A. "Creativity and Nonverbal Communication in Preadolescent White and Black Children." (Unpublished doctoral dissertation, Harvard University, 1970).

Piestrup, A. *Black Dialect Interference and Accommodation of Reading Instruction in First Grade.* Monograph #4. Berkeley, Calif.: University of California, Language Behavior Research Laboratory, 1973.

Rookwood, J., 1978: personal communication.

Rubin, M., 1975, personal communication.

Silberman, C. *Crisis in the Classroom.* New York: Vantage, 1970.

Wachs, T.; Uzgiris, I.; and Hunt, J., McV. "Cognitive Development in Infants of Different Age Levels and from Different Environmental Backgrounds: An Explanatory Investigation." *Merrill-Palmer Quarterly* 17 (1971): 283–316.

Young, V. H. "Family and Childhood in a Southern Georgia Community." *American Anthropologist* 72 (1970): 269–288.

Zigler, E.; Abelson, W.; and Seitz, V. "Motivational Factors in the Performance of Economically Disadvantaged Children on the Peabody Picture Vocabulary Test." *Child Development* 44 (1973): 294–303.

Zigler, E., and Butterfield, E. "Motivational Aspects of Changes in IQ Test Performance of Culturally Deprived Nursery School Children." *Child Development* 39 (1968): 1–14.

A Child's Right to the Valuing of Diversity

Reaffirmations:

Speaking Out for Children

Mary Lane

Faith Bowlus

In response to today's retrogressive attitudes toward human needs, the U.S. National Committee for Early Childhood Education of the Organisation Mondiale pour L'Education Prescolaire (OMEP), the Association for Childhood Education International, and the National Association for the Education of Young Children urge child advocates to speak out about public responsibility for assuring children's basic rights. This series of statements, compiled by Monroe Cohen, Director of the Queens College Institute for Family and Community Life, is not copyrighted, and may be freely reproduced with credit to the authors.

Great cultural diversity still exists on our planet, even as modern technology pushes for more uniformity and as McDonalds and Coca Cola spread everywhere. In ecological terms, we accept the principle of diversity for plants and animals. We protect endangered species—too late sometimes—in most of the civilized world. But if humankind is to maintain itself, the valuing of diversity must increase in our own lives also.

Indeed, *we* may become an endangered species unless we begin early to help our children learn to value diversity. How? By recognizing the rationale for such a position and then organizing society to achieve this goal.

As our world becomes even smaller, communication can be almost instantaneous. Mobility characterizes families more than stability. People in this kind of world must have these three qualities to succeed: (1) the ability to cope with change; (2) an open, flexible personality that enjoys the *process* of change; (3) the ability to assimilate changes into a satisfying personal lifestyle. Diversity is the touchstone for each of these three qualities.

A child who associates with children who speak other languages, who worship in other ways, who eat other foods, whose skin color differs from one's own, and whose behavior suggests different upbringing, learns about the basic similarities of all people everywhere and can understand and appreciate their fascinating differences. Such children have many points of reference when they meet people with other values and when they encounter new situations.

Many of humankind's great upheavals have been caused by the blindness of those in power to the aspirations of people with whom they disagreed. The value of an open, flexible personality is well established. Closed, rigid individuals are prone to prejudice, biased to the extent that they wear blinders to anything that does not match their early perceptions. On the other hand, children who have learned that people of all races and cultures have high ambitions and feel strongly about the quality of life; that love, peace, and respect are universal concepts regardless of the language used to express them— such children have incorporated the basics of an open, flexible approach to life.

Survival itself may well depend on the right to experience diversity and then to assimilate change. To evaluate the validity of experience for oneself and one's lifestyle is the outcome of thoughtfully charting a life course, as opposed to swaying with the whims of the times.

We who speak out for children must ensure that the nation who "tightens its belt" does not choke its future. We must speak out for the rights of children—to be nourished, to play, to imagine, and to value diversity.

Mary Lane *is the Director of the Oakland Parent Child Center, Oakland, California.*

The Butter Battle Book

The Butter Battle Book

Uses and Abuses With Young Children

Nancy Carlsson-Paige
and
Diane E. Levin

In early 1984, Dr. Seuss, one of the most prolific and best known writers of books for young children, published *The Butter Battle Book,* which is a metaphorical depiction of the nuclear arms race. Soon after, the book appeared on *The New York Times*'s best seller list and made its way into the homes and classrooms of many young children. Teachers, parents, and the media quickly began to debate the appropriateness of using this book with young children. The book has fueled the controversy about when and how children should be exposed to the nuclear arms race and other disturbing issues facing the world in which they are growing up.

The Butter Battle Book tells the story of two fictitious countries inhabited by the Yooks and the Zooks. The Yooks and Zooks are divided by a wall and by a disagreement over which side their bread should be buttered on. The Yooks butter their bread on the top side, while the Zooks butter theirs on the bottom. One day, with the firing of a sling shot, a war begins that escalates into a weapons race. Each side keeps building bigger and bigger

weapons (Dr. Seuss's imaginary machines) only to find the other side has made a similar or bigger one. Finally, the "bright back room boys," who have been developing the weapons all along, come up with a "bitsy big-boy boomeroo" bomb which is smaller than an egg and more powerful that any of the previous weapons. The book ends with a Yook and Zook standing at the wall, each holding one of these bombs, while the text asks, "Who's going to drop it? Will you . . . ? Or will he . . . ?"

Should the book be read to children?

Adults' opinions about whether *The Butter Battle Book* should be read to children will depend on how much and what kind of exposure they feel children should have to such disturbing world situations. Some adults feel the book provides a perfect way to introduce the topic of the nuclear arms race to children (Kronish, 1984). They argue that young children need to become involved in the political process and in solving the problems of the world. Other adults argue against

reading the book to young children. Some find the book offensive; they object both to Dr. Seuss' humorous treatment of such a serious topic and to the unresolved conflict at the end of the book which can leave readers with a sense of hopelessness (Goodman, 1984). Others say that raising nuclear issues with young children is harmful. They believe children should be protected from the disturbing realities of the world as long as possible (Adelson & Finn, 1985).

We feel that *The Butter Battle Book* can serve a very useful function with young children, but that it can also be used in ways which are destructive. Because young children have different understandings and needs with respect to the nuclear arms race (Duckworth et al., 1985; Escalona, 1965; Friedman,

Nancy Carlsson-Paige, M.Ed., is Assistant Professor in the Division of Education/Special Education at Lesley College Graduate School in Cambridge, Massachusetts.

***Diane E. Levin,** Ph.D., is an Associate Professor of Early Childhood Education/Child Development at Wheelock College in Boston, Massachusetts.*

1984; Reifel, 1984), they construct their own interpretations of the story. Some children know about the arms race and need to discuss it with adults. Other children do not know and are perhaps not ready to hear about it. For children who are aware of the issue, *The Butter Battle Book* is a valuable resource for opening up discussions with adults. For those children who have not heard about the arms race, the book can frighten them unnecessarily if used improperly. Adults need to use the book in ways which allow children to make their own meanings out of the story of Yooks and Zooks—meanings which may or may not relate to nuclear weapons and the arms race.

A 5-year-old child's ending to The Butter Battle Book.

How do children respond?

In several classrooms where *The Butter Battle Book* was read to young children (4 to 6 years old) for the first time, we saw children respond to the book in a variety of ways. Some children participated in a discussion immediately following the reading of the book, while others did not. Some children later began incorporating aspects of the story into their dramatic play.

Almost all the children we observed took the bread buttering controversy seriously, as opposed to adults who see this as an absurd dispute, or older elementary children who are often disturbed by the fact that people can argue over such unimportant issues. Many young children focused primarily on the controversy. Some were committed to the butter being spread in the right way (the way they did it) and took the side of the Yooks who did it that way.

Some children thought most about how the conflict should be resolved—either through battle (e.g., finding a way to get the Zooks to conform to the Yooks' way of

buttering bread) or through some compromise solution. Many sought a more concrete ending, saying, for example, "Where is the rest of the book?" For a few children, some connections were made between the book and the real world, such as "There really are bombs like that."

The children responded to *The Butter Battle Book* in their own ways as well as in ways which were characteristic of their general developmental level. All of the children took different pieces of the book—those which were most meaningful to them—and related them to what they already knew. Many related to it egocentrically, taking the point of view which was similar to their own experience. A few were less egocentric, struggling with two points of view. Most children thought in very concrete terms about the book. They focused on the dramatic weapons and the bread and butter. A few children

thought in more abstract terms and were able to see it as having a relationship to their world, although none of the children made all of the possible connections that an adult would (for instance, that the Yooks and Zooks were like the Americans and Russians). These diverse responses to the book could occur because the teachers presented the book in ways that enabled children to construct their own understandings.

How to avoid misuse

Some parents and teachers have reported inappropriate uses of *The Butter Battle Book*. One kind of unintentional misuse occurs when adults expect a typically humorous Dr. Seuss story and are startled when they realize they are, in fact, reading a book about the nuclear arms race to children. They find themselves in a difficult situation.

They may experience intense reactions to the book themselves— about the arms race and the way Dr. Seuss writes about it. The adult's discomfort, even if nonverbal, can be sensed by children and, in some cases, may confuse or even frighten them. In addition, some adults find themselves unprepared to discuss the book with children. Therefore, before you read *The Butter Battle Book* to children, it is essential that you read it yourself first, both to work out your own reactions and to consider how you will talk about the book with children.

A second kind of misuse occurs when adults use the book to introduce the topic of nuclear weapons to children or to directly relate the story to the real world. One teacher, after completing the book, told her class of 4-year-olds about nuclear weapons and their destructive power. At least one child came home from school very distressed, asking his mother if there really were bombs that could "kill all the people and all the children, too." When adults make direct links between the book and the real world, it prevents children from coming to terms with this difficult topic in their own way and according to their own timetable. We also risk

frightening children unnecessarily and undermining their sense of safety. **Children have the best chance of learning to cope with difficult issues when they have some control over the connections they make, rather than having adults make the connections for them.**

A third misuse occurs when teachers introduce the book by telling children that Dr. Seuss is worried about the world, does not have a solution for the problems which plague it, and hopes that the children will be able to end the book for him. This approach not only renders the children's hero, Dr. Seuss, impotent, but, even

worse, it puts the responsibility for solving world problems on the children. The responsibility for finding solutions for world problems lies with adults not with children. **While education plays an important role in helping children learn to become active participants in the political process, it must be done in ways which respect children's need to feel protected by adults.**

Ways to discuss bombs and the arms race

For the few young children who connect the book to the arms race or nuclear threat, adults have a special responsibility. If in a group discussion after reading the book, a child says something that indicates an awareness of these issues, the teacher needs to acknowledge that awareness at the time, but then pursue it individually with the child later. For example, if a child says, "There really are bombs that can blow up everything," a teacher can respond with something like "Yes, there are real bombs in the world that are very powerful" and then go on to discuss other children's comments.

After the group time, the teacher would need to find out what that child knows and feels about nuclear weapons. The teacher might ask the child what she or he knows about bombs and use the child's responses as a guide for deciding to ask additional questions and how to respond. Based on this individual discussion, the teacher has to judge whether or not the child feels anxious about the topic and needs reassurance; whether the child is seeking additional information; or, whether the child just wants to share with a trusted adult what she or he knows. Using this approach the teacher works with children individually so as not to raise concerns for other children who have not yet become aware of the arms race.

Adults also need to be aware that children's connections and possible concerns are not always expressed immediately after the book is read or directly in a discussion. For instance, in one classroom children made no obvious connections during the class discussion following the reading of the book. However, the next day three children built a farm in the block area and put missiles (blocks) on the farmyard wall to protect the animals from their enemies. Following the reading of the book, it is important for parents and teachers to look for signs of children's awareness and concern about bombs and nuclear threat in their behavior and to initiate individual discussions with children who indicate an awareness.

The book as a learning tool

In addition to providing a worthwhile vehicle for allowing children to raise the nuclear issue if they need or want to, *The Butter Battle Book* offers other potentially valuable learning possibilities. One of the roles that education can play in

the lives of young children today is to help them develop the skills they will need as adult citizens of the world: the ability to resolve conflicts nonviolently; the ability to consider points of view other than their own; the ability to appreciate similarities and differences among people; and the sense that they are capable of solving problems they encounter. Caring adults can take

active, specific steps to help children develop these skills (Boston Area Educators for Social Responsibility, 1984; Carlsson-Paige & Levin, 1985; Fassler & Janis, 1983; Myers-Walls & Fry-Miller, 1984).

The Butter Battle Book can be used in homes or classrooms to assist children in developing these skills. In one kindergarten, where children were asking for a concrete

ending for the book, the teacher suggested to the children that they write their own endings. She provided them with blank books. Some children wrote several books (drawings with dictations taken by the teacher) which tried out a variety of endings. Children's completed books were discussed at class meetings. The teacher helped children take on the roles of the

Children learn to cope with difficult issues when they have some control over the connections they make rather than having adults make the connections for them.

Yooks and Zooks in the various solutions. When one child suggested a solution in which the Yooks won and made everyone butter their bread in the "right way," the teacher said to the children playing the role of Zooks, "How does that feel to you?" When the Zooks responded that they did not like it and liked buttering their bread bottom side up, the teacher turned

Understanding children's thinking

A cognitive-developmental perspective can help us understand how young children make sense out of what they hear about war and the nuclear arms race. Such an approach involves three steps.

1. Take the children's point of view as you listen to their comments about war.

2. Consider the characteristics of children's general stage of cognitive development when you make hypotheses about what their understanding might be.

3. Consider the active process involved as children transform what they hear about war in their own unique ways.

(Carlsson-Paige & Levin, 1985, p. 16)

back to the Yooks and said, "They don't like it. What are we going to do?" For several days, the children, with the teacher's help, explored numerous solutions to the problem. Gradually, the solutions began to change from those which involved violence and winners and losers, to those which were nonviolent and involved compromises satisfactory to both Yooks and Zooks. One of the later solutions was, "Let's everybody butter the bread on the top one day and on the bottom the next day." The children had an opportunity to try out this solution at snack time for the next 2 days and then discussed how it worked at group meeting again.

When children have the opportunity to work to resolve conflicts through firsthand experience and to create a variety of solutions themselves which can be tested out directly, they learn conflict resolution skills that are appropriate to their level of development. They also are challenged to begin to think about more than one perspective in a situation. While this can be very diffi-cult for young children to do, it is most possible when it occurs in concrete situations in which they are actively engaged. In working out solutions to conflicts in this way, children are also gaining a sense of their own empowerment: that they can solve difficult problems; that they can construct solutions which are successful, that are their own, and that are not those of adults. Building children's self-esteem in this manner is a good way to help children gain a sense of how to control their lives and to help them grow up feeling that their actions can make a difference in the world.

Conclusion

Young children look to adults for assistance in understanding the world in which they are growing up. Because many young children do learn about nuclear war and weapons despite adults' attempts to protect them, parents and teachers need to think about how to approach this topic with children. Our responsibility as adults is not to teach children about war and nuclear weapons directly, but to provide opportunities for children to work out, with our assistance, their own ideas and feelings. *The Butter Battle Book* is one of the few resources that acknowledges a world situation which many children know about, and it provides a way for sincere and reassuring adults to set the stage for children to raise the issue. As we support children's healthy development, we need to find more resources which will help children work out their own ideas and concerns about living in a nuclear age.

References

Adelson, J., & Finn, C. (1985). Terrorizing children. *Commentary, 79,* 29–36.

Boston Area Educators for Social Responsibility. (1984). *Taking part.* Cambridge, MA: National Educators for Social Responsibility.

Carlsson-Paige, N., & Levin, D. (1985). *Helping young children understand peace, war and the nuclear threat.* Washington, DC: NAEYC.

Duckworth, E., Engel, B., Lerman, B., Schirmer, P., & Steinitz, V. (1985, August). Letters from readers. "Nuclear education." *Commentary, 79,* p. 7.

Escalona, S. (1965). Children and the threat of nuclear war. In M. Schwebel (Ed.), *Behavioral science and human survival.* Palo Alto, CA: Science and Behavioral Books.

Fassler, J., & Janis, M. (1983). Books, children and peace. *Young Children, 38*(6), 21–30.

Friedman, B. (1984). Preschoolers' awareness of nuclear threat. *CAEYC Newsletter, 12,* 4–5.

Goodman, E. (1984, April 23). Dr. Seuss the pessimist. *The Boston Globe,* p. 17.

Kronish, M. (1984, November). *Empowering children to take hold of their future.* Paper presented at the New England Kindergarten Conference, Randolph, MA.

Myers-Walls, J., & Fry-Miller, K. (1984). Nuclear war: Helping children overcome fears. *Young Children, 39*(4), 27–32.

Reifel, S. (1984). Children living with the nuclear threat. *Young Children, 39*(5), 74–80.

Seuss, Dr. (1984). *The butter battle book.* New York: Random House.

"It'll be a challenge!"

Managing Emotional Stress in Teaching Disabled Children

Barbara Palm White with Michael A. Phair

"It'll be a challenge and I'm sure you'll manage!" With those words, three severely handicapped children were enrolled in my kindergarten class 4 years ago. The experience has been a challenge, and we have had some success. Although my staff and I expected to learn and understand a great deal more with experience, we were surprised to spend so much time and energy on our *feelings* about our work with the children and their families. We were not ready for the challenge to our emotions!

Our goal is to provide an appropriate long-term program for special needs children, so personal involvement with the children and their families is crucial, as it is in any program serving young children. How we as teachers feel about that involvement can be critical to our effectiveness. Our emotions, when suppressed or denied, can result in exhaustion and depression. We hope that by sharing our experiences, other early childhood educators will prepare for and better understand their emotional involvement with all children and their families.

What kinds of emotional crises have we encountered? How have we turned our negative feelings into positive directions for ourselves and the children? We can identify 11 feelings that we may encounter when working with handicapped children. These feelings can lead to dead ends if they are not dealt with positively. These emotions, and signals of their presence, are summarized in Table 1. For each emotion, we have found constructive ways to channel our thinking and energies to better serve all the children in our care.

Denial and avoidance

At first we tended to overlook the handicapped children's many minor problem areas because we did not understand the difficulties and avoided coping with them. As a result, we offered simplistic solutions like "cut out the sugar and she'll be fine" or referred the problem back to the parents, health nurse, or speech therapist.

Unfortunately, this technique increased our sense of guilt. As professional teachers, we are responsible for providing the best services possible. We must discipline ourselves to recognize handicaps quickly, fill the gaps in our knowledge, and request help and support when faced with a problem we do not understand. Denial and avoidance resolve nothing for the child, for the family, or for ourselves.

Sadness

As a teaching staff, we have felt profound sadness upon meeting a disabled child. The helpless and hopeless feelings we witness in those close to the child are even further discouraging.

To enable us to turn this sorrow into joy, we record every child's success, however small. We post photographs and large charts around the room to remind ourselves and others of each child's achievements. We have developed ways to share the child's progress with our peers, administrators, and especially the parents. For example, we keep a daily journal that everyone, including parents, has access to. Everyone

Barbara Palm White, B.Ed., *teaches and coordinates an integrated program for handicapped children at Winfield Kindergarten, Winfield, Alberta, Canada.*

Michael A. Phair, M.Ed., M.A., *is an education consultant with the Edmonton Regional Office of Education, Edmonton, Alberta, Canada.*

involved with the program is expected to read it and write notes and comments as appropriate.

As we recognize and communicate the children's successes, we progress as a team of educators. We accept new resources and discover personal strengths that lead to a sense of competence and self-assurance. We challenge sadness by proclaiming "We've come a long way!"

Anger

It is so easy to feel angry
- with the child ("Why are you my responsibility?")
- with the parents ("Why don't they do their part?")
- with our supervisors ("How can they expect me to handle all of this?").

We record every child's success, however small.

These feelings and the myriad pressures, annoyances, and frustrations that are typical every day when dealing with all young children can increase our anger. Speaking in anger to another staff member—when what we really want to do is relieve tension—can create rifts that mushroom out of proportion. Our anger can eat away at personal satisfaction if we do not find an outlet for it.

The anger may subside somewhat as you come to accept the children and become actively involved in planning for and evaluating their growth. However, most of us have found that we also need a friend, someone not involved in the program, to listen to our frustrations and help us relax so that we can explore some alternatives.

Guilt

Everyday we encounter feelings of not being good enough, not working hard enough, or spending too much time and

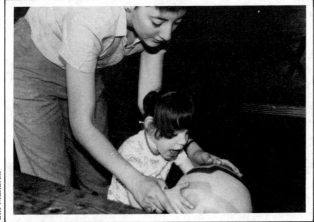

Ann Manzick

We must keep our expectations in line with the child's potential.

Table 1
Negative Emotions and Signals of Their Presence

Negative emotions and related behaviors	Signals of negative emotions in speech
Denial to overlook mild or moderate handicaps	*"No problem really—just shy."*
Sadness sorrow, disappointment about the child and circumstances	*"This deaf child will never know how beautiful music can be."*
Anger directed at child, parents, supervisors	*"If it wasn't for the handicapped child, I would have a good year."*
Guilt especially at the end of a year with few measurable gains	*"If only I knew more." "If only I worked harder."*
Fear of the unknown, of personal inadequacy or inability to cope, of the child or handicapping condition	*"I'm afraid I won't know how to act." "I'm scared she may hurt me/herself/another child."*
Overprotection to exclude or restrict handicapped children from activities or services available to other children	*"She'll eat the sand." "He can't go to the museum. He might get too tired."*
Defensiveness to block ideas from others, to tend to see suggestions as criticism	*"I'm doing all I can and you want me to do more?!"*
Jealousy/competition between staff members or with staff and parents	*"Why don't I ever get any credit for success with this child?"*
Frustration feelings of overwork that can lead to divisiveness	*"I never seem to make any progress." "I want to quit."*
Exhaustion can lead to physical illness	*"I can't face today." "Another meeting?!"*
Fatalism overwhelming hopelessness	*"I can't win, whatever I do." "Nothing I do will make any difference."*

energy at the expense of the children without special needs. Guilt is especially high at the end of the school year when the goals we have set for the children have not been reached. "If only we had worked harder," "If only we had tried . . . ," "If only we had taken that other course."

If we are to keep guilt from overwhelming us, we must keep our expectations in line with the child's potential. Realistic goal setting and good record keeping are crucial. We must be specific and remember that it is no disgrace to admit our limitations or the limitations of the program. Only then can we think creatively about how to improve our work, perhaps by asking a parent to help or by setting up a summer program. When we think and share responsibility for each child's education, we do not need to feel guilty about our own inadequacies.

Fear

We often find ourselves afraid, even though we do not always know why. At times we are afraid of the child or the handicapping condition ("I am scared she may hurt herself/ another child/me.") What can generate more fear than the medical reports and assessments we read before we meet the child?

At other times we are afraid of our inadequacy as a teaching staff and our personal inability to cope. What is my tolerance level when faced with a child who does not use language? Who is not toilet trained at age 5? Who is not mobile? How will the other children and parents react to a severely handicapped child in the class? What will the rest of the staff think? These fears too often cripple our efforts.

When we share information we share power.

We found that we can help conquer our fears by becoming familiar with medical terms and learning about new teaching ideas from books, journals, classes, and conferences. Even more important is our teamwork with other adults, including parents, in which we share our fears, support each other, and compliment each other's roles.

Go beyond the labels to see the child as a wonderful, growing, and challenging person.

The best way to combat fear, however, is to go beyond the labels to see the child as a wonderful, growing, and challenging person.

Overprotection

"He can't play in the sand because he'll eat it." We ponder whether the children should go on the field trip, and if we take them whether classroom staff or parent volunteers should accompany them. In our sincere desire to ensure safety we can too easily exclude handicapped children from activities and services available to others.

Other children in the group follow our cues. If we limit a child's activities unnecessarily, then so will the child's peers. How do we balance the need to integrate children and at the same time provide adequate protection?

The key to success in our program has been to encourage handicapped children to engage in a variety of experiences with others. In a summer program we watched the handicapped children ride horses, swim in a lake, ride in a canoe, and bounce on a trampoline with no detrimental effects. As a result of seeing less restrictive adults working with these children, we became less overprotective. In addition, the other children responded by initiating appropriate and challenging activities with their handicapped peers.

Rose C. Engel

Defensiveness

The specialists, parents, and administrators who work with our program each have their own concerns and goals. Any one of these people might say "Do this, it is important." Another person might suggest something else that is essential. Added together, the list of essential things can become so long that it overwhelms us. Such lists also lead us to approach the child and the program in a piecemeal fashion.

Our reaction to so many directives was to reject all ideas and view any suggestions as criticism. Unfortunately, our defensiveness blocked valuable input from others since we tended to view their ideas as personal criticism.

When we reached this point, we evaluated and restructured our conferences. We now listen to everyone's ideas. Together we set priorities that will result in a balanced program. To achieve this, we draw on all agreed-upon resources. This approach reduces confusion and has helped us come to terms with several different (and sometimes conflicting) directions. Copies of the conference plans and priorities are circulated to everyone involved because as we share information we share power. This process helps us guard against defensiveness and build a more unified program.

Jealousy and competition

Unchecked defensiveness can lead to unhealthy jealousy and competition between staff members. It seems incongruous that professionals and parents might compete over the merits of programs for handicapped children, but it happens. Such conflict is much more difficult to deal with than the problems discussed here. Sometimes jealousy arises because we find it difficult to rejoice in a workable idea that originated from someone else. Maybe we need more positive feedback than we receive. Whatever the reasons, jealousy and competition are very divisive factors.

To combat the problem, we try to encourage all personnel involved with the handicapped children to observe one another as they work with each child. Case conferences, while valuable, lack the insight into personal styles that interaction with the child reveals. Through observation we can develop a healthy mutual respect for other staff and parents and their areas of expertise. We can then express appreciation to each other in case conferences and collectively rejoice in the child's progress.

Frustration

The goal-setting sessions, case conferences, meetings with specialists, and administrative work involved in offering a good integrated program for handicapped children can be very time consuming! Staff often feel overworked and overextended so that little problems and minor difficulties can lead to major crises and frustrations. As the lead teacher, the phone calls, reports, and meetings required to supervise and coordinate the program often leave me angry, frustrated, and immobilized.

To restore balance for all of us and to reduce frustration, we refocus our time and attention back on the children and forego administrative tasks. If possible, I delegate administrative and coordinating responsibilities to nonteaching staff. By reaffirming our commitment to the handicapped child we can put other problems in perspective.

Exhaustion

Burnout is a common phenomenon among people in the helping professions, and probably more so for those in spe-

By reaffirming our commitment to the handicapped child we can put other problems in perspective.

cial education. We all feel tired at times and may even work or worry ourselves into physical illness. Our response to the morning alarm may well become "I don't want to go to work today" and we may only find enough energy to drag ourselves through a superficial day.

To deal with the problem of exhaustion, each day we consider the pace of the program and build in breaks for the staff. One child goes home at 2:30 instead of 3:30 to allow for an extra hour for record keeping and planning. An older child reads to a physically handicapped child while the other children play at recess. Headphones with music or a story might free a staff person for a quiet cup of coffee.

Holidays and breaks are extremely important. Find a different interest to pursue when you are not at work. Disconnect the phone for an evening or do something completely different for a day. Rejuvenation for the body and soul is important for children and adults!

Fatalism

Frustrations, failures, setbacks, anxiety, and a host of similar feelings can occasionally build to the point where we become overwhelmed by our hopeless perspective of the future. We retreat into fatalism, feeling nothing we do will make any difference. The child's limitations, as well as our own, seem formidable.

A child who is blind will never be able to understand, do, or enjoy so much. What will life for these children be like? Will our efforts really matter?

As the year's end approaches, we see a child who cannot walk scheduled to attend a school with hundreds of stairs and no special bathroom facilities. How can we prepare the child for these obstacles?

Just when we think we are breaking through, we are told that a severely disturbed foster child may be placed in another home, the 15th in 5 years. What chance does this child have?

Our work and efforts seem doomed as we get caught up in the arbitrary nature of life. Fatalism overwhelms us most often when we concentrate only on the future and all the things that are beyond our control. Teachers, however, must look at the present and the possible. We must make sure we exercise what power or influence we do have. We must insist that our educational program is as effective and well planned as possible, and then look beyond to what else we might do. Have we made the receiving school aware of the needs of this child? If the disturbed child leaves can we maintain contact? Will our advocacy on behalf of children give us some control on the future? The children's separation from our classroom does not doom them or their future. We must re-explore and find our sense of hope!

The open road

Today, when we see the continuing progress of the hand-icapped children we used to work with, we are always amazed and delighted! I make it a point to tell our current staff and parents how much their children have developed because I know how important that kind of feedback is for them. At the same time, it gives all of us a good feeling about our past commitments and hard work.

Even in this small rural community, our advocacy has been successful. The school with so many stairs received money from a local service club to help with mobility renovations. There have been summer community programs for handicapped children. We see these as healthy and rewarding signs.

Perhaps our greatest accomplishment has been our progress as a staff in grappling with our feelings. Honestly looking at our emotions not only benefited our work as a team but forced each of us to examine our own feelings and grow and develop as adults and educators.

The roads we traveled and the directions we suggest in this article are not new. However, we know that our suggestions offer an open road for dealing with young children, all of whom have some special needs. We can meet the challenge!

Part 4.
Review of stress research

If you are especially curious about the theory and research that led to the recommendations in Parts 1 through 4 of this book, make sure you read this chapter first. Everyone interested in helping young children cope with stress owes a great deal of gratitude to Alice Honig for her ambitious review of the most current research. In addition, she offers 20 succinct ways for teachers (and all parents are teachers, too) to help children cope with stress. This monumental work is a fitting finale to a book on a topic of critical importance to each of us.

Research in Review. Stress and Coping in Children— *Alice S. Honig*

Stress and Coping in Children

Alice Sterling Honig

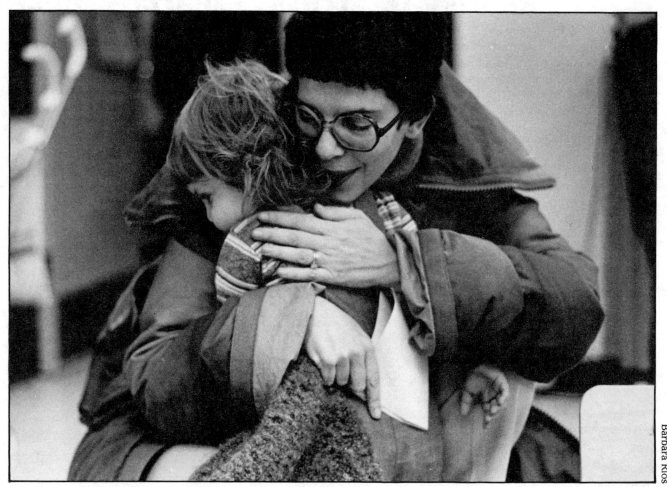

Teachers and parents can act as protectors to create environments low in stress and as facilitators to help young children cope better with stress.

Barbara Rios

Stress is to be expected in the course of human development. The very act of being born includes a stressful and sometimes perilous journey for a baby, even an infant seemingly untouched by genetic, prenatal, or perinatal risk factors. Some newborns have neurological immaturities that lead to chin trembling and long bursts of crying. Some infants' digestive systems do not work well and colic stresses them for months (Honig, 1985a).

Inevitably, in the course of their first years in human society, children will be socialized, gently or more harshly, into acceptable toileting habits, civil (*please* and *thank you*) forms of getting needs met, and table manners that make public eating experiences less stressful for adults.

Stress continues to mark the achievement of developmental milestones. How often an infant, on the verge of toddling, stumbles, lurches, falls, crashes, and recommences bravely. Not all stresses are harmful. The struggle to learn to walk is a good example of how some stresses can be perceived as challenges that impel a child to strive toward more mature forms of behavior.

What is stress? Selye (1982), the father of stress research, defines stress as a *stimulus event of sufficient severity to produce disequilibrium in the homeostatic physiological systems.* Stress also has been conceptualized variously as a *nonspecific response of the body to any demand that exceeds the person's ability to cope,* as a *person-environment relationship that threatens or taxes personal resources,* and as a *mental state in response to strains* or daily hassles (Lazarus & Launier, 1978; Lazarus, DeLongis, Folkman, & Gruen, 1985; Rutter, 1983).

A variety of dissimilar situations that happen to children can produce stress, including physical illness; pain; concentration; overexertion; anxious anticipations of failure due to overly strict or high parental expectations; fear and tension before a test or during a visit to the dentist; being a latchkey child after school; being teased about facial features, allergies, or asthma; humil-

---

Adults need to be sensitive to the *meaning* of a particular stressor for a child.

---

iation; fear of abandonment; feelings of being unloved; racial slurs; living in a dangerous neighborhood; heavy doses of violent television; physical abuse; and even joyous overstimulation. Witness the temper tantrums that some small children burst into on a too-exciting Christmas morning (Grune & Brooks, 1985).

Different kinds of stress situations vary in their outcomes. In a study of behavioral stress responses of public school children, Felner, Stolberg, and Cowen (1975) found that children who had lost a parent through death increased in timidity, shyness, and withdrawal. Children from separated or divorced families more typically increased aggressive, antisocial behaviors. Stress is difficult to research, partly because of the wide variety of stimuli that are potentially stressful, their differential intensity, duration, and the *interactions* of different stressors in a child's life.

Stress can arise from *internal* factors. A young baby with severe gas pains from colic cries miserably

as she flexes her tiny legs. Stress can arise from illness or from the painful stomach aches of a young child lying in bed and listening each night to his parents' violent quarreling in the next room. Stress can arise from *external* factors, too. A kindergarten child, forced by a recent family move to attend a new school, finds walking the new route alone a terrifying experience. He may arrive home with soiled pants because he loses bowel control.

Some stresses are *acute* in a child's life. They arise suddenly, are isolated instances, and their impact may not last long. An infant's sudden fever after a DPT shot or a preschooler's first days of adjustment to a high quality nursery school program are examples of acute stress. Some acute stresses, if isolated, such as a single hospitalization for a child, are associated with short-term emotional disturbance, but *not* with long-term upset years later.

Other stresses are *chronic.* Their impact may be cumulative even for the most well-adjusted child and can lead to long-term disturbances. An alcoholic, an unpredictably abusive parent, or bitter family recriminations long after parental divorce—these are chronic stresses that may impair even the psychologically sturdiest child's functioning.

This two-part review will first examine the components and stages of stress. Then, research findings will be used to illustrate varieties of intrapersonal, ecological, catastrophic, and interpersonal stress factors in the lives of children.

This is one of a regular series of Research in Review columns. The column in this issue was written and edited by Alice Honig, Ph.D., Professor, Department of Child, Family, and Community Studies, Syracuse University, Syracuse, New York.

Some measures of stress will also be noted. Research on children's coping skills and on "invulnerable" children will be cited. Finally, suggestions will be offered that can help caregivers recognize, prevent, and alleviate child stress as well as enhance children's coping skills to deal with stress.

Components and stages of stress

Researchers have focused on several components of stress: a *stressor;* how a child *perceives* that stressor; the *coping resources* a child has; the *support systems* available internally and externally for the child; and the child's *skill* in making coping or adjusting responses when stressed.

A *stressor* is "an acute life event or a chronic environmental situation that causes disequilibrium" (Blom, Cheney, & Snoddy, 1986, p. 9). The severity of stress consequences depends partly on how a child understands and feels about the stressor. Some children are born with temperamental and neurological vulnerabilities that impair their ability to think about and deal adaptively with even small stressors in their lives. Teachers and parents need to be sensitive to the *meaning* of a particular stressor for a particular child. Circumstances change meanings. What would seem to be a stressor for one child, such as father leaving home, may be a relief for another child who has been tyrannized and abused by that parent.

The stress response, seen as an "imbalance between requirements to make an adaptive response and the repertoire" of the stressed person (Zegans, 1982, p. 140) shows several stages:

1. Stage of alarm

Selye's early research (1936) into the initial alarm reaction of the body referred to a "general adaptation syndrome" of stress. Heart rate increases, hormones such as ACTH (adrenocorticotrophic hormone) are discharged, and the galvanic skin response changes. Adrenaline is secreted to make energy available to the body. High blood pressure, bleeding stomach ulcers, and, ultimately, feelings of exhaustion, are body alarm reactions to stress. Thus, life situations which threaten a child's security and evoke attempts at adaptive behavior also evoke significant psychosomatic alterations in the function of bodily tissues, organs, and systems. "These physiological changes, in their turn, will lead to a lowering of the body's resistance to disease" (Rahe, Meyer, Smith, Kjaerg, & Holmes, 1964, p. 42). As a result, stressed children may get sick more often.

2. Stage of appraisal

Many parents and teachers assume that stressors in a child's life can be easily identified. Yet differences in the *cognitive appraisal* of stressors lead to marked individual differences in children's reactions to potential stressors. Appraisal refers to the evaluative process that imbues a situational encounter with meaning for the person. Some children's psychological makeup or value system (such as beliefs, commitments, and goals) may predispose them to perceive particular events as highly threatening to personal security (Lazarus & Folkman, 1984). Other children may react with zest to unknown or unexpected life challenges.

Madeleine's father invited her friend to go sledding with them in the deep snow of a local park. On the way home, the car had a flat tire. The children had to get out of the car and wait in the fast-falling snow as dusk fell, while papa changed the tire. Madeleine held the metal nuts and handed them to papa as he needed them. She felt they were having an adventure and was proud of being a good helper. Her friend, however, became very worried. What if they could not fix the car? How would they ever get home? Her mother might be very angry with her. Such fears became overwhelming, and the little friend started to sob.

Darren was always ready to fight physically if another child at his center touched him. Even if the child just brushed past Darren while running excitedly toward a friend, Darren would whirl, put up his fists, and hit out at the perceived assaulter.

Arthur moved a great deal because of financial troubles in his single-parent family. Arthur, the youngest of four children, felt a sense of high adventure every time he woke in a new apartment. He felt special, for he got a chance to live in many different places compared to other children. Arthur felt special-privileged, rather than special-unfortunate.

3. Stage of searching for a coping strategy

Coping resources young children possess include tears, tantrums, thinking skills, and the ability to become absorbed in play with peers. Ability (1) to ignore unpleasant situations, (2) to find compromise solutions to social conflicts, and (3) to find and accept substitute satisfactions and comforts when stressed are *adaptive* coping resources.

If children have had inappropriate or ineffective caregiver models for coping, their particular strategies may only result in increased stress. In one family, where cursing and lashing out physically were typical parental responses to family frustrations, the child learned well the familiar strategies of cursing and kicking. But these brought only more grief and stress when applied to his first-grade teacher.

4. Stage of implementing coping responses

Coping responses are attempts to resolve life stresses and emotional pain (Billings & Moos, 1982). Some coping responses are *defensive* processes. These may distort or even deny a disturbing reality. Compulsive behaviors, such as insisting rigidly on certain ritualistic actions over and over or on certain room arrangements only, may be ways a child tries to ward off anxiety.

> Adrien's parents fought violently at home. In the child care center, he pushed a toy car across a low table and watched it crash down as it tipped over the far edge. Then he picked up the car and rode it across the table again and again to let it fall precipitously over the edge of the table.

> Eight-year-old Danny pulled the window shades up and down many, many times each evening before bedtime until he got them just so, to a particular level above the window sill. He opened and shut his closet door over and over in getting ready for bed.

Some children cope by *internalizing*. Children with internal controls are more likely to accept responsibility for their actions. If caught misbehaving, such children may honestly face up to their misbehavior, feel contrite, and realize the consequences of the unacceptable behavior.

Some children are *externalizers*. They attribute control to fate or to others. Garmezy (1981) compared children with these different behavioral processing styles. Externalizers are more likely to act surly or angry, fight with others, accuse others when they themselves misbehave, and show little empathy for children they may have hurt. Behavioral adjustments of children who cope with stress by externalizing are less favorable than for children who are internalizers.

George and Main (1979) observed that abused toddlers who were enabled in group care not only hit their peers more than nonabused toddlers did, but they showed no empathy for peers who were stressed by physical hurt or psychological upset. They did not react with concern, nor did they offer help. Too much stress in these toddlers' lives had left them emotionally unresponsive to others'

troubles. They ignored friendly adult overtures in the classroom.

Strong emotional responses to stress may or may not be negative. A strong emotional response may reflect a child's determination to deal with the stress as a challenge to be surmounted rather than a threat that leads to panic or emotional disintegration. Some coping

---

Male children are more vulnerable to stress than female children.

---

strategies include *problem-solving* responses to deflect pain or lessen stress. In *instrumental coping,* a child uses skills and knowledge to make a stressful situation better.

Successful coping involves a pattern of behavioral responses to novel situations, obstacles, and conflicts in which there is an effortful searching for solutions, direct action, and shaping of events. Haan (1982) has identified five properties of successful coping:

- flexible and inventive creation of response options
- open consideration of options and choices
- orientation to reality and to the future implications of situations
- rational, conscious consideration and purposeful thinking
- governance and control over one's disturbing negative emotions

Every caregiver experienced with infants, toddlers, and preschoolers will note that very young children (as Piagetian theory would predict) will not yet have the sequential logical thinking skills nor the cognitive classification skills to permit such optimal coping processes in responding to stress. Does this mean that teachers should always expect

young children to fall apart in the face of daily or long-term stressors? Indeed not. Successful coping also depends on internal personality strengths and external supports. Teachers and parents can effectively act as *protectors* to create environments low in stress and as *facilitators* to help young children cope better with stress.

What do we know about the variety of stressors in children's lives?

Personal child variables

Variables such as prematurity, sex, temperament and neurological sturdiness, age of child, and intellectual capacity are associated with different kinds of stress in children's lives.

Prematurity

Prematurity has been associated with severe stress in infant state management. Brazelton and others caution that when such babies are sent home from intensive care, parents must be alerted to the possibility that overstimulation in loving interactions can lead to acrocyanosis (a condition, associated with pain and numbness, that causes the extremities to turn bluish) and other dangers (1979). Lack of recognition of infants' active self-organization efforts may force premature babies to expend too much energy shutting out stimuli or using poorly modulated sensorimotor responses to cope (Als, 1985; Honig, 1984).

Additional stresses for preterms may arise from parental expectations. When mothers of 18-month-old infants, born preterm, were asked to record their expectations for achievement of developmental milestones, their expectations *lagged* for the first 2 years in comparison with mothers of normal babies. But after that, the mothers of preterms expected precocity in development. "Mothers of preterm infants may harbor unrealistic expectations for their young children" that can cause later dysfunctional family stresses (Leiderman, 1983, p. 151).

Sex

Male children are more vulnerable than female children. Boys have higher rates of bed wetting, dyslexia, and delinquency. In a study of metropolitan child care centers serving low-income families, male toddlers made significantly more distress bids and sought help more than females from their caregivers (Honig & Wittmer, 1982). In an ecological study of multiple factors influencing child abuse, "the most salient characteristic of the abusive families was that 75% of the target children were male compared with 56% for nonabusive families" (Conger, McCarty, Yang, Lahey, & Kropp, 1984, p. 237).

In 1975, Seligman proposed the concept of "learned helplessness," a cognitive style which differentiates people who perceive coping outcomes as within or outside of their own control. Feelings of helplessness about their fate make children less able to deal with stress.

When children in elementary classrooms received feedback from adults that they were failing, boys tended to respond with greater efforts. Girls tended to give up and attributed their failing to their own lack of ability (Dweck, Davidson, Nelson, & Enna, 1978). Rutter has suggested that in classrooms there is a sex differentiated pattern of feedback from teachers. "Boys are given the message that their failure is a consequence of their misbehaving or not trying hard enough and hence that they *could* cope if they chose to do so" (1983, p. 27).

Certain stressors may differentially affect boys and girls. Significantly more negative behaviors were found for 24 nursery-school-age boys and 24 girls from white, middle-class families of divorce in comparison with children from intact families. Two years later, the *boys,* but not the girls, in divorced families were still having adjustment problems (Hetherington, Cox, & Cox, 1978).

Temperament

Three major child temperament patterns have been described: easy-to-adapt, slow-to-warm-up, and irritable/irregular (Thomas & Chess, 1977). Does temperament modify a child's ability to cope with stressful events? No research has found a correlation between security of attachment of infants with mothers and infant temperament classification. Yet Rutter (1978) has found that in families of mentally ill patients, children with adverse temperamental characteristics were twice as likely to be criticized by parents (Werner, 1986). Temperament vulnerabilities will be discussed later in relation to disturbances in mother-infant attachment.

Age and intellectual capacity

Different kinds of stressors affect children at different ages. For example, Grune & Brooks (1985) found that older children were distressed by anticipation of tests, by

---

If children have inappropriate models, their coping strategies only result in increased stress.

---

report cards, and by their personal appearance. Infants in the first year of life, particularly if they are born with medical problems, will be more stressed simply in trying to maintain physiological well being or homeostasis. Also, since stranger anxiety sets in at about age 8 months, infants who enter group care at about that time will be particularly stressed.

In Project Competence, interactive effects of life stressors and personality variables were studied from third to sixth grade in three groups of children: normal, heart-defect, and mainstreamed physically handicapped. Among the two stressed and one normal group, boys had significantly higher classroom disruption scores (Garmezy, Masten, & Telleger, 1984). IQ functioned as a protective factor. High IQ children scored higher on an academic achievement test despite higher or lower levels of personal or family stress in their lives as measured by Coddington's Life Events Questionnaire.

Ecological stressors

Housing and neighborhood

The living environments of some children seriously increase the risk of stress because of increased neighborhood crime; criminal and antisocial role models; and unesthetic, dreary, or garbage-cluttered streets. Some apartments are very crowded, so that the number of persons per room (household density) does not permit the privacy and play space children need (Zuravin, 1985). In the United States, high household density seems to increase both the extent to which parents hit their children and the number of verbal quarrels (Booth & Edwards, 1976). In Hong Kong however, high density does not act as such a stressor. Therefore, cultural accommodations and attitudes must be taken into account in assessing the extent to which household factors may be stressors. Also, a child's *privacy* requirements increase from infancy to adolescence, so the age of the child may be a factor in whether or not high density is perceived as a stressor.

In a study of immigrant North African mothers and toddlers living in Paris, Honig, and Gardner (1985) found that density *per se,* and even total number of persons in the apartment, did not differentiate families where mothers reported feeling overwhelmed with stress. However, significantly more overwhelmed mothers *lacked two or more facilities* such as toilet, kitchen, or bathing facility, in comparison with nonstressed mothers.

Childrearing stress is greater in high-rise apartment houses. Children's play is often restricted to the apartment interior, since parents fear accidents or crime if children are allowed outside on their own. This can create tensions, aggravate conflict among family members, and decrease neighborliness (Becker, 1974). Parents also restrain noisy play to decrease their own and neighbors' stress in high-rise apartments with poor sound-proofing. In low-rise housing, children often combine outdoor play with frequent trips indoors to see parents who can then get their own housework done.

Socioeconomic status as a stressor

Poverty

Poverty as a chronic family stressor may intrusively interfere with effective family functioning. When stress is severe in the lives of low-income mothers of infants, then attachment is more likely to change from secure to insecure between 12 and 18 months (Vaughn, Egeland, Sroufe, & Waters, 1979).

In the Oakland Growth study, Elder and colleagues (1985) found that when fathers lost jobs they became pronouncedly more severe, tense, explosive, and rejecting with their *less attractive* daughters. Mothers did not change in supportiveness. Attractive daughters, however, were not likely to be mal-

---

T he stress of poverty can be mitigated by programs that nourish the social and motivational roots of early learning.

---

treated by fathers during adolescence, no matter how severe the economic pressures.

The Infant Accident Study included 24 infants (less than 12 months old) who had either been hospitalized for child abuse *or* accident (Elmer, 1978). Children were matched on age, race, sex, and socioeconomic status. All the infants were from low socioeconomic status families. As infants, the problems suffered by the abused babies marked them as more stressed. More of the abused infants were below the third percentile in height and weight, had significant health problems, and were below norms developmentally. When followed up 8 years later, however, the effects of poverty proved almost as pernicious as earlier abuse or accident status in infancy. Aggression was pronounced in 6 abused and 8 accident children. Language and communication problems existed for 11 of the 12 abused and 6 of the 12 accident children. Eight of the abused and 3 of the accident children were not performing up to

their ability in school. Half of each group was reported to have nervous mannerisms (by the teacher, pediatrician, or parent).

What was grievously apparent was that *all* of the children were damaged: psychologically, in language development, in the ability to achieve and learn in school. None seemed free to enjoy, learn, and grow in a reasonably healthy manner. They displayed a pervading sense of sadness, anxiety, and fear of attack by others.... We must inquire whether membership in the lower classes is itself dwarfing the potential of young children (p. 18).

During the 1960s and '70s, programs proliferated that offered enriched early child care to poverty families. Children who participated in such preschool enrichment, regardless of form of program delivery, showed better cognitive achievement and positive social behaviors (Honig, 1979, 1983). Ten or more years later, low-income children whose families had received these services had been held back in school less frequently, spent fewer years in special education classes, and had less delinquency than children without such programs (Consortium, 1983).

Low-income single mothers with normally born infants were given medical and social services, including child care. Increased parental nurturance was the main goal of the program. Ten years later, the poverty children with intervention had better school attendance, and the boys were less likely to require costly special school services in comparison with the control group. Control boys were also rated much more negatively than intervention boys by their teachers and, to a serious degree, they were described as more disobedient (Seitz, Rosenbaum, & Apfel, 1985).

Thus, poverty as a stressor in the lives of children can be mitigated by social programs that *nourish the social and motivational roots of early learning* and provide nourishing food and cognitive activities.

Catastrophes and terrors

Figley and McCubbin (1983) have addressed ways in which families face and resolve the effects of catastrophes like hospitalization, natural disasters, childhood illness, and war. Some of these stressors are discussed here.

Hospitalization

Whether parent or child is hospitalized, age of the child is strongly related to the degree of the child's stress. Stress from separation is more upsetting from about 6 months to 4 years (Schaffer & Callender, 1969). Interference with an infant's development of a strong attachment to a parent leads to severe infant disturbance. The Robertsons (1971) found that stress was reduced when individualized, loving family care was provided for toddlers whose mothers were hospitalized. If parents are allowed unlimited access to hospitalized babies, separation stress may be much reduced.

Hospitalization experiences can be fearful in their own right. When researchers attempted to decrease such fears through prior home visits, peer modeling, films, and reading books to children about going to the hospital, children thus prepared before a tonsillectomy, for example, showed decreased emotional disturbance during and immediately after admission (Ferguson, 1979; Wolfer & Vistainer, 1979).

A single hospitalization does not seem to cause long-term noxious outcomes (Rutter, 1979). But two or more hospitalizations for a child who, in addition, comes from a deprived or disturbed family, have been found to result in more long-term, persistent child disturbance

after discharge. Rutter comments, "It was not just that the adverse effects summated, but that they potentiated one another so that the combined effects of the two together was greater than the sum of the two considered separately" (p. 22).

Societal disasters

Disasters like the 1985 earthquake in Mexico can leave hundreds of infants and young children homeless and orphaned. Other potential disasters, such as the threat of nuclear warfare, are more amorphous but may increase anxiety and fearfulness in children. Clinical interviews reveal that specific trauma, such as the Chowchilla kidnapping in California, result in nightmares and emotional disturbances for several years. In that event, 26 children on a school bus were kidnapped and held hostage underground for 27 hours by three masked armed men. Several years later, stress symptoms remained moderate for 6 of the children and severe for 17. The children had kidnap-related dreams and felt guilty for their lack of awareness of preparedness for the trauma that had occurred (Terr, 1981).

Other disastrous traumas, like the assassination of President Kennedy or the explosion of the Space Shuttle Challenger, may preoccupy children with nightmares, worries, and gory imagery in their drawings. After the Challenger disaster, the New York Times conducted a poll with 1,120 families, of whom 175 had children 5 through 8 years of age. Older children, 9 through 17, 224 were also interviewed. According to the poll, girls were more likely than boys to say they had been upset a lot. Thirty percent of the parents of the younger children said the children were upset by the shuttle accident, and slightly more

than half said that they thought it was because a teacher had been on the flight. After the tragedy, 40% of the younger children, as opposed to over 80% of the older children, watched a lot of television coverage. This difference may account for the lowered upset of the younger vs. older children polled (Clymer, 1986).

Nuclear war threat. Awareness and fear of the threat of nuclear war are infrequent among preschoolers but rise as children's cognitive sophistication increases. In a study by Beardslee and Mack (1986), about 40% of students between 5 and 12 years of age were concerned about or afraid of the nuclear threat. Older children, such as adolescents, "begin to have the capacity to understand the (nuclear) danger as well as the fact that people are doing something about it ..." (Yudkin, 1984, p. 25). During the World War II blitz in London, children showed *more* severe neuroses when separated from their parents and sent to safe foster homes in the country than children left with their parents in the city. When adult caregivers are calm and provide security, young children will not pick up fears that cause deep concern in older children.

War and terrorism. Radio and television have brought global terror intimately into the lives of young children. Many a preschooler eats dinner with family, while on the TV screen all are watching someone in a far away land blow up or shoot at human beings. One can only wonder at either the stress *or* premature insensitivity to cruelty that is engendered when very young children see that their family seems unperturbed by these bloody events on the TV screen.

In Israel, in border communities where terrorism has been a pervasive threat, children's nervousness, nightmares, and sleep difficulties have necessitated the active intervention of child psychologists in child care centers. This story was repeatedly told to me during 1985 visits to child care centers near the Lebanese border. Children in border kibbutzim (collective agricultural settlements) who lived under terrorist attacks and shelling showed more teeth grinding than children on kibbutzim farther inland, out of range of attacks (Ziv & Israeli, 1975).

Community cohesiveness and strong social support networks increase child stress resistance. Kibbutz methods of rearing children in group care with calm daily routines, beloved stable caregiving persons, and close relationships with peers and caregivers have been found to buffer children from war anxiety (Milgram, 1982). During a period of heavy artillery shelling of a particular kibbutz on the Lebanese border in 1970:

The preschool children had become visibly distressed and their *metaplot* (caregivers) were uncertain as to how to handle the situation. The consultant held group discussions with these women and quickly identified the problem: the underlying anxiety of some *metaplot* and preschool charges. Once they were able to acknowledge their concerns for their husbands and their own children, they could begin to draw upon the resources of the kibbutz to bolster their flagging confidence. Thereafter, they could develop teaching and training strategies to enhance the sense of security of the children under their care. They set up telephone communication between their charges and their mothers and also communicated with their own children elsewhere on the kibbutz. They encouraged the children to decorate the shelters in which they had to sleep. They permitted expression of apprehension through class discussions and through drawing. In sum, group work with the outside consultant enabled the child care workers to cope more effectively with their own fears and to help their preschool charges cope more effectively with theirs. (p. 662)

Unfortunately, in many war-torn communities, such as sectors of

Northern Ireland, psychological services for young children are not widely available. One can only guess at the stresses suffered by children in displacement camps or starving persons in drought countries where famine strikes.

War orphans invariably suffer a painful experience. A recurring problem in Israel revolved around how and when to tell children about their father's death (Milgram, 1982).

It became clear that mothers who were

evasive or who lied altogether only confused and upset their children. One four-year-old child was told that his father was in heaven. He subsequently became anxious whenever he heard an airplane overhead because he feared (it was learned subsequently) that the airplane might run his father over. He also got upset whenever it rained because the rain would make his father cold and wet. Another child of three years was told that his father had fallen. The word "fall" in Hebrew clearly implies death, but this child became disturbed whenever he went up or down stairs, fearing, as he later explained, that if he were to fall on the stairs, something terrible would happen to him as it had to his father who had fallen. (p. 663)

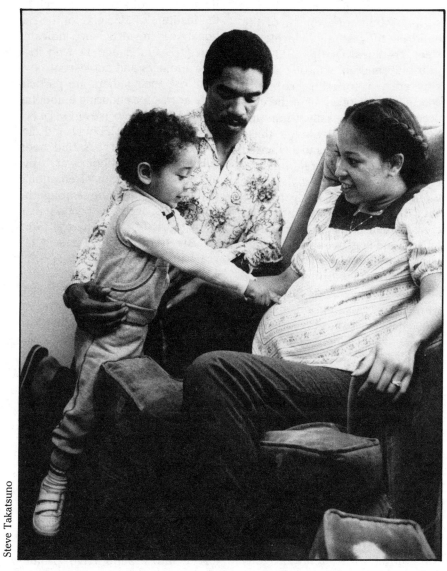

Steve Takatsuno

If loving child care workers, parents, and other family friends increase positive attention paid to older children, then the new baby may not turn out to be the severe stressor that it sometimes has been found to be for siblings.

Family events as stressors

Birth of siblings

For some children, the birth of a new baby into the family can be a stressful occasion. Moore (1975), in a study of London children, found that 15% of the children he studied developed difficulties, predominantly through a disturbed mother-child relationship or acting out behaviors, after the birth of a new baby in the family.

Dunn and her colleagues (1981) reported that after the birth of a sibling, about one fourth of the children they studied developed sleep troubles. Of the 40 2-to-3-year-old children, almost one half showed new toileting problems, and more than one half of the children cried more easily. Dunn and Kendrick (1980) attributed these child stress responses to a changed mother-oldest child relationship. Following the new baby's birth, mothers were less likely to play with the oldest child, and they increased their prohibitions, confrontations, and negative verbal interactions with the older children. Thus, the birth of a sibling can be a stressor. But if loving child care workers, parents, and other family friends increase positive attention paid to older children, the appearance of a new baby may not become the severe stressor that it sometimes has been found to be for siblings.

Bereavement and loss

Death of a parent. Loss of a parent is perhaps the greatest stress a child must cope with. Death of a parent increases a child's sense of profound helplessness and loss, particularly when mental resources are not equipped for coping with such a tragedy (Furman, 1974). Researchers have reported that loss of a parent "creates profound reactions, in-cluding: denial, reversal of affect, identification with the parent, an intense attachment to the lost parent, fantasies of the parent's return, idealization of the parent, persisting demands to be cared for, a vindictive rage against the world, efforts to force the parent to return by suffering, and a self-inflicted repetition of the loss via other relationship" (Adams-Greenly & Moynihan, 1983).

The age and sex of the child at the time of a parent's death affect the intensity of stress. Research by the Institute of Medicine of the National Academy of Science indicates that girls under age 11 who lose their mothers and adolescent boys who lose their fathers are particularly at risk for enduring emotional problems all their lives (1984). For 47 children, both kibbutz and city reared, whose fathers had been killed in the Yom Kippur war, a significantly higher rate of emotional pathology was found among the young boys, aged 3 to 6 years, than among girls of the same age (70% vs. 20%) both at 1 year and 1½ years after the father's death (Elizur & Kaffman, 1983).

Rutter's research (1983) on children of sick, dying parents revealed that immediate grief reactions of young children were both milder and of shorter duration than those of adolescents. Yet the long-term consequences in terms of psychiatric disturbance were greater for the young children. Stress factors *consequent* upon the bereavement may, however, account for the long-term severity of loss for young children. For example, after a parent's death, a child may be forced to undergo a move to new housing, may be cared for by many others, live impoverished, and be forced into a supportive, prematurely responsible role by the grieving, surviving parent.

Bowlby's attachment theory sug-gests that early loss of a parent sensitizes a child, who then becomes more vulnerable to later stresses, particularly later losses and threats of loss. For children who lose a mother before they are 11 years old, later stress events are more likely to provoke depression (Brown & Harris, 1978).

Of 2,000 murders in this country each year, 10% involve children as witnesses. Poussaint studied 10 Black and Hispanic children where family death had occurred through murder. For these bereaved children, rage was overwhelming. "They felt violated, like rape victims—they wanted to seek revenge, hunt for the killer, and exhibited terror of their environment" (cited in Turkington, 1984, p. 16). Emotional pathology was likely when the killer was not caught, and the children became obsessively preoccupied with thoughts about the murder rather than able to go through the grief work that leads to more normal personality reorganization.

Psychiatric symptoms in death of a parent. Arthur Kemme (1964) looked at the symptoms of 23 emotionally disturbed children who had lost a parent. The children showed severe psychiatric symptoms that included:

● deep insecurity and inability to trust
● narcissistic self-involvement
● extreme impulsivity
● unprovoked violence toward peers, adults, and property
● overtly seductive invitations for sexual contact
● nightmares, night terrors, and phobic reactions
● guilt toward the dead parent and reactive depression episodes

A more recent study randomly selected bereaved spouses and control families with children at a mean age of 10 to 11 years. Child age, sex, number of children, and the socioeconomic status of the family were carefully controlled. One year after the death, according to the bereaved parents who were interviewed, the children showed a greater frequency of sadness, crying, irritability, sleep and eating troubles, temper tantrums, and bedwetting. During the first year after parental death, bereaved children were reported to fight more with siblings and be more disinterested in school than control children. None of the control children, but almost one fifth of the bereaved children, reportedly were doing worse in school.

Death of a sibling. A dying sibling represents a severe shock for a child (Rosen, 1985). Family members experience fear, guilt for resenting the disruption in their lives, and anger and sorrow at the impending loss. Bewilderment and isolation increase for the healthy sibling. In a study of therapeutic work done with children dying of cancer and their families, Sourkes has noted the typical effect of the stress of a sibling dying on younger children in the family:

> Parents learn to recognize and interpret stress reactions in the siblings. Susan's little brother began to wet the bed nightly during her prolonged hospitalization (for cancer). The mother thought that bedwetting was his means of delaying her daily departures to the hospital, since she would wash and change his linens before leaving. The mother thus understood the enuresis as a symptom of the child's stress, rather than as an annoying additional burden. (1977, p. 67)

Handicapped sibling: A stressor?

Research prior to the past decade tended to show that siblings of a handicapped child were more likely than other children to suffer from emotional or behavioral disorders, especially if the normal sibling was close in age. Recent research has not found a difference in the proportion of emotionally disturbed children whose siblings are handicapped (Breslau et al., 1981). Where support services are low, the siblings of autistic children have been found to be more poorly adjusted and family stress higher (Bristol & Schopler, 1984). Male siblings may be more vulnerable. Breslau (1982) found that boys with handicapped brothers and sisters

---

When adults are calm and provide security, young children will not pick up fears.

---

suffered greater psychological difficulties than did girls. Normal siblings coped best when their parents spoke openly about the child's handicap, included the normal child in the family decision-making process, and asked for the child's help in integrating the handicapped sibling into the community (Garland, Swanson, Stone, & Woodruff, 1981). Thus, open communication, support, and parental sensitivity can diminish the potentially stressful impact of a handicapped sibling on a normal child.

Spouse problems: A child stressor

Separation and divorce

Like bereavement or loss of community imposed by war and dislocation, separation and divorce are devastating stress situations for children. Schools have reported higher rates of disrupted learning, erratic attendance, increased tardiness, school dropout, and social misbehaviors among children from divorced families.

Wallerstein and Kelly (1980) car-

ried out extensive clinical investigations of 131 children and parents from 60 middle class, mostly White California divorcing families. Approximately one third of the children continued to experience overt parental discord even 5 years after the divorce. Stress thus can be severe and even terrifying for children not only when parents fight prior to a divorce but long after a marriage is dissolved.

The patterning of divorce-as-stressor is different from the long-term chronic stressor poverty or from an acute stressor, such as a single hospitalization. Family instability generally lasted in this sample for 3 to 5 years—well over half the lifetime of a preschool child. Long-term effects may well be more serious than recovery from acute/immediate postdivorce griefs would suggest. Compared with loss through death, divorce stress "is greatly increased by the child's accurate perception that the parents are the agents of his distress, and that they have become such agents voluntarily" (Wallerstein, 1983, p. 272). "Anger at parents and guilt-restoration fantasies may even be more powerful and longer lasting" (p. 273) for children of divorce compared to bereaved children.

Wallerstein conceptualizes several different stages of the adjustment to divorce process:

1. *Acute Phase.* Precipitated by the decisive separation of the married couple, and (usually) the father's departure from the home. Verbal violence, rages, and evocations of hurt and sense of loss of internal control often characterize this phase.

2. *Transitional Phase.* Economic hardship, moving, and radically altered parent/child relationships may occur.

3. *Stabilizing Phase.* The postdivorce family is reestablished as a stable, functioning unit.

In the acute phase, the custodial parent tends to be less competent. Hetherington and his colleagues, (1978), in a longitudinal study of children after divorce, noted that household disorder increases. New patterns of mother-work often result, with young children having to put themselves to bed and to spend a lot of time with sitters as the now single parent tries to create a new social/sexual life. Wallerstein has also observed "greater disorder, poorly enforced discipline, and diminished regularity in enforcing household routines. The root causes underlying the deteriorating household's order (were), in addition to fatigue and overloading, the mother's fear of rejection by her children" (1983, p. 277). During the first postdivorce year, children were more irritable, edgy, accusatory, and rebellious.

Age was an important variable in delineating the effects of divorce stress. The preschool child is

more likely to regress behaviorally; more likely to worry about being abandoned by both parents; more likely than the older child to feel responsible for causing the divorce; is likely to become intensely aware of all separations and to be very frightened at routine separations during daytime and especially at bedtime; is likely to be tearful, irritable, and more aggressive; and is likely to suffer an inhibition of play.

Children in the early school-age group are likely to show moderate depression; to be preoccupied with the father's departure from the home; to grieve openly and to long intensely for his return; to fear replacement ("Will my daddy get another mommy, another dog, another little boy?") and to experience the father's departure as a rejection ("If he loved me, he would not have left"). Approximately half of the children in this age group experienced a disruption in their learning at school as well as deteriorated relationships with their peers during the year following the decisive marital separation. (p. 280)

Sex of child. Both of the investigators cited have found that compared with sons, girls in mother-custody homes adapt significantly better after the divorce for the first couple of years, in their overall adjustment and in cooperation with their mother.

Wallerstein notes six tasks children have in coping with divorce. The first two are: *acknowledge the marital disruption* and *regain a sense of direction and freedom to pursue customary activities.* The next four tasks become more salient for adolescents than for younger children: *dealing with loss and feelings of rejection; forgiving the parents; accepting the permanence of the divorce;* and *resolving issues of relationship.*

The first task is very difficult for small children, partly because fantasy and reality are so hard for preschoolers to separate. Fears were rampant. One half of the children in Wallerstein's study feared that their father would totally abandon them; one third expected the mother would do so; a few feared they would be placed outside the home. Fears and anxieties "evoked by visions of a cataclysmic disaster" (p. 285) decreased over the first postdivorce year particularly as children were assured of continued love and care. These absurd fears are typical when children have experienced loss:

Kim, a Korean 6-year-old child who had been adopted 2 years before, seemed very worried and sad as his adoptive family excitedly prepared to move into the new house they had recently purchased. When questioned, the child explained, "But I don't know how to cook and I won't have anything to eat." He assumed that when the adoptive family moved to the new house, he would be left behind in the old house and would starve alone, since he could not cook for himself.

Caregivers need to realize the full extent of such child terrors in order to become more sensitive and attuned to the dimensions and intensity of divorce and other disturbances, as they may be acted out in group care. Teachers can be particularly helpful with Task 2. Master teachers can refocus and sustain children's interest in play activities, help children commit energy and persistent interest to appropriate learning tasks. *Empathy* rather than exasperation (with children's mood swings, agitated tensions, and disruptions in concentration) can energize caregivers. Adults need to galvanize their energies to help provide nurturant, stable, secure, curiosity-challenging play opportunities and interactions at a level that encourages stressed children to cope.

Wallerstein notes that the most difficult task for many children to master is "assimilating the grief over the departure of one parent from the home, and coming to terms with the partial or total loss of that parent" (p. 285). Where visitation patterns did not live up to the child's yearnings, an intense sense of suffering loss, of dejection, and of being unlovable or unworthy continued. Low self-esteem then interfered with effective learning and with friendships. Teachers may want to give priority in program planning to building secure self-esteem, and devising cooperative games to enhance peer pleasures for stressed children of divorce.

Some children in this study failed to achieve the special coping tasks for dealing with divorce. Developmental arrest was evident in the continuation of intense sorrow, anger, feelings of rejection, and the never-ending search for the absent parent combined with poor self-esteem. Divorce stressors added heavy burdens to the children's regular developmental tasks. Successful resolution *did* occur for many children 5 to 10 years after the divorce, as revealed in increased children's pride in independence and in their mastery of divorce stress.

Stepfamilies

The Vishers (1983) have noted that "many stepfamilies seem to start with the assumption that the new parent and the stepchildren will come together and love one another at once, as though they had grown up together. This unrealistic expectation can lead to deep disappointment and guilt in the family and stress for the parents and children" (p. 137). Based on their work with stepfamilies, the Vishers counsel that settling basic custody and visitation issues, developing more courteous relationships with ex-spouses, and finding social support networks can ease stressful tensions for children in stepfamilies.

Working mothers: A source of stress for children?

Research on the effects of other-than-mother care for children with working parents has proved inconclusive. Some studies show no negative effects, especially where the mother's attitude toward her work is positive (Yarrow, Scott, de Leeuw, & Heinig, 1978). Others have shown that boys are differentially stressed when their mother works; their school achievement suffers, and their fathers have less positive regard for them (Gold & Andres, 1978).

In a study of toddlers of working and nonworking mothers, the toddlers of nonworking mothers possessed significantly higher IQs (Schachter, 1981), but children of employed mothers were more peer-oriented and self-sufficient.

Vaughn and colleagues (1985) studied 90 mothers with 24-month-old children, who represented these three groups, respectively: one where the mother returned to work/school early and placed the child in group care prior to 12 months; one "later work" group where infants were placed between 12 and 18 months; and one "no-work" group of mothers. All the infants were observed at both 12 and 18 months in the Ainsworth Strange situation. [This is a procedure that consists of 8 three-minute episodes

Betty C. Ford

Empathy for, rather than exasperation with, children's mood swings, agitated tensions, and disruptions in concentration can energize caregivers.

involving the presence and absence of mother and stranger for a baby left in a room with toys. Attachment is coded as secure, avoidant, or ambivalent/anxious depending on how positively the baby accepts comfort upon reunion with mother (after two episodes of her departure) or whether the baby ignores mother

or squirms away from her attempts to comfort baby upon rejoining him or her.]

At 2 years of age, the children were asked first to participate in toy play, then cleanup, and finally in solving difficult tool-using tasks without adult help. The results of this study were dramatic and suggest that early return to work was stressful for these young children.

Babies who had been identified as securely attached at 18 months and whose mothers had returned to work early showed more oppositional behaviors when mothers gave directives than did the children previously identified as insecure. They also had "a less optimal experience during the problem-solving tasks than the insecure children" (p. 131). Securely attached children in the late-work group ignored fewer of their mothers' directives and were rated as better able to cope with the stresses of the difficult problem-solving tasks.

Children in the "no-work" group showed the most optimal responses. The no-work group yielded numerous significant differences between children identified as securely versus insecurely attached. In this group, secure children were less likely than insecure children to behave in an oppositional way, to say no, to whine, or to display frustration behaviors in the face of maternal directives. In addition, the secure children were less likely than their insecure counterparts to ask for mother's help. These securely attached children were rated as more persistent, as better able to cope with the stress of the problem-solving procedure, as showing more positive affect (and less negative affect) during the procedures, and as being more enthusiastic in approaching the problems. Further, the secure children were rated as less noncompliant, frustrated, and angry than the insecure children were. Finally, mothers of securely attached children (in the no-work group) were rated as being better able to structure and control the situation for the child. (pp. 131–132)

Thus, in this research, when mothers went to work early (before 12 months), there was a deterioration in the quality of adaptation over the period of 18 to 24 months for toddlers rated as securely attached, so that by 24 months, the formerly secure children were no longer distinguishable from insecure children in their adaptations. It should be noted that all groups of anxiously attached children were rated as somewhat maladaptive in the 24 month tasks. Thus, the *timing* of mother's return to work, if too early, may serve as a stressor to interrupt continuity in positively adaptive organization for infants who have been up to then securely attached. Much more research is needed to give us a more complete understanding of the effects of maternal employment on child development.

Mental illness in parents

Even tiny infants are attuned to the emotional availability and status of their parents. When mothers were instructed to act depressed and look solemnly or indifferently, babies showed disorganized, distressed behavior, often averted their gaze, protested, looked wary, and attempted to elicit responses from the "depressed" parent before withdrawing into apathy themselves. Field (1984) videotaped 24 mothers (one half "depressed" and one half nondepressed) with their 3-month-old infants. A split-screen technique focused on the baby *and* on the mother's face. The heart rate for both was also recorded. Mothers were instructed in three face-to-face, 3-minute interactions: first, playing with a baby as if at home; next, looking at a baby as if in a depressed, too-tired-to-play mood; third, playing naturally again.

Overall, infants of nondepressed mothers showed more frequent positive facial expressions and vocalizations, less frequent negative facial expressions, and higher activity and heart rate levels. During the "depressed" situation, infants of nondepressed mothers, compared with infants of "depressed" mothers, showed more frequent negative facial expressions, more protesting behavior, and looked more wary. The babies of nondepressed mothers seemed to be trying to overcome the stress of the "depressed mother" situation by protesting. Infants of "depressed" mothers changed little during the "depressed" interaction. Their lower heart rates, however, may need to be examined in light of research that shows that lower heart rate may be associated with helplessness and passive coping. Field suggested that these babies appeared to "mirror" their mothers' behavior. "By experiencing frequent lack of control during early interactions, they have developed a passive coping, depressed style of interacting" (p. 521).

These data suggest that the stress of coping with emotional difficulties in maternal personality may be communicated extremely early to infants. Enriched environments with more opportunities for positive feedback from loving responsive adults seem urgent for infants who lack control over emotional interactions because of maternal depression or other personality disturbances. Greenspan and Weider (1984) described the importance and efficacy of providing such therapeutic encounters for infants in a special nursery when life stresses have made mothers emotionally unavailable, abusive, or both.

Child psychiatric disorders

Rutter (1979) identified six family variables strongly associated with children's mental illness:
- severe marital discord
- low social status
- overcrowding or large family size
- father's criminality
- psychiatric disorder of the mother
- care through a local authority such as foster care.

Among a large sample of 10-year-old children, *one* of these risk factors alone did not increase children's chances for psychiatric disorder, but when two risk factors occurred together, then problems doubled. When four or more of the risk factors occurred together, children's psychiatric problems were

10 times as likely. Rutter observed that *a combination of chronic stresses had much more serious probability of resulting in psychiatric illness* than if a child had but one of the stresses. One out of five children who had four or more stresses became seriously emotionally disturbed.

In the Rochester Longitudinal Study, a mother's severe and chronic mental illness was a better predictor of child disturbance than any specific category of mental illness (Sameroff & Seifer, 1983). At 30 months, children of mentally ill mothers showed very poor socioemotional competence on the Rochester Adaptive Behavior Inventory compared to children from families with no parental mental illness. Children from low socioeconomic status (SES) families also showed some of the same symptoms: more fearful, less cooperative, more timid, more depressed, and more likely to engage in bizarre behavior than the comparison group. By 48 months, however,

> there was a separation between the risk-group behaviors. The children of mentally ill mothers continued to show the same deficits they had at 30 months compared with children of healthy mothers, but many of the differences among children in different social status groups became less pronounced. The 48-month data alone suggest a greater role for mental illness than for social status. (p. 1259)

Mental illness *combined* with lower SES resulted in the most disturbed outcomes for children, particularly in emotional problems and lowered IQ scores for children by 4 years of age.

Inept parenting practices: Stressors for children

Inappropriate parenting and poor parenting skills markedly increase stress levels in children. When mothers overuse aversive consequences, as in giving constant threats or nagging commands, they stress children significantly. In microsocial studies of children with high social aggression rates, Patterson (1980) observed that their mothers could not perceive child deviance as well and were more *coercive* than mothers of nonaggressive children. Mothers who were under stress were more likely to use disapproval, negativism, and yelling, and less likely to use talk, laughter, and approval.

Patterson (1983) describes mothers with high *irritability* scores as more apt to "blame, command, complain, criticize, disagree, disqualify, [place] guilt-trip[s], [ask] leading question[s], mind-read, and threaten" (p. 258). The families in this research were asked to plan an activity together for 10 minutes. Also, for 10-minute sessions they were asked to discuss something the parents wanted to change in the family, and next, something that the children wanted to change in the family. These laboratory exercises revealed that parents lacked the skills in: 1) setting up household rules to reduce the likelihood of conflicts (such as sibling fights); 2) making clear what punishments would follow the breaking of rules; and 3) following through in behavioral management. Specifically, antisocial, disruptive children had mothers with high irritability and poor parent negotiation skills, and chaotic quality of parent-child interactions. Stress is greater for children whose parents lack problem-solving skills in coping with crises outside and inside the family.

Two-parent, poor, immigrant North African parents living in France were interviewed about family stresses and childrearing with their 24-month-old children (Honig, Gardner, & Vesin, 1985). Out of 191 mothers, 36 reported feeling overwhelmed. Significantly more of the overwhelmed versus nonoverwhelmed mothers reported severe behavioral problems in their toddlers such as aggression, shyness, and jealousy. They also reported poorer interpersonal relationships between both parents and the toddlers than mothers who did not feel overwhelmed.

Parental discipline techniques: A source of stress

Even in normal families, Patterson (1980) has suggested that childrearing is stressful for mothers, and that ineffective child management practices may produce maternal feelings of anger and depression. Baumrind (1983) characterizes parental discipline methods as authoritarian, permissive, and authoritative. The first two methods are stressful to children because through adult coercion or overindulgence they take away opportunities for children to make responsible choices and to become more mature, well-socialized people. In contrast, authoritative parents produce children who work well in classrooms, get along with peers, and are more pleasant in the family. High standards coupled with consideration, helpfulness, and commitment from parents create more stress-free environments despite the parent's firm rules and high expectancies. Thus, some family discipline techniques can be more appropriate and helpful in socializing children into cooperative and mature behaviors (Honig, 1982a).

Child abuse: An unsecret stress. Four kinds of abuse occur with children: Severe *physical abuse* leaves bodily scars and results in death for several thousand children annually; some children suffer from *psychological unavailability* of the mothering one; some are *neglected* and hungry; and some are emotionally scarred by bitter *hostility,* shaming, chronic verbal abuse, and criticism.

In a prospective study of the developmental sequel of different kinds of abuse among urban poor mothers of infants, Egeland and Sroufe (1981) found that of 19 hostile mothers, 15 also abused their infants physically. Of the 19 psychologically unavailable mothers, 12 also severely physically abused their infants. Thus, multiple abuse is frequent and makes strict comparisons of abuse types difficult. Feeding and play interactions were observed at 3 and 6 months. Quality of infant attachment was assessed at 12 and 18 months with the Ainsworth Strange Situation procedure.

At 18 months, the majority of infants whose mothers had been hostile and physically abusive were anxiously attached. Children of psychologically unavailable mothers who had not been physically abusive were overwhelmingly avoidantly attached at 18 months. None was securely attached.

At 24 months, the toddlers were observed in the tool-using, problem-solving situations devised by Matas, Arend, and Sroufe (1978). Toddlers who had been physically abused acted significantly more aggressive and frustrated, and had lower scores on positive affect during the problem-solving situation, than secure control toddlers. Whining, frustration, and negative affect in the problem-solving situation was greater for the children of psychologically unavailable mothers. They showed anger and frustration *earlier* than the other children.

The most marked and stunning effect of having a psychologically unavailable mother was evident on developmental quotients. At 9 months, the average mental score for these children was 118. By 24 months, their mean mental score had declined to 87. Mean mental

Some discipline techniques can be more appropriate and helpful in socializing children into cooperative and mature behaviors.

developmental scores for infants whose mothers were psychologically unavailable *and* who also physically abused their babies was 121 at 9 months, but had declined to 83 by 24 months.

Attachment patterns of neglected infants were markedly different from normal infants'. Only 27% and 29% (respectively) of infants who had been neglected, with and without physical abuse, were securely attached to mother at 12 months. This figure should be contrasted with national United States norms of about 67% secure attachment for infants at 1 year. Neglected babies who were not physically abused changed from inse-

cure/ambivalent at 12 months to insecure/avoidant attachments by 18 months. At 24 months, both groups displayed high noncompliance, anger, and frustration with mothers during the problem-solving situation.

The researchers concluded that for the children with psychologically unavailable mothers, the outcomes were "severely malignant, pervasive, and pernicious. Having a mother who is chronically unavailable and unresponsive has devastating consequences on the child that touch every aspect of early functioning" (p. 89). *Early, positive, responsive care is crucial for children's emotional well being.* "At a time when most children are engaging the environment on their own and falling back on caregivers when their own resources are exhausted, maltreated children are locked in an angry struggle with their caregivers or are unable to engage the environment effectively" (p. 91).

Stressors that cluster with child abuse. In a study of 74 low SES families, both abusive and non-abusive, Conger, McCarty, Yang, Lahey, and Kropp (1984) examined intersecting sets of ecological and personal variables that might predict child abuse. Demographic factors associated with abuse were first birth, economic distress, more children, less education, and lower occupational status.

Maternal values were assessed. High authoritarian values (for example, where child obedience was considered extremely important, even for babies) and negative perception of child were associated with maternal abuse. Mothers were observed in preschool and six times at home while playing simple bean bag, Lincoln logs, or construction toy games with their children. The ratio of positive to total maternal behaviors was computed. Stressful life circumstances had an influence *independent* of maternal personal values and perceptions. Poverty and early parenting as well as maternal psychological variables *both* had direct and indirect influences on abusive or positive maternal behavior.

In a study of nearly 400 Wisconsin families with child abuse, more than two thirds of the parents were perceived as having strong emotional difficulties. In addition, two out of five families had marital stress. One third of the children were removed from the home, although for 10% foster care placement was temporary. The families

were overwhelmingly poor, and in about one half the cases the father had not finished high school. Thus, not only was child abuse *per se* a stressor in such families, but clusters of other difficulties were also inherent in these children's lives. Stress factors were a part of the family's functioning, particularly in their personal interaction styles.

Trickett and Kuczynski (1986) asked 40 families of children aged 4- to 11-years-old to keep careful records of daily misbehaviors, such as fighting with others, breaking things, and whining, and to record how they handled the misbehaviors. One half of the parents had a long history of child abuse; the others were matched to this sample's demographic characteristics. Contrast in the *stressfulness* of the discipline techniques used by the two groups was evident; 80% of the abusive parents and 65% of the control parents reported using physical punishment at least once during the 5-day period. However, 40% of the abusive parents and 0% of the control parents reported using *severe* forms of physical punishment (such as striking with an object, hitting in the face, or whipping) at least once during this 5-day period. Parents in both groups reported feeling dissatisfied after punishing, but twice as many abusive parents reported feeling angry or irritated. When children's misbehaviors were conventional (for example, violating family rules about leaving clothes around) rather than highly arousing (such as fist fight with brother), abusive parents were significantly more likely than control parents to punish; control parents were more likely to use reasoning. In high-arousal situations, all parents were likely to use punishment.

Abused children were more likely than control children to refuse to

comply and get angry when disciplined. Thus, the researchers note that "the failure of abusive parents to use reasoning after moral and conventional social transgressions may have been maladaptive, because they used strategies for gaining short-term immediate compliance rather than long-term compliance strategies that would increase chances for children to learn internal controls. Such aversive responding may escalate to the point of actual abuse of a child once an interaction begins" (p. 122). Specific parent training in child management skills and in *using different techniques for different goals* (short- or long-term compliance) *may be helpful in reducing stress* for children in abusive families.

These researchers suggest that we need to give high community and civic priority to educational preparation for parenthood, supports for new parents, and to training pediatric clinic staff to become alert to the grim potentials for child abuse in unavailable, neglecting, and physically abusive parents. As a society, we also need to support high quality group care to enhance education prospects for low-income children at risk for abuse, and as a respite for chronically stressed parents.

Invulnerability and coping

Despite some adults' wishful thinking, there are no super children who are impervious to all stresses in life. Even Garmezy (1985), who had earlier written about the remarkable coping skills of some children he labeled *invulnerable,* acknowledges regret at having given the impression that some children are impervious to all stressors. Children *do* differ in resilience, but unless adults are careful, they may tax the resources of even the most resilient child.

Garmezy (1981) has defined coping as a pattern of behavioral response to novel situations, obstacles, and conflicts in which occur search, effort, direct action, and shaping of events. Blom, Cheney, and Snoddy (1986) listed the behavioral characteristics of stress-resistant children with effective coping skills. They noted:

> Behaviors such as empathy, understanding the points of view of others, helping others, good verbal skills, good attentional processes, reflectiveness, problem solving, inner locus of control, frustration tolerance, and success appear possible to teach. Other behaviors seem to be more complex and global and do not easily lend themselves to an instructional or training approach. These include the ability to detach from the dysfunctional behaviors of others, being personable and well liked, creative thinking, autonomous thinking, optimism, having a sense of humor, being aware of personal power, having a future orientation, and having a well-developed value system. (p. 156)

Catalytic variables that *increase* the effect of stressors are known as *vulnerability variables*. Variables that *decrease* stressor effects are called *protective factors* (Rutter, 1979). In the families of psychiatric patients where there was discord, *one good relationship with a parent protected the children*. Only one fourth of these children showed a conduct disorder. In discordant homes where there was no buffering good relationship with a parent, three fourths of the children showed conduct disorders.

Heightened awareness of the buffering effects of a nurturant parent-child relationship came from the evacuation studies of children during the London blitz bombings in World War II. Anna Freud and Burlingham (1943) reported no traumatic shock for young children who were in their own mother's care or the care of a familiar mother substitute as a re-

sult of the German bombing of London. Yet almost one half of the children evacuated to rural areas for protection from air attacks developed neurotic symptoms. A close mother-child attachment was a powerful buffer even against wartime stresses.

Caring adults give purpose and direction to traumatized children's lives and help them to develop what Sheehy called the "victorious personality." Sheehy (1986), who herself adopted an orphan of the Pol Pot Massacres in Cambodia, uses the term "polestar" to describe an adult mentor who "endorses the youngster as worthy, who may offer a goal that is healing and who helps feed the future with the hope that things will get better" (p. 47).

Locus of control and self-esteem

Perceiving yourself in control of your life and having self-esteem are factors that help you cope adequately with external stressors. People with low self-esteem are "unable to count on positive self feelings as a resource and feel trapped by their own ineffectual attempts to adapt, frequently responding with depression" (Lee, 1983, pp. 3–4). Lee studied families that had a teenage parent in the family. For 46 blue collar, mostly rural families, items from the Schedule of Recent Life Events (Holmes & Rahe, 1967) were used. This scale measures the magnitude of adjustment required for each of 42 life events such as illness in the family, bills to pay, car broken down, and family arguments. Patterson has revised and extended this checklist to 101 items rated for intensity on a scale from -3 to $+3$. Additional items were added that reflected stressors and hassles the mothers anticipated for their adolescent daughters with babies.

Women who experienced the greatest number of stressors and who received higher levels of social support had the lowest depression scores. Those with high internal (rather than external) locus of control scores believed that they were able to master life circumstances. They fared much better in terms of mental health, with fewer illnesses, fewer sleeping and eating disorders, and less sadness, despite having many life stressors. "Faith in the ability to master life problems served as the protective buffer in the onset of depression for those who reported the most life problems in the two years prior to the interview" (Lee, 1983, p. 12).

Although carried out with adults, this research has strong implications for teachers of young children. Teachers have priorities in their goals for children. They may emphasize cognitive skill acquisition, polite manners, or learning classroom rules. Yet Lee's research suggests that *when teachers help young children feel they have more control over important life aspects, the children may develop sturdier coping skills*. For example, in infant care, prompt pickup and comfort when an infant is distressed leads to feelings of effectiveness and to secure infant attachment. Secure versus insecure infant attachments significantly differentiated toddlers who coped from those who crumpled into temper tantrums, oppositionality, and giving up early rather than attempting to solve difficult tool-using problems in a laboratory situation (Matas, Arend, & Sroufe, 1978). Securely attached toddlers (in contrast to anxiously attached toddlers) persevered, and mastered the stressors of frustration when faced with tool-using tasks too difficult for them to solve alone.

Martin (1981) found that a sense of control (as reflected in mutual involvement of mother with infant interactions) was crucial for the later social adjustment of preschool boys. If boys had received responsive maternal care as infants, then at 42 months they were more compliant and noncoercive with their mothers, more bravely willing to explore a toy hidden behind a barrier out of mother's sight, and more interested in a strange experimenter. Lack of control may be a greater stress factor for male than female infants. Martin notes that "without having acquired this sense of mastery over the interpersonal environment in the mother-child relationship, a boy is likely to become a relatively timid and socially imcompetent child" (p. 47).

Cognitive skills and coping

Coping skills may be more effective among older children because of their increased *ability to think about problems*. Schultz and Heuchert (1983), argue that children need certain mediational skills in order to adapt to the stresses of schooling. Teachers are advised to make schools more exciting and rewarding places in order to help children feel positive about school experiences.

Yet even preschoolers can find coping mechanisms that may not depend on cognitive sophistication. Murphy and Moriarty (1976) examined children with severe family stresses, such as a chronically ill mother, or an infantilizing parent, and found some children coped well. The first child found a "second mother" in a next-door neighbor. The second child devoted all his energy to sports in order to cope with his mother's wish to keep him a baby. However, when support systems are missing in preschoolers' lives, the lack of abstract, consequential thinking combined with life circumstances may intensify the effects of stressors. Very young children cannot autonomously move about in the wider community to seek out supportive adults. Caring preschool teachers can be particularly significant in these children's lives.

Coping skills are being assessed and taught in some intervention programs. Coping Through Personalized Learning is a decision-making model used to plan early intervention services for young at-risk children. The Early Coping Inventory (Zeitlin, Williamson, & Svcvepanski, 1984) measures infant sensorimotor responsiveness and adaptive behaviors. Handicapped infants are encouraged to manage routines, opportunities, and frustrations in daily living. A 6-month-old Down Syndrome infant with low muscle tone that interfered with head and trunk control gained control through carefully programmed exercises. *Self-initiated coping* and independent behaviors markedly differentiated normal infants from handicapped infants (80% versus 25%). Handicapped infants needed specific help in balancing independent and dependent behaviors.

Emotional skills as buffers

Empathy as a buffer against stress

Studying two groups of mothers, 30 of whom had been abusive and 30 nonabusive, Letourneau (1981) used the Hogan Empathy test to distinguish parents who could be empathic. Mothers were also asked to respond to a role-play inventory. A series of situations in which a child sought comfort or help or became angry was presented to the parent by means of a recorded voice. The mother's immediate responses were coded as help-withholding, comfort-withholding, sensitive to the child's needs, or ag-

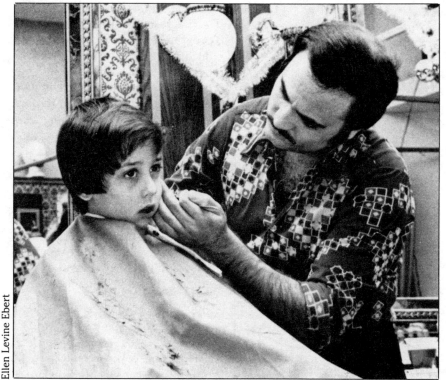

Ellen Levine Ebert

When adults help young children feel they have more control over important life aspects, the children may develop sturdier coping skills.

Table 1

Telltale signs of stress in young children

Doesn't respond to friendly caregiver overtures

Daydreams frequently

Has grave, solemn face; rarely smiles or laughs (check first for iron deficiency; see Honig & Oski, 1984)

Has frequent prolonged temper tantrums

Cries a great deal for months after entry into group care (even though caregivers have been gentle and responsive)

Acts sullen, defiant (says "I don't care" frequently when caregiver explains how misbehavior has hurt another)

Punishes self through slapping, head banging, or calling self bad names ("bad boy")

Is overly sensitive to mild criticism

Flinches if teacher or visiting adult approaches with caressing or reassuring gesture of outstretched arm

Reports proudly to teacher that he or she has hurt another child

Is overly vigilant about others' misdeeds, tattles, or jeers

Is highly demanding of adults although usually fairly self-sufficient

Bullies or scapegoats and may get other children to join in

Carries out repetitive, stereotyped play that may have destructive aspects

Clings to, shadows caregiver, although in group for months

Is unable to carry out sustained play with preschool peers

Has constant need to sleep although physically well

Is preoccupied with frightening images of monsters or other violent, threatening figures

Has dull, vacant expression, as if trying to ward off thinking about stressful trauma or tries to deny stressful feelings

Is hyperactive or restless, wanders around room, touches and disturbs toys and games, cannot settle into constructive play

Displays disturbed bodily functions, has trouble with feeding, constipation, or diarrhea, soils self frequently months after toilet training is completed

Has trembling of hands or facial twitches although apparently well

Talks compulsively about physical dangers and threats

Grinds teeth during naptime

Has rigid facial expressions from taut muscles

Displays loss of perceptual acuity

Displays reduced attentional capacity; even though caregiver is very clear in communicating, the child cannot focus well on activity or request

Stimulates self constantly (by prolonged thumb-sucking, masturbation, rocking body back and forth, or other such behaviors), which children normally do occasionally for self-comfort

Feels jittery

Stutters, uses disfluent speech, or refuses to talk in group (older preschooler)

Is clumsy on easy manual tasks due to muscular tensions

Frequently acts aggressively against others, even adults

Has nightmares

---

gressive. Each mother was asked to imagine she was busy in the kitchen next to the room where her 1-year-old and her 4-year-old were playing with a puzzle.

The mean Hogan empathy score of 29.3 for the abusive mothers contrasts with the score of 40.8 for the nonabusive mothers. Abusive mothers were significantly more aggressive than nonabusive mothers in their responses to the taped child's negative behavior. Both groups of mothers were highly stressed, but *mothers high in empathy were able to adapt.* For example, in response to the taped child's statement, "I don't like this game—you're stupid, Mommy," 63.2% of the abusive mothers versus 6.6% of the nonabusive mothers gave a physically punishing response. When the child said "Mama, it hurts," 83.3% of the nonabusive mothers (as opposed to 36.6% of the abusive mothers) gave a comforting response such as "I know it hurts. Let Mama kiss it."

The researchers suggest that a program aimed exclusively at reducing stress would not prevent the occurrence of child abuse. They conclude that in addition, *empathic skills need to be developed through role-modeling and role-taking work* with abusive parents.

Humor

The National Center on Child Abuse and Neglect suggests humor as a buffer. Their comic book "Dennis the Menace: Coping with Family Stress" is a good example of how families can grin rather than grimace at many child mishaps.

Protective factors: Intersections

Particularly noteworthy in invulnerability research is how *intertwined* the buffering factors are that help children avoid the troubling consequences of stressors such as early high-risk status. The Kauai study (Werner & Smith, 1982) is a good example of such intersection. Low-income Hawaiian children were followed from birth, with assessments at ages 2, 10, and 18. Children with initial birth trauma frequently showed no later deficits *unless* their difficulties were compounded by continuous environmental stressors, such as a mother being mentally ill, an unstable family, or chronic poverty.

Targeting those children who had not developed *any* problems by 18 years of age as *resilient,* Werner and Smith identified the protective factors that buffered these children compared to children with problems. Resilient children had affectionate, good-natured temperaments and elicited positive responses from their families and from strangers. They often found "refuge and a source of self-esteem in hobbies and creative interests" (Werner, 1986, p. 189). Resilient children (despite parental lacks) were more likely to have a close bond with at least one person (such as an aunt or grandparent) from whom they received lots of attention during the first year of life. More often they had structured, rule-oriented households and assigned chores. They themselves often did useful work—babysitting, supporting the family with part-time earnings, and carrying out other caring, helpful acts. When mothers were steadily employed, they appeared to be powerful role models for resilient girls reared in poverty. Low levels of family conflict, smaller family size, and some counseling or remedial assistance were factors that also contributed to resilience in these children's lives.

These findings increase our awareness of the difficulty in understanding stress factors, whether acute or chronic. We need to consider variables such as age and sex at time of stress, possible potentiation of negative effects years later in life by additional stresses, person-situation interactions, intrapersonal vulnerabilities, and how cultural contexts lessen or increase the effects of stressors.

Stress mediators and buffers

Social supports: A key ingredient for coping

Family supports have frequently buffered children against the severe effects of stressors. Crockenberg (1981) assessed high or low irritability in newborn babies with the Brazelton Neonatal Behavioral Assessment Scale. The 48 high school educated mothers were then observed at home with their 3-month-old babies and were later interviewed about family and friend supports. From home observations, *high-responsive* mothers were those who responded more promptly to infant distress. *Low-responsive* mothers fell below the me-

Teachers of young children can mediate family stress by the quality and stability of child care they provide.

How teachers can help children cope with stress

Considering the large number and variety of stressors that children's lives entail, and considering the fragility of coping skills and the scarcity of buffering supports in some children's lives, what can parents and teachers do to help children cope with stress? Most of the suggestions given here focus on preschoolers and school-aged children rather than infants. Some will be useful for caregivers of children of all ages. Adults who care for children in stressful life situations need to have a *wide* variety of techniques and ideas to help young children adjust better in classrooms, at home, and in stressful situations such as temporary foster care or hospitalization.

1. Fundamental to helping children cope with stress is the development of well-honed adult **noticing skills.** Recognize when a child is stressed. Be alert to changes in behavior (more quarrels with playmates, bedwetting, poor concentration) that signal stress. Parents and teachers who are sensitive to telltale signs of stress can tune in more effectively. Learn the signs of stress (see Table 1).

2. **Demonstrate self-control and coping skills yourself.** Be fair and sensitive to differences and problems. Demonstrate brave behaviors: Keep calm even when classroom problems arise and stresses (such as crying, diarrhea, acting-out) seem to be especially prevalent or aggravating on a particular day. If a teacher's voice is exasperated, whiny, disappointed, aggrieved, or angry fairly often, then young children learn that these are acceptable models of coping with stress.

As a parent or teacher, **find social supports in your own life** so that you are energized for adaptive coping with problems that arise with young children. Your "feeling of confidence or faith that things will work out as well as can be reasonably expected and that the odds can be surmounted" contributes to children's effective coping (Werner, 1986, p. 192).

3. **Enhance children's self-esteem** wherever and whenever possible through encouragement, caring, focused attention, and warm personal regard. You are the mirror that reflects the personal worth of each child (Briggs, 1970).

4. Encourage each child to develop a special interest or skill that can serve as an **inner source of pride and self-esteem** (Werner, 1986).

5. **Use proactive intervention to avoid unnecessary stress.** Give children plenty of time before a transition. For example, use verbal, musical, or light-dimming signals so children can gradually put away toys and get ready for lunch. Anticipate stressful occasions.

Preventative actions lessen the possibility and impact of stressful events. Frequent fire drills make children less terrified of loud alarms or sudden commotions. Children who have experienced drills and other such procedures become used to their occurrence and the rules to be followed, so that a fire drill does not become an occasion for panic.

6. Help children understand the consequences and implications of negative, acting-out behaviors on others and on themselves. Shure and Spivack (1978) provide daily activities to help young children improve **skills in consequential thinking.**

7. **Acknowledge children's feelings and encourage verbal mediation.** Help children learn that they are not alone in having uncomfortable feelings. Give them permission to feel scared, lonely, or angry (as when a peer squashes their sandpie). Help them *decenter*—become able to see how others also feel upset if their play or rights are interfered with. Give children *words* to express their negative feelings so that they will not have to be aggressive or disorganized when stressed. "I" statements help a child communicate personal upset and strong wishes rather than accusing, hurting, or threatening others (Gordon, 1970).

Impulsive behavior often causes peer troubles. Help children think about the situation and their impatient feelings so they can avoid a fuss with

dian in promptness of responding. At 1 year of age, infants and mothers were videotaped in the Ainsworth Strange Situation play and separation episodes. Most of the babies (71%) were securely attached to their mother. They sought and accepted comfort upon reunion and then settled into play. About 20% of the infants were *anxiously attached—resistant* to accepting comfort on reunion. About 10% of the infants were *anxious/avoidant*—showing little upset when the mother left the room and ignoring her upon her return.

Mothers with high social supports had fewer babies classified as resistant or avoidant. High irritability was significantly associated with anxious infant attachment *only* when mothers lacked social supports. *Social supports served as a critical buffer against stress when infants were highly irritable.* For less irritable infants, even if social supports for mother were in short supply, secure attachment was more likely. Babies who are easygoing may demand little of stressed caregivers with low supports and they calm more quickly once their needs are tended.

Rooming-in as a buffer against child abuse

Extended maternal contact with newborn babies (rooming-in) can help prevent inadequate mothering patterns. Vietze (1978) provided rooming-in for one half of 291 infants and their undereducated, low-income, teenaged mothers. The other mothers received routine hospital care. Seventeen months later, only 2 out of 146 babies in the rooming-in group had been neglected or abused. In contrast, 10 out of 145 routine-care babies were either hospitalized, referred to, or placed by protective services because of abusive or inadequate maternal care. Early contact, even though not sought by these mothers, may have served as a protective buffer to enhance their early relationships with their infants.

Father interactions as a buffer

Father presence during childbirth has been associated with more positive mother-infant interactions, whether or not early extended contact has been provided.

Where child care quality was poor, Howes and Olenick (1984) found that increased father-toddler interactions were associated with more positive toddler behavior, despite the fact that toddlers in low quality child care centers were generally less competent and less cooperative.

Schools as protective buffers

Although families are significant in furnishing both stresses and supports in children's lives, other people and settings can also be crucial, particularly as buffers. Rutter (1984) followed into adult life 90 girls who spent much of their childhood in institutions because their parents could not cope and had either abandoned or abused them. Despite the lower competence of some of the girls, about one third functioned well. These girls reported positive experiences in school, such as "success in sports, achievement in music, getting positions of responsibility in the school or developing a good relationship with a teacher" (p. 62). The *most* important protective factor for these girls, in general, however, was a harmonious, secure marriage to a nondeviant man, whom they had known for at least 6 months and had married planfully, and not to escape a bad situation. The girls who had had good experiences in school were more likely to be planners. Good school experiences gave the girls a feeling that they were able to succeed at some-

friends. Use Gordon's (1970) active listening: "You wish you could have the new trike all morning, but other children want to ride too, so we need to take turns." "You are trying so hard to sit still until the crackers are passed to you. You are wiggling and *waiting*. Good for you."

The "Think Aloud" lessons (Camp & Bash, 1981) teach children to deal with cognitive and interpersonal problems through verbal mediation. Children learn to talk to themselves in effective and skillful ways to identify their problem, to make plans for coping, and to weigh the merits of different solutions.

8. **Help children distinguish reality from fantasy.** Having strong angry wishes about a brother did not cause that brother to become ill. Papa did not leave home because you were a sloppy eater or were mad at him for not buying you two ice cream cones.

9. **Use gentle humor** when possible to *help children reframe* their negative thoughts and feelings. Then they can perceive mild stressors as possible opportunities or challenges. For example, if Jonathan accidentally knocked down his own block tower, you could comment matter-of-factly with a smile, "Jonathan, your elbow sure was a giant tower-smasher. Now you have a chance to design your next tower even fancier and taller."

10. If the stressor on a child is peer aggression, **focus directly on the stressor.** If a class bully gets others to tease or jeer at a child, *you must stop the bullying.* Talk to the children in your class about attitudes and values that permit bullying or threatening. Speak with the children and their parents separately. Aggression that is not addressed does not go away (Caldwell, 1977). Teachers need to be brave and direct in handling hurting. Children cannot be allowed to hurt others. A child who scapegoats needs to have other ways to feel good about herself or himself.

11. **Help children view their situation more positively.** Some stressors make a child feel ashamed as well as hurt. *Shame eats at a child's self-esteem.* Having a single parent can be such a stressor. As Blom, Cheney, and Snoddy (1986) have noted in their excellent resource for teachers: "A child can be helped to view the single-parenthood status of his mother as acceptable, not uncommon, and preferable to having both parents together and quarreling. [The child's] perception can be altered and the impact of the stress thereby reduced" (p. 82).

12. **Structure classroom activities to enhance cooperation** rather than competition. A cooperative climate in the classroom can help reduce stress. Children will flourish where they can grow and achieve at a pace comfortable for each. Required helpfulness has been found to increase children's sense of effectiveness and coping. Devise cooperative games to play (Honig, 1985b; Honig, 1985c; Honig, Wittmer, & Gibralter, in press; Sobel, 1982).

If a child is unpopular with peers, arrange for *cooperative activities* that require children to work together. When you provide friendly younger peers as companions in mixed-age classes, unpopular children increase their social skills (Roopnarine & Honig, 1985).

13. **Modify classroom situations and rules.** Make choices and expectations easier to understand and to meet. *Rearrange environments to decrease stress.* Quiet reading corners should not be set up adjacent to tricycle riding or block building areas. Define activity areas with clear rules so that fewer tensions will arise in play.

14. **Find individual talk time** with troubled children. Find out how children perceive threats or stresses. A child may feel picked on or that nobody likes her or him. Help children think of a variety of possible solutions for their problems. *Generating alternatives* will increase a child's coping resources.

15. **Mobilize other children to help.** For example, if a handicapped child is entering a preschool class, talk with the children about strengths and troubles every child, and particularly the handicapped child, might have in

making friends, using materials, or negotiating spaces. Honig and McCarron (1986) have shown that normal preschool children in a mainstreamed classroom can be very helpful, empathic, and prosocial toward handicapped peers. If a child has a seriously ill sibling, *enlist classmates* of the well child to provide peer support and attention.

16. **Use bibliotherapy.** Adults can find many materials to read aloud with children to help them identify with stressed characters and how they cope. Some representative titles from the Human Sciences Press are *My Grandpa Died Today, The Secret Worry, Two Homes to Live In: A Child's Eye View of Divorce,* and *Dusty Was My Friend.* Walker Publishers have books such as *That New Baby* and *About Handicaps.* Sunal and Hatcher (1985), Jalongo (1983), and Fassler (1978) provide guides to the use of such books when children are having troubles in their lives.

17. **Have regular classroom talks, in a safe calm atmosphere,** about different stressors. Ask children who are comfortable about their experiences to share what it was like: to go to the hospital for surgery; to move to a new house or school; when a new baby was born in the family; when a parent had to go away for a long while; when there was a violent storm; when a fierce-looking dog barked at them; and when a child thought she or he was lost while shopping with a parent.

Arent (1984) has written a guide to symptoms, situations, and strategies for dealing with child stress, which can stimulate your ideas for talks. Such talks give courage to a child who may be hiding secret sorrows, thinking she or he is all alone with these troubles, or the only one scared by them.

In the Bessell and Palomares "Magic Circle" program (1973), children sit in circles and share pleasant and unpleasant feelings, secure that they will not be judged.

Provide verbal stems for children who may find it difficult to talk in circle time: "One time when I really felt scared, I. . ."; "My friend made me feel really good when. . ."; "One time I was very worried when. . . ."

Such openers help a teacher evaluate the appraisal reactions of young children to stressors and to learn the range and efficacy of coping strategies that children have used.

18. **Use art.** Many young children cannot verbally express fears and anger about the painful stressors in their lives. Paint, clay, and other art tools allow a child to express upsets and act out private feelings. A big, brown, smeary painting can be the way a child feels about the ambulance that came to take Papa away when he suddenly became ill.

19. **Encourage children to act out coping skills** with doll and other dramatic play. For example, if a particular child is stressed because of a recent or future move, "doll houses, housekeeping equipment, and boxes are good for helping a child act out a moving experience. Toy telephones allow imaginary communication with friends in other places and friends that the child would like to know better" (Long, 1985, p. 8). Early in the school year, doll play can help children deal with separation from home.

Use puppets to act out positive problem-solving responses to ordinary daily stressors that a child might encounter. Some sample topics might be forgetting to bring lunch or lunch money to school; wanting a turn on the slide and finding a lot of children ahead of you; wanting a teacher to read to you right away when she or he is busy helping another child; feeling another child unfairly got a bigger portion than you.

20. **Involve parents.** Recommend good books about recognizing and managing child stress (Arent, 1984; Brenner, 1984; Kersey, 1985; Wolff, 1969). Remind parents about how important rest and good nutrition are for coping with stressful situations (see Honig and Oski, 1984, for a discussion of iron deficiency symptoms of irritability and solemnity in infants and young children).

Listen empathetically if parents are able to share some of their life stresses. Together, you and the child's family can be a mutually supportive human system to reduce stress effects and to enhance the security of a child who is troubled.

thing and they were more in control of their own lives, so maybe they could succeed at other things.

Enriched child care as a special support for families. When risk factors are multiple, quality early childhood programs can enhance children's lives. Ramey and Gowan (1984) provided enriched infant/toddler care for low-income children with fetal malnutrition, as measured by a low Ponderal Index (ratio of birthweight to length). Their mothers were undereducated and unresponsive. Yet by 3 years of age, these children had mean IQ scores of 96.4. Control children, equally at risk at birth, but without this cognitively enriching program, had a mean IQ of 70.6. Group care workers need to be aware of how important their role is. Not only do they directly build secure positive relationships with young children, but in addition, caregivers provide a buffering social support for families. Nurturant high quality child care can lessen family stress. Parents nurture their young better when they feel less stressed. Teachers of young children can mediate family stress by the quality and stability of the child care they provide.

Transition to new teacher: Buffering ideas. A change in teachers can produce stress for some children. Children may worry about whether expectations for them and classroom routines will be very different. Some children withdraw attention and affection as a response to loss of a well-liked former teacher. Stress management skills are suggested to help new teachers cope with the change. One suggestion is to have the outgoing teacher participate in the transition phase.

If the present teacher points out some positive aspects of the incoming teacher, she can assist the children in making adjustments. For example, the teacher may say, "She likes books and is a good storyteller" or "She has worked with children before; you will like her" or "She likes our kind of music".... The current teacher needs to remind the children of her departure day and of the arrival date of the new teacher, "who is looking forward to being with you." On the last day, she should explain to the group where she will be going and reaffirm that each child will be missed. A positive follow-up such as a card or letter to the children will be appreciated. (Lawhon & Krishman, 1986, p. 12)

The new teacher can help smooth transitions if she or he looks over the outgoing teacher's plans and schedules, talks with director and parents, recognizes that children will need time to adjust, uses humor to help children relax, and sets expectations about rules and consequences through group discussions with the children.

At the Children's Center, the teachers and preschoolers had discussed together in a group meeting the staff's concern about children hitting or hurting each other. Children and adults spent time discussing *other* ways a child could behave if he or she becomes mad or upset at another child. Staff gave clear indications of the "time-out from play" procedures that would instantly follow any hurting behaviors. Next day, Johnny, impatient at Jimmy's long turn with a desired toy, raised his arm. [The] teacher, in turn, raised her eyebrows at him. "I wasn't going to hit him," Johnny explained, "I was just raising my arm." And he waited patiently. [The] teacher smiled.

References

Adams-Greenly, M., & Moynihan, R. T. (1983). Helping Children of fatally ill parents. *American Journal of Orthopsychiatry, 53*(2), 219–229.

Als, H. (1985). Patterns of infant behavior: Analogues of later organizational difficulties? In F. H. Duffy & N. Geschwind (Eds.), *Dyslexia.* Boston: Little, Brown.

Arent, R. P. (1984). *Stress and your child: A parents' guide to symptoms, strategies and benefits.* Englewood Cliffs, NJ: Prentice-Hall.

Arthur, B., & Keeme, M. L. (1964). Bereavement in childhood. *Journal of Child Psychology and Psychiatry, 5,* 37–49.

Baumrind, D. (1983). Rejoinder to Lewis's reinterpretation of parental firm control: Are authoritative families really harmonious? *Psychological Bulletin, 94,* 132–142.

Beardslee, W. R., & Mack, J. E. (1986, Winter). Youth and children and the nuclear threat. *Newsletter of the Society for Research in Child Development, Inc.* 1–2.

Becker, F. D. (1974). *Design for living: The residents' view of multifamily housing.* Ithaca, NY: Center for Urban Development Research.

Bessell, H., & Palomares, U. (1973). *Methods in human development: Theory manual.* El Cajon, CA: Human Development Training Institute.

Billings, A. G., & Moos, R. H. (1982). Stressful life events and symptoms: A longitudinal model. *Health Psychology, 1,* 99–117.

Blom, G. E., Cheney, B. D., & Snoddy, J. E. (1986). *Stress in childhood: An intervention model for teachers and other professionals.* New York: Teachers College Press, Columbia University.

Brazelton, T. B. (1979, December). *Assessment techniques for enhancing infant development.* Paper presented at the meeting of the National Center for Clinical & Infant Programs, Washington, DC.

Brenner, A. (1984). *Helping children cope with stress.* Lexington, MA: D. C. Heath.

Breslau, N. (1982). Siblings of disabled children: Birth order and spacing effects. *Journal of Abnormal Child Psychology, 10*(1), 85–96.

Briggs, D. (1975). *Your child's self-esteem.* New York: Doubleday.

Bristol, M., & Schopler, E. (1984). A developmental perspective on stress and coping in families of autistic children. In Blacher (Ed.), *Severely handicapped young children and their families: Research in review.* New York: Academic.

Brown, G. W., & Harris, T. (1978). *Social origins of depression: A study of psychiatric disorder in women.* New York: The Free Press.

Caldwell, B. M. (1977). Aggression and hostility in young children. *Young Children, 32*(2), 5–14.

Camp, B. W., & Bash, M. A. (1981). *Think aloud. Increasing social and cognitive skills—A problem solving program for children.* Champaign, IL: Reseach Press.

Clymer, A. (1986, February 2). Poll finds children remain enthusiastic on spaceflight. *The New York Times,* pp. 1, 16.

Conger, R. D., McCarty, J. A., Yang, R. K., Lahey, B. B., & Kropp, J. P. (1984). Perception of child, child-rearing values, and emotional distress as mediating links between environmental stressors and observed maternal behavior. *Child Development, 55,* 2234–2247.

Consortium for Longitudinal Studies. (1983). *As the twig is bent: Lasting effects of preschool programs.* Hillsdale, NJ: Erlbaum.

Crockenberg, S. B. (1981). Infant irritability, mother responsiveness, and social support influences on the security of infant-mother attachment. *Child Development, 52,* 857–865.

Dunn, J., & Kendrick, C. (1980). The arrival of a sibling: Changes in the pattern of interaction between mother and first-born child. *Journal of Child Psychology and Psychiatry, 21,* 119–132.

Dwick, C. S., Davidson, W., Nelson, S., & Enna, B. (1978). Sex differences in learned helplessness: II. The contingencies of evaluative feedback in the classroom, and III. An experimental analysis. *Developmental Psychology, 14,* 268–276.

Egeland, B., & Sroufe, A. (1981). Developmental sequelae of maltreatment in infancy. *Directions for Child Development, 11,* 77–92.

Elder, G. H., Van Nguyen, T., & Avshalom, C. (1985). Linking family hardship to children's lives. *Child Development, 56,* 361–375.

Elizur, E., & Kaffman, M. (1983). Factors influencing the severity of childhood bereavement reactions. *American Journal of Orthopsychiatry, 53*(4), 668–676.

Elmer, A. (1978). Effects of early neglect and abuse on latency age children. *Journal of Pediatric Psychology, 3*(1), 14–19.

Fassler, J. (1978). *Helping children cope.* New York: Free Press.

Felner, R. D., Stolberg, A., & Cowen, E. L. (1975). Crisis events and school mental health referral patterns of young children. *Journal of Consulting and Clinical Psychology, 43,* 305–310.

Ferguson, B. F. (1979). Preparing young children for hospitalization: A comparison of two methods. *Pediatrics, 64,* 656–664.

Field, T. M. (1984). Early interactions between infants and their postpartum depressed mothers. *Infants Behavior and Development, 7,* 517–524.

Figley, C. R., McCubbin, H. I. (Eds.). (1983). *Stress and the family. Vol. 2: Coping with catastrophe.* New York: Brunner/Mazel.

Freud, A., & Burlingham, D. T. (1943). *War and children.* New York: Medical War Books.

Furman, E. (1974). *A child's parent dies.* New Haven, CT: Yale Univ. Press.

Garland, C., Swanson, J., Stone, N., & Woodruff, G. (1981). *Early intervention for children with special needs and their families.* WESTAR Series Paper #11, Westar States Technical Assistance Resource. Monmouth, OR (ED 207–278).

Garmezy, N. (1981). Children under stress: Perspectives on antecedents and correlates of vulnerability and resistance to psychopathology. In I. A. Rabin, J. Aronoff, A. M. Barclay, & R. A. Zucker (Eds.), *Further explorations in personality.* New York: Wiley.

Garmezy, N. (1985, April). Introduction. In N. Garmezy (Chair), *Stress, coping and development.* Symposium conducted at the meeting of the Society for Research in Child Development. Toronto.

Garmezy, N., Masten, A. S., & Tellegen, A. (1984). The Study of Stress and Competence in Children: A Building Block for Developmental Psychopathology *Child Development, 55,* 97–111.

George, G., & Main, M. (1979). Social interactions of young abused children: Approach, avoidance and aggression. *Child Development, 50*(2), 306–318.

Gold, D., & Andres, D. (1978). Developmental comparisons between 10-year-old children with employed and non-employed mothers. *Child Development, 50*(2), 306–318.

Gordon, T. (1970). *Parent effectiveness training.* New York: Wyden.

Greenspan, S. I., & Weider, S. (1984). Dimensions and levels of the therapeutic process. *Psychotherapy, 21*(1), 5–23.

Grune, A. L., & Brooks, J. (1985, April). *Children's perceptions of stressful life events.* Paper presented at the meeting of the Society for Research in Child Development, Toronto, Canada.

Haan, N. (1982). The assessment of coping, defense, and stress. In L. Goldberger, & S. Brezner (Eds.), *Handbook of stress: Theoretical and clinical aspects.* New York: The Free Press.

Hetherington, E. M., Cox, M., & Cox, R. (1978). The aftermath of divorce. In J. H. Stevens, Jr., & M. Mathews (Eds.), *Mother-child relations.* Washington, DC: NAEYC.

Holmes, T. H., & Rahe, R. H. (1967). The social readjustment rating scale. *Journal of Psychosomatic Research, 11,* 213–218.

Honig, A. S. (1979). *Parent involvement in early childhood education.* Washington, DC: NAEYC.

Honig, A. S. (1982). Research in review. Prosocial development in children. *Young Children, 37*(5), 51–62.

Honig, A. S. (1983). Evaluation of infant/toddler intervention programs. In B. Spodek (Ed.), *Studies in educational evaluation* (Vol. 8) (pp. 305–316). London: Pergamon.

Honig, A. S. (Ed.). (1984). Risk factors in infancy [Special issue]. *Early Child Development and Care, 16*(1 & 2).

Honig, A. S. (1985a). High quality infant/toddler care: Issues and dilemmas. *Young Children, 41*(1), 40–46.

Honig, A. S. (1985b). Research in review. Compliance, control, and discipline. (Part 1). *Young Children, 40*(2), 50–58.

Honig, A. S. (1985c). Research in review. Compliance, control, and discipline. (Part 3). *Young Children, 40*(3), 47–52.

Honig, A. S., & Gardner, C. (1985, April). *Overwhelmed mothers of toddlers in immigrant families: Stress factors.* Paper presented at the biennial meeting of the Society for Reseach in Child Development. Toronto, Canada.

Honig, A. S., Gardner, C., & Vesin, C. (1985, July). *Stress factors among overwhelmed mothers of toddlers in North African immigrant families in Paris.* Paper presented at the meetings of the International Society for the Study of Behavioral Development, Tours, France.

Honig, A. S., & McCarron, T. A. (1986, July). *Prosocial behaviors between handicapped and nonhandicapped peers in an integrated preschool.* Paper presented at the meeting of the International Congress of Child and Adolescent Psychiatry, Paris, France.

Honig, A. S., & Oski, F. A. (1984). Solemnity: A clinical risk index for iron deficient infants. In A. S. Honig (Ed.), Risk factors in infancy (Special issue). *Early Child Development and Care, 16*(1&2), 69–83.

Honig, A. S., Wittmer, D. S., & Gibralter, J. (1987). *Discipline, cooperation, and compliance: An annotated bibliography.* Urbana, IL: ERIC Clearinghouse on Elementary and Early Childhood Education.

Howes, C., & Olenick, M. (1984, April). *Family and child care influences on toddler's compliance.* Paper presented at the meeting of the American Education Research Association, New Orleans.

Institute of Medicine. (1984). *Report on bereavement.* Washington, DC: National Academy of Sciences.

Jalongo, M. (1983). Using crisis-oriented books with young children. *Young Children, 38*(5), 29–36.

Kersey, K. (1985). *Helping your child handle stress: The parents' guide to recognizing and solving childhood problems.* New York: Acropolis.

Lawhon, T., & Krishman, B. (1986). New teacher: Avoiding stress overload. *Dimensions, 14*(2), 11–14.

Lazarus, R. S., DeLongis, A., Folkman, S., & Gruen, R. (1985). Stress and adaptational outcomes: The problem of confounded measures. *American Psychologist, 40*(7), 770–779.

Lazarus, R., & Folkman, S. (1984). *Stress, appraisal and coping.* New York: Springer.

Lazarus, R. S., & Launier, R. (1978). Stress-related transactions between person and environment. In L. A. Pervin & M. Lewis (Eds.), *Perspectives in interactional psychology.* New York: Plenum.

Lee, D. M. (1983). *Mediators of the stressor-depression relationship.* Paper presented at the 36th annual meeting of the Gerontological Society of America, Chicago.

Leiderman, P. H. (1983). Social ecology and childbirth: The newborn nursery as environmental stressor. In N. Garmezy & M. Rutter (Eds.). *Stress, coping and development in children.* New York: McGraw-Hill.

Letourneau, C. (1981, September). Empathy and stress: How they affect parental aggression. *Social Work,* pp. 383–389.

Long, S. M. (1985). Mobile lifestyles: Creating change and adaptation for children and adults. *Dimensions, 13*(2), 7–11.

Martin, J. A. (1981). A longitudinal study of the consequences of early mother-infant interaction: A microanalytic approach. *Monographs of the Society for Research in Child Development, 46*(3, Serial No. 190).

Matas, L., Arend, R. A., & Sroufe, L. A. (1978). Continuity of adaptation in the second year: The relationship between quality of attachment and later competence. *Child Development, 19,* 547–556.

Milgram, N. A. (1982). War related stress in Israeli children and youth. In N. Garmezy & M. Rutter (Eds.), *Stress, coping, and development in children.* New York: McGraw-Hill.

Moore, T. (1975). Stress in normal childhood. In L. Levi (Ed.), *Society, stress and disease: Childhood and adolescence* (Vol. 2), London: Oxford Univ. Press.

Murphy, L. B., & Moriarity, A. E. (1976). *Vulnerability, coping, and growth: From infancy to adolescence.* New Haven: Yale University Press.

Patterson, G. R. (1980). Mothers: The unacknowledged victims. *Monographs of the Society for Research in Child Development, 45*(5, Serial No. 186).

Patterson, G. (1983). *Coercive family process.* Eugene, OR: Catalina Publishing Co.

Rahe, R. H., Meyer, M., Smith, M., Kjaerg, G., & Holmes, T. H. (1964). Social stress and illness. *Journal of Psychosomatic Research, 8,* 35–44.

Ramey, C. T., & Gowan, J. W. (1984). A general systems approach to modifying risk for retarded development. In A. S. Honig (Ed.), Risk factors in infancy (Special issue). *Early Child Development and Care, 16*(1&2), 9–26.

Robertson, J., & Robertson, J. (1971). Young children in brief separation: A fresh look. *Psychoanalytic Study of the Child, 26,* 264–515.

Roopnarine, J., & Honig, A. S. (1985). The unpopular child. *Young Children, 40*(6), 59–64.

Rosen, H. (1985). *Unspoken grief: Coping with childhood sibling loss.* Lexington, MA: Lexington Books.

Rutter, M. (1978). Early sources of security and competence. In J. Bruner & A. Garton (Eds.), *Human growth and development.* New York: Oxford Univ. Press.

Rutter, M. (1979). Protective factors in children's responses to stress and disadvantage. In M. W. Kent, & J. A. Rolf (Eds.), *Primary prevention of psychopathology: Vol. 3: Social competence in children.* Hanover, NH: University Press of New England.

Rutter, M. (1983). Stress, coping, and development: Some issues and questions. In N. Garmezy & M. Rutter (Eds.), *Stress, coping, and development in children.* New York: McGraw-Hill.

Rutter, M. (1984). Resilient children: Why some disadvantaged children overcome their environments, and how we can help. *Psychology Today, 18*(3), 57–65.

Sameroff, A. J., & Seifer, R. (1983). Familial risk and child competence. *Child Development, 54,* 1254–1268.

Schachter, F. F. (1981). Toddlers with employed mothers. *Child Development, 52,* 958–964.

Schaffer, H. R., Callender, W. M. (1969). Psychologic effects of hospitalization in infancy. *Pediatrics, 24,* 528–539.

Schultz, E. W., & Heuchert, C. M. (1983). *Child stress and the school experience.* New York: Human Sciences Press.

Seitz, V., Rosenbaum, L. K., & Apfel, N. H.

(1985). Effects of family support intervention: A ten year follow-up. *Child Development, 56*(2), 376–391.

Selye, H. (1936). A syndrome produced by diverse nocuous agents. *Nature, 138,* 32.

Selye, H. (1982). History and present status of the stress concept. In L. Goldberger & S. Breznitz (Eds.), *Handbook of stress: Theoretical and clinical aspects.* New York: The Free Press.

Sheehy, G. (1986, April 20). The victorious personality. *New York Times Magazine,* pp. 24–26, 43–47, 50.

Shure, M. B., & Spivack, G. (1978). *Problem solving techniques in childrearing.* San Francisco, CA: Jossey-Bass.

Sobel, J. (1982). *Everybody wins.* New York: Walker & Company.

Sourkes, B. (1977). Facilitating family coping with childhood cancer. *Journal of Pediatric Psychology, 2*(2), 65–67.

Sunal, C. S., & Hatcher, B. (1985). A changing world: Books can help children adapt. *Day Care and Early Education, 13*(2), 16–19.

Terr, I. C. (1981). Trauma: Aftermath: The young hostages of Chowchilla. *Psychology Today, 15*(4), 29–30.

Thomas, A., & Chess, S. (1977). *Temperament and Development.* New York: Brunner/Mazel.

Trickett, P. K., & Kuczynski, L. (1986). Children's misbehaviors and parental discipline strategies in abusive and nonabusive families. *Developmental Psychology, 22*(1), 115–123.

Turkington, C. (1984, December). Support urged for children in mourning. *APA Monitor,* pp. 16–17.

Vaughn, B. E., Dean, K. E., & Waters, E. (1985). The impact of out-of-home care on child-mother attachment quality: Another look at some enduring questions. In I. Bretherton & E. Waters (Eds.), Growing points of attachment theory and research. *Monographs of the Society for Research in Child Development, 50*(1–2). Serial No. 209.

Vaughn, B., Egeland, B., Sroufe, L. A., & Waters, E. (1979). Individual differences in infant-mother attachment at twelve and eighteen months: Stability and change in families under stress. *Child Development, 50,* 971–975.

Vietze, P. M. (1978, August). *Effects of rooming-in on maternal behavior directed toward infants.* Paper presented at the meeting of the American Psychological Association, Toronto.

Visher, E., & Visher, J. (1983). Stepparenting: Blending families. In H. I. McCubbin & C. R. Figley (Eds.), *Stress and the family (Vol. 1): Coping with normative transitions.* New York: Brunner/Mazel.

Wallerstein, J. S. (1983). Children of divorce: Stress and developmental tasks. In N. Garmezy & M. Rutter (Eds.), *Stress, coping and development in children.* New York: McGraw-Hill.

Wallerstein, J. S., & Kelly, J. (1980). *Surviving the breakup: How children and parents cope with divorce.* New York: Basic Books.

Werner, E. E. (1986). Resilient children. In H. E. Fitzgerald, & M. G. Walraven (Eds.), *Annual editions: Human development.* Sluice Dock, CT: Dushkin.

Werner, E. E., & Smith, R. S. (1982). *Vulnerable but invincible: A longitudinal study of resilient children and youth.* New York: McGraw-Hill.

Wolfer, J. A., & Vistainer, M. A. (1979). Prehospital psychological preparation for tonsillectomy patients: Effects on children's and parent's adjustment. *Pediatrics, 64,* 646–655.

Wolff, S. (1969). *Children under stress.* Baltimore, MD: Penguin.

Yarrow, M. R., Scott, P., deLeeuw, L., & Heinig, C. (1978). Child-rearing families of working and non-working mothers. In H. Bee (Ed.), *Social issues in developmental psychology* (2nd ed.). New York: Harper & Row.

Yudkin, M. (1984). When kids think the unthinkable. *Psychology Today, 18*(4), 25.

Zegens, L. S. (1982). Stress and the development of somatic disorders. In L. Goldberger & S. Breznitz (Eds.), *Handbook of stress: Theoretical and clinical aspects.* New York: The Free Press.

Zeitlin, S., Williamson, G. G., & Svcvepanski, M. (1984). *Early coping inventory.* Edison, NJ: Pediatric Rehabilitation Dept., John F. Kennedy Medical Center.

Ziv, A., & Israeli, R. (1973). Effects of bombardment on the manifest anxiety levels of children living in the *kibbutz. Journal of Consulting and Clinical Psychology, 40,* 287–291.

Zuravin, S. (1985). Housing and child maltreatment: Is there a connection? *Children Today, 14*(6), 8–13.

Index

Neglect
emotional 78
physical 78, 79
"self care" 77
See also Child Abuse

Obedience *see* Discipline

Parenting practices 113–114, 155–157
Parents
mental illness in 154
teacher work with 17–18, 23, 31, 37–38, 39–40, 48–52, 54, 55, 67, 74–75
See also Family
Peace education 130–135
Peer interaction 62, 110–115
friendships 113
Performances by children 109
Personality *see* Temperament
Physical development 9, 32, 127
Play
benefits of 22–23, 91
child's right to 91
mastery 9
pretend 6–12
symbolic 6–12
Popularity 110–115
and parenting practices 113–114
Poverty 147–148, 155
Powerfulness 8
See also Control
Prematurity 145–146
Protective factors
father interactions 163
rooming-in 162–163
schools 163–165
social supports 161–162
See also Coping

Reality, distortions of 84–90
Research about stress 142–167
Resilience *see* Coping
Responsibility
for action 93–95
for choices 96–98
for household tasks 48–52
Reward and punishment 93–94
Rough-and-tumble play 9, 11

Self-care 77
Self-confidence 48
Separation
anxiety 38
during hospitalization 26
from friends 30–33
from preschool 30–33
on death of loved one 35–40
with divorce 65
Sex as a factor in degree of stress 146, 152
Sex education 13–19, 43
correct vocabulary 13–14
genital differences 13
guidelines for teachers and parents 13–17
masturbation 16–17
opportunities to observe each other 14
parental involvement 16, 17–18
reproduction and birth 15
Sexual abuse 44, 78, 79
Sibling
birth of 44, 150
death of 39, 151
handicapped 151
Signs of stress 160
Social
development 8, 110–115
skills 114–115

Social service agencies 82
Societal disasters 148
Socioeconomic status as a stress factor 147–148, 155
Sources of stress 58, 143
Stages of stress 144–145
Stepfamilies 70–76, 153
complexities of 72
research findings 70–73
stepchildren 72
stepfathers 71
stepmothers 71–72
teacher involvement 73–75
Superhero play 6–12
adult management of 9–12
aggression in 9, 11
benefits for children 8
nature of 8–9
Support, sources of 161–165

Teacher techniques for helping children cope with stress 162–165
Temperament 116–121, 146
characteristics of 118–119
difficult 116
easy 116
slow-to-warm-up 116
Transitions
between activities 103–104
See also Continuity; Separation

Unpopularity 110–115

War 131–135
nuclear 133, 148
terrorism 148–149
ways to discuss 133–155
Working mothers 153–154

Information About NAEYC

NAEYC is . . .

. . . a membership-supported organization of people committed to fostering the growth and development of children from birth through age eight. Membership is open to all who share a desire to serve and act on behalf of the needs and rights of young children.

NAEYC provides . . .

. . . educational services and resources to adults who work with and for children, including

• *Young Children,* the journal for early childhood educators

• **Books, posters, brochures,** and **videos** to expand your knowledge and commitment to young children, with topics including infants, curriculum, research, discipline, teacher education, and parent involvement

• An **Annual Conference** that brings people from all over the country to share their expertise and advocate on behalf of children and families

• **Week of the Young Child** celebrations sponsored by NAEYC Affiliate Groups across the nation to call public attention to the needs and rights of children and families

• **Insurance plans** for individuals and programs

• **Public affairs** information for knowledgeable advocacy efforts at all levels of government and through the media

• The **National Academy of Early Childhood Programs,** a voluntary accreditation system for high-quality programs for children

• The **National Institute for Early Childhood Professional Development,** providing resources and services to improve professional preparation and development of early childhood educators

• The **Information Service,** a centralized source of information sharing, distribution, and collaboration

For free information about membership, publications, or other NAEYC services . . .

. . . call NAEYC at 202-232-8777 or 800-424-2460, or write to . . . National Association for the Education of Young Children, 1509 16th Street, N.W., Washington, DC 20036–1426.